Glimmerings III

Glimmerings
III

The Third Collection
Of Thoughts, Ideas,
Observations, Musings,
Reflections, and Comments
On Whatever Comes to Mind

Robert A. Harris

.:Virtual**Salt**
Publishing
Tustin

Glimmerings III
The Third Collection of Thoughts, Ideas, Observations,
 Musings, Reflections, and Comments
 On Whatever Comes to Mind

ISBN 978-1-941233-24-5 (Paperback)

Scripture quotations are from the New American Standard
Bible, Updated (NASB) unless otherwise specified. © 1971
The Lockman Foundation.

VirtualSalt® Publishing
Tustin, California

www.virtualsalt.com

VirtualSalt® is a registered trademark of Robert A. Harris

Nothing so enlarges the mind as this ability to examine methodically and accurately every one of life's experiences, with an eye to determining its classification, the ends it serves, its worth to the universe, and its worth to men. . . .
        — Marcus Aurelius, Meditations *3.10*

[Francis Bacon] pleased himself [by expecting that his essays] will live as long as books last. It may, however, satisfy an honest and benevolent mind to have been useful, though less conspicuous; nor will he that extends his hope to higher rewards, be so much anxious to obtain praise, as to discharge the duty which Providence assigns him.
        — Samuel Johnson, Rambler *106*

But examine everything carefully; hold fast to that which is good.
        —1 Thessalonians 5:21 (NASB)

Introduction

Glimmerings III is the third collection of thoughts and observations from my personal notebook, this portion ranging from 2014 to 2019, written between my ages of 63 and 68.

Glimmerings I consists of my thoughts recorded between the ages of 23 and 31. Apparently I was a late bloomer, because the reviews have been about as warm as a glass of iced tea on a porch rail in a Montana winter.

Glimmerings II, written between my ages of 31 and 63, apparently demonstrates a bit more understanding of the world, since it has received warmer reviews.

So, here is *Glimmerings III*, supposedly containing my most mature thinking (ages 63 to 68). I notice that over the years I have gotten increasingly verbose: *Glimmerings I* required only 189 pages to record my first 1000 thoughts; *Glimmerings II* required 217 pages; and *Glimmerings III* has pushed up against 300 pages. (And this in an age when fewer and fewer people want to read lengthy material. And this from a man known for his clear, concise prose style.)

Once again, my hope is that you will enjoy many of these ideas and comments, think about some of them, learn from a few, and share one or two with someone. Perhaps a few of these can serve as conversation starters. (Please don't prefix your quotation with, "Can you believe this guy?")

Finally, remember that an idea might not be true or useful in itself, but it can serve to stimulate thinking that will result in a truly good idea. If I must be wrong, may I be wrong in an interesting way.

Glimmerings III

[January, 2014; age 63]

2004. Many people are afraid of truth because truth is authoritative and people hate authority because it conflicts with their personal goals or wishes. If you can believe (or at least claim to believe) that "there are many truths," or "truth does not exist," you can liberate yourself from responsibility for lying, deceiving, cheating, and so forth. Both positions are weak, however. If there are many truths, that represents an acknowledgement that truth does exist. If you assert that truth does not exist, you are caught in a logical fallacy — for the assertion itself cannot be true if truth does not exist.

So, aha, we now understand why so many professors and intellectuals say that they cannot know what is true. However, to claim not to know what is true is to claim to know something true — you know that you cannot know truth. That, too, is a self-referential absurdity.

2005. Your values and beliefs are among your tools for understanding. Therefore, keep your principles clear and well defined, so that when you want to understand another person's actions, or a temptation you face, or an idea you read, you will be ready with your touchstone to test and gain insight.

2006. How many concepts there are that we no longer think about because we no longer discuss them or see them discussed, as if they have been relegated to the trashcan of time. *Virtue, chastity, honor, duty* — all would be mocked if someone mentioned them in most circles today. And only slightly less scorned would be *integrity, sacrifice,* and *commitment.*

1

2007. Why do so many of those in charge of media, those who shape our cultural values, want us to view virginity as a defect, to be cured as quickly as possible? Is this what we call cultural progress?

2008. The only change most people like is what the clerk gives them when they hand him a dollar bill for a fifty-cent candy bar. (Rewritten from a comment by Dewey Wilson.)

2009. What tool is it that we use every day because it is an essential resource, yet that we seldom want to learn more about or learn how to use better? The mind. We are prone to cognitive biases, logical fallacies, irrational thought, confusion between the wisdom of the mind and the urges of the brain—yet we don't take the time or expend the energy to learn how to avoid these weaknesses of thinking or how to improve our intellects.

Most of us are so conceited and smug about our own thinking ability that we reject the idea that learning how to think would be helpful. I remember teaching my course on critical thinking one semester, when I was reading the syllabus to the class and we came across a passage that said the goal was to learn how to think better. One student raised his hand and asked, "What if you already know how to think?"

2010. When you think about your life in the context of eternity, or even a few thousand years before you were born and a few thousand after you die, the words *puny* and *petty* seem always to come to mind. So why are we so anxious to be honored, celebrated, revered? Even "lasting fame" is ephemeral by comparison. We are so worried about what half a dozen (or if you're a movie star, half a million) people will think of us, and yet out of the billions of people on earth and the grand timeframe of eternity, how justified can we be to grow arrogant and prideful over being remembered by handful of people for a dozen years?

2011. Vanity: The desire—the hope, the conviction—that strangers will pronounce your name with admiration long after you are dead.

2012. They spent their hours and days in pursuit of ephemeral pleasures, in pursuit of more and more things, heaping their barns of goods up to the rafters. They invested their lives in the pursuit of stuff — and ended up with a handful of sand.

2013. We sit in boats at different places on the river of time, and we cannot change our relative position, but must ride along wherever we are. We can't row back to our childhood, nor forward into a technological era that will have some tool we could use. We can't marry the girl born 200 years ago, nor be friends with the man born 200 years from now.

2014. We live what we know. We have certain technologies and we use them unselfconsciously. But only a few people want to use what they can imagine.

"Let's cook the food."

"That will take 30 minutes in the oven."

"What we need is an oven that will cook the food in one or two minutes."

"That's impossible. It can't be done."

"Your definition of *impossible* is *cannot be done*. My definition is *cannot currently be done*. There's a huge difference."

"Yeah, but two minutes, twenty minutes, what's the difference? In two minutes you might turn a chunk of frozen glop into an airline meal."

2015. Conservatives are often wrongly accused of opposing change, period. But there is a difference between change that involves a moral step backward or the loss of treasured values and change that involves technological progress or effective problem solving. Change for its own sake is questionable: hemlines go up and down as fashions change, but to what end? Your closet fills with clothes you no longer wear. Isn't it interesting, too, that we see lots of advertisements shouting, "This will change your life!" But almost none of them say, "This will *change your life for the better!*"

And by change, some people mean that constant loosening of moral and ethical constraints that society has used as glue for so many years. But as T. S. Eliot notes, there is no clearly identifiable end point for this loosening. Once you start down the slope of loosening, there is no turning back.

2016. How biased we are toward ideas or literary works created by someone famous or whom we honor. Just as some studies have shown that wine and liquor tasters are influenced by the brand, the shape of the bottle, and the color of the booze, so critics and readers alike are influenced by the fame or ethos of the author, the cover of the book (never a truer cliché), or the publisher.

Try this experiment. Ask a friend to comment on a point of interpersonal advice. Tell your friend the advice is: "When someone hurts you, the faster you forgive the person, the faster the hurt will go away."

Next, with one friend, say that the advice came from Mahatma Gandhi. With another friend, say that it came from a former US president or some famous football player. See if you get different responses.

Another way to test this is to quote the saying and ask your listener to pick from a list the person most likely to have originated the saying. Gandhi? Jesus? Oprah? Dr. Phil?

2017. Kindness is the right arm of love.

2018. The opposite of kindness is not cruelty. The opposite of kindness is thoughtlessness.

2019. What we have lost with the busyness of modern life (in spite of all our "labor saving" devices) is time to think. We're so busy we can't pause to ruminate, to assess, to evaluate, to contemplate the meaning of it all.

- Meaning comes from connecting activity with values.

- Understanding comes from overlaying context on specific events or experiences.
- Thoughtless experience prevents a meaningful life.
- A life of purpose comes from aligning your choices and actions in a consistent direction, toward coherent goals.

2020. Mental maps require time to form. When you move to a new neighborhood, you only gradually start putting the streets together in your mental geometry. "Let's see. I can go down this street, turn left on the next street, and be at the house. Or, I can follow this diagonal and make a right turn after the shopping center." Sometimes we get stuck in a mental rut and always take the same route from A to B—until one day, it suddenly occurs to us that we've been taking the long way and that there is a shorter way.

Our moral and philosophical mental maps act in the same way. Sometimes many years of thinking are required before we can see the connections, the pathways, the shortcuts, through our own ideas. As we gain understanding about ourselves and our thoughts, our maps become more interconnected, more detailed, and clearer.

2021. Something intrepid learners understand that insecure learners do not is that often a broader context is needed before clarity and understanding can occur. An insecure learner reads a page or two of some new and complex work and comes across a word or sentence he doesn't understand and gives up. "This is too deep for me," he says, or "I can't understand this." Reading a Shakespeare play for the first time, or even the King James Bible, are examples of engaging initially daunting works. Another type of off-putting work for the insecure reader is one whose vocabulary is easy but whose concepts are challenging. "I don't know what this author is talking about," the insecure learner says. "So I stopped reading."

The intrepid learner continues reading, knowing that clarity will come out of a deeper exposure to the material, or perhaps through a second or third reading.

This observation fits in well with the previous comment about mental maps. Difficult material requires time (and thought) and offline processing (read: sleep). I might have mentioned in a previous entry that when I was teaching syllogisms, some students had blank looks, followed by looks of confusion for several days, until suddenly one day the lights came on. They finally got it.

Moral of the story: Don't give up on a tough book, difficult idea, or challenging problem, just because you don't understand it right away.

There is a *Calvin and Hobbes* comic strip where Calvin says something like, "Anything I can't understand in five seconds isn't worth knowing." That's not an uncommon attitude today, and the result is the loss of much valuable thinking and good decision making.

2022. Why is it that when many people undergo a fundamental change in their worldview (a "worldview reset"), the change is often accompanied by bitterness and resentment toward the people or organizations that promoted the "old" worldview? Think of the response to divorce, the loss of faith (in God or an organization or person), the disillusionment over a political ideology. All of these events involve a loss of trust, confidence, and security. The result of bitter resentment comes from the feeling of being played for a fool, for being duped. The spouse was unfaithful, one's faith now seems to have been a confidence scheme, the trusted organization took advantage of one's belief in its integrity—now shown to have been hypocritical—and the friend was just using the now disillusioned person.

And, of course, the follow-on to resentment is the desire for revenge, starting with the public exposure of the wrongdoer. Hence, exes speak to everyone about their former partner's crimes and misdemeanors, the new agnostics evangelize for faithlessness, organizations perceived as culpable are sued, and so on.

2023. One of the tradeoffs or penalties for our busyness is that we don't have the time to investigate the reliability of sources. Instead, we adopt a short cut and indulge in "book cover judgment." If the book or Web site or brochure or ad looks sophisticated and reliable, we assume that it is so. Hence we are more regularly deceived than ever.

2024. Yes, I know we like to smirk at the clichés about suffering for art and the tortured soul of the artist. But I think there sometimes is a connection between pain and beauty, or beautiful art. The singer who can feel the emotions of a song about lost or unrequited love usually produces a more moving performance than the singer who can't put feelings into the words.

Now that I think about it, the same is true of songs of worship. Some worship songs are played either so bloodlessly, rigidly, and formally, or else are rocked out so whammity bam bam, that little emotional connection or response is made available to the worshipper. The singers who can truly worship the Lord when they sing, and who can express that feeling of love and adoration in their voices — they are the better singers.

2025. **Thoughts After Looking at a University Literary Magazine Written by Undergraduates.**

1. It must be difficult to be a creative writing teacher, knowing how fragile the egos are of those who have literary aspirations but little talent and less skill. Criticism crushes them.

2. It must be difficult to teach poetry writing because there are no standards of quality now, and any comment, such as "The poem lacks compelling imagery," or "The point of the poem is unintelligible," can be rebutted by appealing to dozens of critically approved examples.

3. What does a teacher in a creative writing class tell a student whose work is bald, banal, and boring?

I would enjoy presenting my (antiquated) views about how to write good poetry, but I've always disliked offering advice because in every case so far, the poor would-be poet has gone away despondent and (1) never returned and (2) never attempted to improve by deliberate study and practice of the poetic craft.

2026. If I might offer a tentative definition of an *ideologue*, it is someone who will not even for a moment seriously consider any argument or data that disconfirms his belief.

2027. We are plagued by so many costly debacles because they are dreamed up by people with "Utopia Now!" bumper stickers pasted on their brains.

2028. When something bad happens to you, don't worry about whether or how much you are going to suffer. Instead, ask yourself whether this event will prevent you from living rightly, or diminish who you are. If not, then take courage and be thankful.

2029. Getting married reveals many mysteries that few men ever could have predicted. Today's amazing fact is that rags belong to different social classes. The first clue a husband gets into this seemingly secret hierarchy comes when he, under the car or under the sink or on his knees attempting to mop up a spill with a paper towel, shouts out to his wife, "Honey, I need a rag!" Naturally, he in his cluelessness expects his bride to answer, "Of course, sweetheart. Here are several." Instead, he is surprised to hear her ask, "What kind of rag?"

To save my readers the embarrassment of answering, "You know, just a rag," thereby provoking an argument that will likely end in his sleeping on the sofa for the next several weeks, here is the explanation.

At the top of the social hierarchy are the Royal Rags, often indistinguishable from Guest Towels. They are frequently folded neatly, stacked together in a pile of half a dozen or so, and ensconced in cute little ceramic holders in the bathroom. But beware, O man, Royal Rags are not to be used under any circumstances. Pity the husband who dries his hands on one. And should he wipe his greasy hands with one after changing the oil in his wife's car, well, that thought cannot be completed. Just remember: Royal Rags are part of the decor, not part of your toolkit.

Next are the Good Rags. These rags often have all four edges sewn, are nicely rectangular, and have no holes or rips. Good Rags may be used for light jobs such as wiping the bathroom mirror, cleaning one's glasses, drying the dishes, and so forth. It is not a good idea to take some of these to the garage or workshop, because they will be in danger of getting soiled. If you have a dirty job, you need to use Worker Rags.

Worker Rags supply the backbone of household cleaning tasks. They can be used to mop floors, wipe the mud off shoes, apply some preserve-and-shine treatment to tires, clean the dust off neglected book shelves, scrub the shower pan, and perform other elbow-grease-required tasks.

Finally, at the bottom of rag society—and ironically enough, the most useful and hardworking in the rag hierarchy—are the Kamikaze Rags. Kamikaze Rags can be identified by their often irregular shape, frayed edges, stains, and evidence of a former life as a bath towel, bedsheet, T-shirt, or dog bed pillowcase before being cut or ripped into rags.

These rags can be used for anything—wiping greasy hands, cleaning up after an event by Junior or Fido, applying some strange chemical to clean some rusty tools, wiping the runs off a paint can, removing the grease from a lawnmower, or helping with any truly yucky task. Unfortunately, Kamikaze Rags are used only once. So husbands, take note: Always keep a supply of Kamikaze Rags on hand. The ones you use and hand to your wife are headed for the trash, not the washing machine. Those super handy little red rags you can get in the automotive department of hardware stores are perfect for grimy use. Just remember that they are mortal and will not be reincarnated. No woman wants to launder her delicate unmentionables in a washing machine that has been used to clean filthy rags. (Ever wonder why auto repair shops have their own washing machines?)

In addition to a personal supply of Kamikaze Rags, every husband should ask his wife to identify the various living accommodations of each of the other classes of rags, in order to avoid issues (as they are called). Pay special attention to the domicile of Worker Rags, since these are the ones you are least likely to get into trouble if you use them.

2030. Myth: My spouse should make me happy. Fact: Sadly, the universe was not created just for you and your happiness. You were not put on Earth for your spouse or anyone else to cater to your every idle whim or impulsive desire. Your happiness is on your own task list.

2031. Thucydides says that we use hope to convince ourselves that we will get those things that reason tells us we can't, and we use reason to explain away the objections to our hopes.

2032. The difference between a philosophy and an ideology is that a philosophy is interested in truth and wisdom (*philo* = love, *sophos* = wisdom). An ideology is interested in its ideology, and in securing political power for its followers, quite apart from truth or wisdom.

2033. Acts 2:13 is an example of how we interpret new experience through the framework of past experience. Some of those who witnessed the apostles speaking in tongues simply could not comprehend the possibility of a manifestation of the power of the Holy Spirit because they had had no experience of such an event. But they had encountered babbling drunks, so that is the interpretive frame they put on this situation.

2034. Why is ugly, repulsive art celebrated these days? Why is cacophonous music touted? Is it because of the invention of photography that art has taken such a turn? Is it because the only alternatives in music are classical, pop, and advertising jingles; and none of these forms can be considered high art or sophisticated? So, we have atonal grinding and screeching noise, or rap music.

Possible reasons are (1) the basic rebellion in the human heart, the desire to destroy one's surrounding culture as a proof of individuation or ego strength, or (2) the need to do something new and different so that one can avoid being labeled common, a copycat, typical, trite, "so yesterday," etc., or (3) a pretense to sophistication, someone who can appreciate what others cannot. Yes, push the envelope to be *avant garde*, a thought leader, moving into the future incomprehensible by the Philistine conservatives—or I mean, reactionaries—who declaim the new and hate what they cannot understand.

2035. Why are the utopians so dangerous? They sit in their offices in academia or government and draw lines on a map of territory they have never seen or are barely aware of. Then they start the bulldozers and let the destruction begin. Necessary consequences, they say, as families are corrupted, ruined, or even killed. "Unfortunate collateral damage."

Had they looked at the situation from ground level, from a study of individuals, they would have had a slower but more humane approach. Oh, but I forgot. Utopians are not big on compassion—in practice—as opposed to compassion in theory.

2036. When preaching the Gospel, or teaching anything, do you start with truth or with relationship? It depends on the audience. Most people want to know who you are before they will listen to what you have to say. But, however you begin, you must at some point get to truth, because without truth you cannot have a genuine relationship. And in the case of a relationship with Christ, our erosive culture can all too often wear away any relationship that is less than strong and mature—which almost implies one that includes the incorporation of truth.

2037. **The Kind-Hearted Crazy Man.**
I recently came across a check that my mentally ill brother had taped to the front door of the house. (It's an old check, dated

May 19, 2003, when he still had a checking account.) He had the account put in the name he said was his new name (quite an accommodating bank), Auy Poll Axils. The check's "Pay to the Order of" line says, "Get them out of Jail," for $100. The memo line says, "Getting brothers and kids out." He was under the delusion that he had other brothers and children. But even in his insanity he was compassionate.

2038. I know I sound like a broken record, but please don't tell me that evolutionism/scientism/naturalism isn't a religion. The evangelists of this superstition have just rebaked Carl Sagan's TV series, *Cosmos*, for a new generation of unsuspecting young people, and they are putting it on ten — yes, ten — channels: Fox, National Geographic, Nat Geo Wild, Nat Geo Mundo, Fox Life, FX, FXX, FXM, Fox Sports 1, Fox Sports 2. You read it right: The program is on two sports channels as well as eight others.

Is it science or religion? The first episode begins with, "The Cosmos is all there is, or was, or ever will be." That's philosophy — or religion — and not science.

Then there is the hypocritical blather about science going wherever the truth leads. Then in the first few minutes of the first episode, there are several expressions of what "may" have happened or what might be the case.

Then I go to the bookstore, where I purchase *The Quantum Universe*, and, true to form, the authors do the requisite obeisance to evolution, not too far from the beginning, on page 52: "Darwin's theory of evolution by natural selection provides a simpler explanation [of complex creatures] that fits the available data beautifully." The authors go on to say that "random mutations produce variations in organisms," etc., etc., and "This process alone can account for the complexity we see in life on Earth today."

Hello! The nineteenth century is just so over now. Mutation and natural selection were all fine before we discovered how complex even single celled organisms are, and how uber-complex biological systems such as the blood-clotting cascade are. Evolved one mutation at a time? I don't think so.

And of course, science is so willing to follow truth wherever it might lead that the establishment sues to prevent the teaching of any opposition, criticism, or qualification to evolutionary theory, even if such criticism comes from peer-reviewed articles in the establishment's own journals.

Finally, Inquisition-like, academics are punished by loss of employment if they dare to speak against the holy doctrine.

2039. We gain understanding by the aggregation and processing of items of meaning. We collect data, process it into information, process that information into knowledge, and process that knowledge into both wisdom and decision making. When the knowledge is of ideas and values, the further result is wisdom; when the knowledge is of technique or algorithm, the result is problem solving. Together, wisdom and problem solving produce decision making or action.

2040. As a means of filling in the gaps of ignorance so that we can feel that we understand a new acquaintance, we put the people we meet into rather constrained pigeon holes. This habit becomes evident when the new person does or says something our predefined pigeon-hole didn't include. Then we say, "I can't believe he said that! What is he thinking?" or "How could she do that? It's so unlike her."

2041. I wonder if rebels and nonconformists realize that they are really conforming to a type after all. Rebels who decide to oppose authority in a reactionary way simply conform to custom in a negative way. They conform to anti-authority. There's no originality there.

The rebel asks, "What are others doing, so that I can do the opposite?" The truly independent thinker asks, "What's the best thing to do in these circumstances, regardless of whether the answer conforms to or deviates from the established truth or practice?"

Many young people are so worried that they will be viewed as a generic adolescent that they fall into this "prove you're an individual" thinking, and take up some preposterous behavior to show that they are their own person. Boys grow their hair long, girls get their belly buttons pierced, both get tattoos, and so on. But then, much of their peer group is doing these things, too, so such actions are really quite conformist after all.

2042. It has been said, and even I have said it, that when you oppose something, it's important not only to say what you are against, but also to say what you are for. Of course, some people who are rabidly against something don't really know what they are for, other than some pleasant abstraction (justice, fairness, equality). However, it now occurs to me that others know indeed what they are for, but what they are for is so radical or offensive that they dare not articulate it at the current moment.

2043. University professors are something of a mystery. On the one hand, they are eager to advance the most bizarre of theories and argue for the most preposterous interpretations (of literature, data, human behavior, and so on). Yet, at the same time so many profs seem unwilling to commit to any idea, at least not without infinite qualification. Perhaps they were attacked in graduate school for making unsupportable generalizations. So now, instead of telling his Introduction to Literature class, "John Keats wrote 'Ode on a Grecian Urn,'" the professor will remark, "A person believed to have gone by the name of John Keats is usually credited with part or all of the authorship of a poem that has become known as 'Ode on a Grecian Urn.' Of course, the title might seem to imply that an actual urn and the art on it were referenced during creation of the poem's original ur-text, but whether or not such an object ever existed cannot be known." And so forth.

I might have mentioned this elsewhere, but I had a professor once who was so careful a thinker that he found it nearly impossible to express an idea. He would say, "This passage predicts—no, that's not the right word—this passage foreshadows—no, that isn't really it—the passage hints—no, not so much hints as suggests—well, what I'm adumbrating here is the sense of warning—no, the sense of ominousness—or better, the—you know the feeling you have when you drive down the street and suddenly can't remember whether you closed the garage door? Well, it's not like that exactly, but—" and so on.

I recall how difficult it was to take notes in that professor's class. I wonder what he said when his wife asked, "How did you like my soup?"

2044. You can read with your mind closed, but you can't read with your eyes closed. Okay, so someone can read to you or you can use Braille or listen to an audiobook. Sure, destroy my offering of wisdom with a few silly truths.

2045. Evil is a lock picker, ever trying to break in and steal values and standards, and then abuse, pervert, or kill them. Much of the abuse and perversion is accomplished by manipulating the language. See newspeak, propaganda, equivocation, etc.

2046. In classical art and literature, Truth is depicted as a naked woman. It's not because men lust after truth, but because Truth does not disguise what she really looks like. Whether you like her body or not, what you see is what you get. Falsehood, on the other hand, always appears in an alluring costume. In fact, Falsehood will put on any outfit that will attract you to her. A thousand disguises will tempt you. And she always wears plenty of makeup.

2047. What is the appeal of dictators, cult leaders, and powerful ideologues? They act as if they know what they are doing, as if they know what's what. Many people have at least a small degree of uncertainty about life—a degree of insecurity—and the confident, charismatic leader has a lot of appeal for them.

(This fact, by the way, also explains why many young women are attracted to "take charge" young men. Such men appear confident, self-assured, and "in control." Unfortunately, after the relationship gets going, "in control" becomes "controlling.")

2048. **Theory of Mixed Mutations.**

If life on earth developed through the commonly promoted Neo-Darwinian mechanism of random mutations selected by reproductive advantage, why do we not find now living or in the fossil record more life forms with odd features?

While most mutations are harmful and the ones Darwinism proposes are selected because of benefit, we can assume that there is actually a range of fitness from very beneficial through neutral to very harmful. So why don't we see, say, humans with lots of bumps on their arms, or two noses or extra ribs? These would be features that are not so harmful as to be quickly selected out. No one would notice the extra ribs, for example.

And if selection is so exact, why don't all women have large breasts, since that seems to be of such high value in attracting men?

2049. The funeral business is such an exploitation of people's grief. First, you buy a plot for $3,000 to $9,000 or more. That's a 4 by 8 foot piece of real estate. You're paying the equivalent of $4 million to $12 million an acre for that property.

Then "basic services" of $2,500, which amount mostly to the funeral director shaking your hands and cashing your check. I know this fee is high because a few funeral homes charge as little as $300. It's the same with embalming: $250 for some, $800 for others.

And don't get me started about the casket. There's 20-gauge steel for you cheapskates for only $2,500, but who says you have to love your departed? Or you can get an 18-gauge stainless steel casket (that's more than a hundredth of an inch thicker) with a rubber seal to protect your loved one for only $4,500 to $26,000. And of course the casket must be protected by a concrete vault, the cheapest of which is $1,200. But you want the copper lined, neoprene sealed, memorial tagged version for $5,000.

But wait a minute. We're not protecting Uncle Joe or Aunt Mary. They are dead. (Dead meaning their soul and body have separated.) We're talking about protecting a corpse. From what?

Trying to thwart natural decay processes is a game you can't win. I remember a mortician once telling me, "We have your father here." I should have answered, "No you don't. All you have is his body."

2050. Each of the Seven Deadly Sins derives from the failure to consider other people. They are seven aspects of selfishness. Thinking only about oneself gives rise to Pride, Anger, Greed, Envy, Gluttony, Lust, and Sloth. Interestingly, the Seven Virtues are all other-directed: Prudence (Wisdom), Temperance, Justice, and Fortitude (Courage), Faith, Hope, and Charity (Love). Therefore, sin is "all about me," whereas virtue is all about what I can do for you.

2051. Marcus Aurelius notes that "to pursue the unattainable is insanity" (5.17). But there is a slight problem. Too often we can't distinguish between the attainable and the unattainable from the front end, before the attempt. It's only looking back that allows us to discover the difference. So we still must hope; we still must try.

2052. That God works through people is evident from Acts 10 where he tells Cornelius to "send some men to Joppa," and then tells Peter that "three men are looking for you," and that "I have sent them myself." God allowed Cornelius the freedom to pick the men, but ordered the scene. Or to put it the opposite way, God directed the event, but that still involved the free choice of Cornelius in selecting the people to send. God uses a management technique now recognized as a best practice: he tells Cornelius what to do but not how to do it.

2053. Faith necessitates having sufficient room for choice so that free will can operate. If there were no room for doubt, belief would be required and not chosen. Trust, the basis of faith, would be eliminated. However, as the world grows more sophisticated and unbelief and disbelief grow more strident, the support for faith also grows. The design and complexity of the creation is increasingly revealed.

2054. Some of the materialists/naturalists are attempting to use fields such as chaos theory and fractal algebra to argue that the creation is the result of a bunch of simple equations, elaborated into apparent complexity. But is the Author of a set of simple equations that can explain roses and mitosis any less to be revered than One who produced them with fancy integrals?

2055. **Ideas from *Too Big to Know* by David Weinberger.**
    1. We can know but not act. There are many reasons for this:
- social proof (others are not acting or are doing something in conflict with what the knowledge tells us)
- institutional, cultural, legal barriers
- we are waiting for more information (another source, confirmation, details)
- fear, bribery, threats, letting an enemy fail

    2. Too much information is bad because it confuses the issue. We can process only a limited amount of information. Give us too much, and decision making or even mere apprehension of the facts diminishes.
    3. No matter how much information we get, we remain skeptical and look at it with suspicion because of possible
- selection, slanting, filtering
- distortion, counterfeiting
- degradation, dilution

    4. There is a tension and a continuum between guarantors of quality information (editors, peer reviewers) and censors of the "wrong ideas."
    5. A plausible argument can be made both for and against pretty much any idea or fact claim.

2056. Having read the *History of the Peloponnesian War* by Thucydides, I am struck by how much grief there has been in the world, much of it resulting from war. Thucydides reports that larger city states attack smaller or weaker cities, and if they resist, they are conquered, with the outcome that all the men are killed and all the women and children are enslaved. In sea battles, when a ship was overtaken, all the soldiers on board the losing ship were typically butchered.

This behavior goes on for more than 20 years—conquer, kill, and enslave—all for the sake of power and domination. Think how many widows had to grieve over their husbands; not just the widows of soldiers, but the widows of every man in town, from the baker to the mayor. And think of the 7 year-old boys who now were reduced to slave labor, or the 14 year-old girls who were reduced not only to slavery, but to sexual exploitation.

2057. "If I become a Christian or believe in God, I'm afraid I will miss out on some things."

"That's right, you will miss out on some things. But if you don't become a follower of Jesus, you will miss out of some things also."

"What do you mean?"

"Our life is like a stream, with many branches, all leading to different destinations. Our lives are traveling down the stream, and at every branch, we must decide which to choose."

"So what does this have to do with my problem?"

"The point is that any decision you make precludes many other decisions—that's the missing out you fear—but the decision also enables many more decisions.

For example, if you are invited to a meeting in Chicago, you can't also attend a meeting in San Francisco or vacation on the beach in San Diego during the week of the meeting. So some options are indeed precluded.

But if you choose Chicago, other options become available that would have been precluded if you hadn't taken the choice.

There are millions of books to read, and thousands of movies. You must make choices. You can't read every book or see every movie.

The conclusion is that if you accept Jesus, you will "miss out" on some things, but you gain heaven.

2058. The problem of evil is not only that it wants the freedom to wallow in its degradation and rebellion, not only that it wants tolerance for its behaviors, and not only that it wants approval for its debauchery. These things are alone sufficient for us to realize how terrible evil is. But evil also wants to infect every potentially good thing and pollute and corrupt it. For example, it wants to turn the sexual relationship between husband and wife into a degrading, perverted, sick interaction between two disturbed individuals. This so that every time you think of something good, its perversion comes to mind.

2059. When girls are young, they wear long hair and short pants. When girls grow old, they wear short hair and long pants.

2060. **Why You Can't Rely on Reviews or Review Sites.**
1. Disgruntled people are much more likely to post than people who were satisfied.
2. Competitors might post negative reviews to drive buyers or users away. And if there are only a few choices, driving people away from one product will push them toward another product—such as the competitor's.
3. Providers and their allies might post positive reviews to make the product or service appear well liked. Fifty reviews of five stars implies that fifty people have purchased, used, and liked the product very much.
4. There is a tendency for people to generalize from one negative aspect. They see that the carpet didn't get vacuumed and they say, "The whole place was dirty."
5. When making an argument to post publicly, many people hunt around for evidence they can add that will strengthen their case. For example, if their complaint was that the vending machine took their money but didn't deliver the soda, they know that's not enough to sound like a reasonable complaint. So they

ask themselves, "What else could I say that was bad about the place?" The walls were dingy, the windows dirty, and didn't the room have a bad odor? And that free breakfast was just nasty. Now the complaint sounds more reasonable.

6. When posting, people are concerned about how their published (and therefore public) persona will be understood. They don't want to be viewed as a whiner over trivial disappointments. So they write a strong case, as described above.

7. A complaint represents a single experience. Generalizing from it would be risky. Question: How many single experiences do we need before we can generalize reasonably from them?

8. The review sites often publish an average score. But suppose ten people rate the item or hotel as a five-star experience, and ten others rate it as a one-star experience. That's 50 plus 10 or 60 points, divided by 20 reviewers, for an average of 3. What does that tell you?

9. Reviews are a snapshot it time—in other words, they are time bound. What was true six months or a year ago might not apply to the situation now. Things could be better or worse.

10. There is always the personal factor. (1) Some people are simply impossible to please and can find fault with everything. (2) The reviewer's tastes and preferences might be different from yours, and the review's positive or negative comments might be dependent on those tastes. (3) Remember that many, if not most, people evaluate things not by a rational analysis of how well the things meet a set of objective criteria, but by how the things meet or fail to meet their expectations. (Some people are picky and have expectations that are likely never to be fully met, while others are easy going and welcome pretty much whatever comes.)

2061. One of the most shocking things in the arena of human personality is that we adapt our behavior and even our beliefs about who we are to correspond with the judgments of others about us. Pascal says, "Man is so made that if we are continually telling him that he is a fool, he comes to believe it; and by repeating it to himself he makes himself believe it" (Lafuma 189).

This was made manifest once again in the life of a little old woman who was told she had Alzheimer's disease. So she stopped talking, eating, and drinking and tuned out the external world, lost weight and declined rapidly. Then a PET scan revealed that she did not have Alzheimer's. Her brain was normal. Hearing this, she started talking extensively again, regained energy and appetite, and displayed a good memory and a good personality.

2062. Regarding the Pride-Rebellion-Rejection of Authority nexus: "Deconstruction . . . provided a rationale for the busting of canons, the debunking of authority, and the rejection of the concept of meaning" (David Lehman, "Deconstructing the Deconstructionist," *Wall Street Journal*, March 15-16, 2004, p. C5.)

2063. **High Finance.**

So I go to the thrift store and am lucky enough to see that they are having a 50% off sale just yesterday and today. So I look around and find a pair of speakers, each labeled $5. My question is, does this mean $5 a pair or $5 each? Then I find another speaker, labeled "Center Speaker," and discover that it's a set of three. I ask one of the employees about the price and tell her that they should be a set, all three for $5. She goes to check with someone. While she is gone, I look around some more and discover two more, labeled "Left Surround" and "Right Surround," making a set of five from a 5.1 surround setup, most likely.

When the employee returns, I explain that the whole set should be $5, and she says she told the cashier that the three should be $5.

I get to the cashier and tell her that the set should be $5, but she says the speakers say $5 each. She goes to check with someone. When she returns, she says, "The price is $8 for all of them." Now, I'm not sure how five speakers can be priced at $8, but I relent and say okay. Then the cashier rings it up and says, "That will be $4." After all, there is a 50%-off sale going on!

Okay, so I thought it amusing that we had to negotiate a "list price" before we could convert it to the sale price. Anyway, I am now the proud owner of five small speakers, the front three shielded. I opened one up and there is a sizable magnet in it, so we'll see if the sound is any good.

2064. "Hello, Family Funeral Home. Ted speaking."

"Hello, Ted. My brother Harold just passed away. Do you have my dear Harold there?"

"No, madam. Your dear Harold is with the Lord. All we have here is his body, the empty shell of his soul."

2065. "In science, we are eager to pursue the truth wherever it may lead, unless that truth has supernatural implications."

"So, science is the search for truth, as long as it doesn't lead toward God."

"I just said that."

"So then, why do you say, 'wherever it may lead'? You are saying that we are in search of the truth, but only in a certain area."

"You're not paying attention. Listen to me. Science is the search for truth —."

"But only with naturalistic answers."

"That's right. Now you're getting it."

"But that's not the entire truth."

"Listen. If you're some sort of committed religious fanatic, whose doctrines cannot be assailed because you define your terms so rigidly, I will not bother talking to you anymore. Good bye."

2066. A comprehensive explanation of the cosmos must, as Pascal says, "be able to give an explanation both of the whole nature of man in particular, and the whole direction of the world in general" (Lafuma 17).

2067. Pascal says, "Physical science will not console me for my ignorance of moral philosophy in time of sorrow; but a knowledge of moral philosophy will always console me for being deficient in knowledge of physical science" (Lafuma 60). Having scientific knowledge cannot make up for a lack of philosophic, moral, or spiritual knowledge. A scientist with technical genius can still be a moral monster. On the other hand, spiritual knowledge — knowing about God — does more than make up for a lack of knowledge of science. Such knowledge tells us about the connection between physical science and God. By knowing about God first, we can see the creation in the beauty and complexity God designed and created; by knowing about the physical world first, we can learn about God and his creative, artistic, detailed creative care.

2068. It's interesting how readily one can pick up that "polite but cautious" vibe that young women emit when put into the presence of a man under certain circumstances. For example, a man and a woman alone in an elevator, a man asking a young woman for directions (yes, it does happen), or a man driving his son's girlfriend home from visiting in the hospital. What makes that wariness perceptible behind the politeness? Body language? Tone of voice? Facial expression? Connotation?

2069. **Triple Redundancy.**
    Three soap dispensers in a small gas station bathroom with two sinks. It's a good thing, too, since only one dispenser works.

2070. Forget trying to keep track of whose towels are whose when there are four people in the hotel room.

2071. "And those who most despise men and put them on the same level as the animals, nevertheless wish to be admired and believed by them . . . (*Pensees*, Lafuma 91). Why, if evolutionary theory is really true — that we are all products of meaningless, undirected forces in a universe without God, do evolutionists care whether everyone believes that or not? Why get so exercised when some poor, meaningless animal tries to find meaning in his meaningless life? If our existence has no ultimate purpose, who cares who believes what? Specifically, why do scientists care so deeply—even so militantly—that everyone must give obeisance to their ideology? Fear of theocracy, you say? More likely fear of loss of respect for their lives and purpose. But if life is meaningless, why care? "Oh, but we create meaning that matters." And the meaning they create is—? That life is meaningless. Wow.

2072. Imagination bridges the gap between desire and reality. As Pascal says, imagination produces in seconds a greater satisfaction than reason can offer in years.

2073. As we drive on a long journey, why do we concentrate on the boring road instead of the beautiful clouds?

2074. Why We Need Thinking Training #1.

Is the conclusion of this hypothetical syllogism valid or invalid? Explain.

If this secret message contains the code phrase, "Pet the Dog," then the message is authentic and was sent by our operative. However, the message does not contain the phrase, "Pet the Dog," but instead has the secret code phrase, "Eat the apricot." Therefore, the message is not authentic.

2075. Why We Need Thinking Training #2.

Is the conclusion of this hypothetical syllogism valid or invalid? Explain.

If this warehouse is run by the Zambini mob, then we will find illegal drugs here. And look, stacks of cocaine, heroin, and unlabeled amphetamines. So, we can conclude that this warehouse is indeed run by the Zambini mob. There is plentiful evidence.

2076. Why We Need Thinking Training #3.

Is the conclusion of this hypothetical syllogism valid or invalid? Explain.

There are only two possibilities for the electrical short and subsequent fire. Either rats got into the wiring and chewed the insulation off until the wires shorted out, or the wiring was installed defectively and contrary to code. Oh, look. Rat pellets and some rat fur. Well rats must have caused the short and the fire, so we can conclude that a bad wiring job was not the cause.

Answer to Glimmering 2074. Invalid. The argument commits the fallacy of Denying the Antecedent. When the premise of the argument is denied, the argument must stop. "Pet the Dog" might be an alternate authentication phrase.

Answer to Glimmering 2075. Invalid. The fallacy is Affirming the Consequent. Someone else might own the warehouse full of drugs.

Answer to Glimmering 2076. Invalid. The fallacy is Affirming a Disjunct. Both situations (rats and bad wiring) could have existed together.

2077. A History Lesson.
"So, how would you define 'history'?"
"That's easy. History is an account of what happened."
"But no one could give an account of everything that happened."
"Okay, then, history is an account of selected events that happened."
"But if historical events took place in the past, how can we be sure they actually occurred?"
"Okay, then, history is an account of selected events that the historian believes to have happened."
"You say, 'account.' Isn't there some judgment involved about what the events mean? Don't accounts differ?"
"Fine. Then history is an interpretation of selected events the historian believes to have happened."
"But why does he select and present just those events?"

"History is an interpretation of selected events the historian believes to have happened, chosen to support the historian's point of view."

"What's 'point of view'?"

"The argument the historian is advancing about the meaning of the historical events, his ideology, his worldview."

"Conclusion?"

"History is a little less objective than I thought."

2078. If you have ever wondered why the postmodernists are always talking about narrative, as in, "According to the company's narrative, the defect was unknown until three months ago," that's because narrative — telling a story — is the mechanism of persuasion today. Arguments based on evidence or logical connections are not used very much now simply because first, fewer people understand them; second, many people are suspicious of them; and third, stories are a lot more compelling.

Fewer people understand them. Ask a friend to explain syllogisms to you, or to give you an example of the fallacy of accident or affirming the consequent. Unless your friend is an attorney, you might get a blank look. So what? People aren't likely to respond to arguments they can't parse. As mentioned above in Glimmering 2021, the cartoon character Calvin once made a comment to the effect that if he couldn't understand something in five seconds, he didn't care about it.

Thanks to the pomos, who have "problematized reason," logical appeals are viewed with contempt and hostility by lots of people, especially college students. Another comic strip character, whom I have now forgotten, once remarked that reason was "thought control." Once again, those who cannot see the logical fallacies in arguments that draw conclusions they don't like — or who feel oppressed by properly valid logical arguments they don't like — attack the messenger and reject that sort of reasoning altogether. I recall once again a scene from a comedy movie (very roughly paraphrased from long-term memory):

"How can we deal with these people? They will stop at nothing."

"If they will stop at nothing, then if we do nothing, they will stop."

"What? That's preposterous."

"Please show the fallacy."

But the important point is that stories are much more compelling than reasons. Stories mount an argument or frame a moral proposition with all the power of vicarious engagement. We feel along with the characters, experience their issues and discover their successes or failures and the actions they took or decisions they made that brought them success or failure. Samuel Johnson (*Rambler* No. 4, March 31, 1750) has an interesting take on the power of fiction. He says that the verisimilitude of novels (just then being invented) makes them potentially dangerous because readers who have little life experience will be likely "to regulate their own practices" by imitating the fictional examples when confronted with similar situations. Stories, especially in the form of video, but also even in the form of a narrated anecdote, can be intensely compelling.

So, since narratives are more effective than evidence or reasons, and since Big Data is too complex for the ordinary person to figure out, the tale has replaced the head. As a result, business books are increasingly written in novel-like fashion, and those who can tell stories about events are heeded more than those who have only facts. The affective is more effective.

2079. So, what about using stories to persuade? Good or bad?

The good is that stories allow an idea or concept to be rendered in understandable, every day, concrete terms that allow the mind to form pictures, follow a linear plot, and gain easier insight into a situation than would be possible with mere pronouncements of wisdom. And, of course, stories are just more interesting than dry philosophy.

The usefulness and impact of stories for teaching or persuasion is not exactly new. Remember Aesop's *Fables*, stories told by the Sufi, Chinese stories such as the *Celebrated Cases of Judge Dee*, and the parables told by Jesus. A well-liked book is *Chinese*

Fairy Tales and Fantasies, translated by Moss Roberts (Pantheon, 1979).

Stories have immediate appeal. For making an impactful presentation of philosophy, they work very well. And that is also the down side. Stories appear to be representing reality as it is or has occurred. A character gets into difficulty or faces a problem, engages in a strategy to solve it, and comes out a winner (or sometimes, a loser). Stories appeal directly to the emotions. And therein lies the problem. The emotions are much more easily deceived and manipulated than the reason. Sometimes the affective is too effective.

This fact, by the way, explains why some of those who write history make sure that their narrative (there's that word again) presents evidence for the truth of their ideology. History is often presented in the form of a series of narratives — stories — and each one can be spun to favor the writer's preferred interpretation.

2080. One more note on story. Constructing a story from pieces of evidence is the principal way detectives solve crimes. Stories organize the facts of the situation and provide understanding. The story is incomplete but often leads to conclusions that reveal other clues or even the answers.

The broken window, the missing door key, the cigarette butt on the floor, the fact that the homeowner doesn't smoke, the size 12 shoe print, etc., all are combined to create a probabilistic story about what happened and who the likely perpetrator was.

2081. Have you noticed that words that used to describe the normal in an acceptable way have now taken on negative connotations? Anything described as "adequate" is thought of as inferior.

"How do you like your new car?"

"Oh, it's adequate."

"Got a lemon, huh?"

We are led down the path by these terms.

"Brake service special, $79 per axle."

"I'll take your brake special."

"Well, that includes only Standard brake pads."

"So they aren't very good?"

"Well, we recommend the Superior pads."

"How much extra are they?"

"$30. But if your daughter is going to drive this car, why not get the Premium pads?"

"Okay."

"Right. So that's $129 per axle."

Or what about those automatic car wash machines? "Press 1 for Regular Wash, 2 for Deluxe Wash, 3 for Superior Wash, 4 for Ultimate wash."

We are, as Samuel Johnson might have phrased it, in a culture of "exaggeratory declamation," where hyperbole is the norm, and you must amplify from there on up if you are to express enthusiasm for anything.

2082. The deeper you look, the more value you find.

2083. A house is built into a home one kind word at a time.

2084. "Let your one delight and refreshment be to pass from one service to the community to another, with God ever in mind" (Marcus Aurelius, *Meditations* 6.7).

2085. There is no stable and enduring place to stand in the present. We all stand on little chunks of ice in a stormy sea. Yesterday, we gloried in that cell phone or that car and we wanted it to last forever and be an anchor in our lives. But now the new phone and the new car are available, and we want to move on.

2086. One of the things that irritates me substantially is the news or panel-style program where three or four people do nothing but interrupt and talk over each other, jumping on half a sentence spoken by someone they disagree with. A similar kind of disrespectful, instant judgment behavior is increasingly common in our ordinary social interactions.

Suppose we are in a small group and someone says, "Confucius made a significant contribution to Western civilization." Someone else in the group is likely to smirk and step in immediately with, "You mean Eastern civilization. Confucius was Chinese." Or perhaps simply, "Hellooo! Confucius was Chinese you know. From the East, not the West."

A polite audience would have simply waited for elaboration, or perhaps prompted, "In what way?" And here the answer could have been that the speaker thought the Latin translation of the *Analects* that was introduced into Europe in 1687 was influential for its views about the desired behavior of the gentleman.

Too often we jump all over someone's statement before we even know what they are talking about, assuming that we know what they mean. It's also interesting that, since criticism is valued above agreement (because it supposedly shows better analysis or keener insight), hardly anyone interrupts with, "That's very true," or "I really agree." Instead, it's, "That's wrong," or "You don't know what you're talking about," or even, "But that doesn't take into account the price of Lima beans in Australia."

If we were really curious in conversation rather than interested only in "talking for victory," we would encourage those talking to elaborate, specify, exemplify, and delineate their views instead of cutting them off before we know what their views really are. We would seek first to understand. And to understand them, we should let them talk for a while before we make a comment.

2087. Blaise Pascal says that "man wants to be happy and to be assured of some truth" (Lafuma 123). Strange thing about that. It's true even in today's relativistic, postmodern world.

Note how people who argue that there is no such thing as truth (or Truth), that there are many "truths," that our minds cannot know truth but only the epiphenomena of our brain chemistry—all are adamant, even outrageously aggressive—to support and defend the truth of those assertions. Of course, such claims are embarrassed by self-referential absurdity — self-contradiction — but nevertheless it demonstrates how earnestly and how strongly committed so many of these people are.

But Pascal is right. We want assurance of some truth. This explains why so many try so hard to locate evidence for the rightness of their beliefs, whether social, moral, scientific, philosophical, or religious.

"We have no free will or free thought," someone says. "Everything we say or do or think is predetermined."

"So, then, why are you telling me this?"

"To convince you."

"But if all our thoughts and ideas are predetermined, there can be no such thing as a change of mind independent of predetermined changes. Argument, reason, and conviction are illusions. But I guess your need to try to convince me is predetermined, so you can't help yourself. And unfortunately, I'm predetermined not to believe you."

The same comments could be made about man's search for meaning. Some people argue that life has no meaning, and they are earnest to convince everyone else that such is the truth. But if life has no meaning, why bother? Why care? Nor does it help much to say, "Well, we as individuals or societies construct socially agreed upon meanings." Doesn't that sound a bit arbitrary? As the saying is, In a land without steak, cardboard is steak. If the real thing is denied or missing, a counterfeit will be invented.

2088. Suppose I show you some object and say, "This is a flurnitron. Isn't it perfect?" What would you answer?

That's right, you'd ask, "What does it do?" or more skeptically, "What is it supposed to do?" But in either case, you want to know its purpose — why it exists — because you cannot tell whether something is good or bad until you know its purpose and how well it fulfills that purpose.

Thus, your first question about the flurnitron would not be, "How much electricity does it use?" or "Is it made of steel?" or the like. Until you know what it was designed to do, those questions are irrelevant. What we value in an object is not what it's made of or how it's powered—until we understand the relevance of those answers.

So, when we think about our own lives, before we can answer, "Am I a good person, living a worthwhile life?" we have to determine the purpose for which we exist. For if everything exists to fulfill its purpose, we can evaluate things, including ourselves, based on how well they fulfill their reason for being.

If, as the marketers seem to imply, our purpose is to consume products and spend money, then many of us do that really well. If we have no purpose, then it doesn't matter what we do, and there is no estimation of fitness to purpose possible. But if we do have a purpose—to serve God who created us and to be his hands in serving his children—our fellow human beings—then we can adjust our lives to align ever more closely with that purpose. That purpose, to steal a few words from Shakespeare, "is the star to every wandering bark," providing a fixed focal point for our behavior, a star in the heavens by which we can navigate through the wanderings of daily life.

Therefore, we can see that finding the best steak in town or memorizing the names of all the players on a favorite professional sports team or driving the fanciest car on the block are activities that do not really speak to our purpose. I myself am rather embarrassed to think of the highly tangential nature of many of my own pursuits. These comments, then, are addressed to me.

2089. Some people object to being reminded of "obvious" truths, such as are found in proverbs: "A house is turned into a home one kind word at a time." "Knowledge without understanding is a flashlight without a battery." But consider. First, we live in such an overwhelming information tsunami that unless we repeat common truths, they will sink into oblivion under the wash of everything else.

And often that "everything else" includes misinformation, disinformation, lies, half-truths, urban legends, myths, conspiracy theories, faked experiments, cooked data, ideological fabri-cations, spin doctor treatments, invented narratives, and mis-understandings, not to mention simple errors, superfluities, and data smog.

In a word, lies are repeated endlessly and constantly. Lies are shouted from the housetops and pronounced solemnly by pundits and academics with many letters after their names. Lies drone on and on—and, as the saying is, lies repeated often enough become the truth.

So, if we don't repeat true truth, it has no possibility of over-coming the lies. Error will reign and people will congratulate each other that "the controversy has finally been settled" be-cause no one now opposes the ever-repeated wrong conclusion or bad idea.

2090. "The only palliative [to the blindness of shared assump-tions in the modern world] is to keep the clean sea breeze of the centuries blowing through our minds, and this can be done only by reading old books." —C. S. Lewis

"Truth that triumphs over all things . . . seems to remain more usefully and to fructify to greater profit in books. For the meaning of the voice perishes with the sound; truth latent in the mind is wisdom that is hid and treasure that is not seen; but truth which shines forth in books desires to manifest itself to every impressionable sense." —Richard de Bury, *Philobiblon*, circa 1345

Lewis was thinking about really old books, such as those of the ancient Greek philosophers, or even somewhat old books, such as *Philobiblon*, quoted above, but even slightly non-contemporary books can sometimes shed light on the blindness of groupthink that seems to possess every era to some extent. I have in my library an introduction to American literature text-book from the early twentieth century, listing Herman Melville in an appendix as an "also wrote," while featuring now-neglected writers such as Booth Tarkington.

An interesting example of a not-so-old book about the sources of modern and postmodern times is *The Revolt Against*

Reason by Arnold Lunn. It was published in England in 1950 and by Sheed and Ward in New York in 1951. (You can still get copies, though. Just google the author and title.) Here is some food for thought drawn from Mr. Lunn:

"[T]he success and enduring influence of a systematic construction of falsehood depends very largely on *inexact* terminology" (3). Consider how squishy and inexact are many of the terms over which bitter debates are fought: climate change, evolution, social justice, reason and faith, knowledge versus belief, what is fair, legislating morality. And of course we won't even go to love, need, fairness, and so on. When you can use a term, knowing that your definition is different from that of your hearer or reader, but allowing them to assume that their definition is yours too, then all kinds of manipulation are possible.

Thinking about the anti-rationalism of postmodernism, we can find a relevant remark in Lunn: "The revolt against reason is in its ultimate essence the revolt of unbridled individualism against an external and objective code" (50). Reason favors objective measurements, which rely on a code of values and truth, which implies accountability external to oneself. The revolt against reason produces subjectivity of measurement, an existentialist operating method, and a solipsistic view of living for oneself.

But I should let Lunn continue: "The great leaders of this revolt have all been wishful thinkers who contrived to believe that reality could be forced to conform to the pattern shaped by their ambition or by their lust" (59). Doesn't that nicely describe the utopianism of so many of our elites?

2091. To an extent, the so-called culture wars represent a battle between authority and the self, or in starkest relief, between pride and humility, where humility is defined as the recognition of a higher authority than oneself. The message of classical Western philosophy is that happiness comes through the submission of personal desire and appetite to reason, a reason informed by transcendent, objective reality and absolute truth. In other words, self-control for the sake of personal happiness and the social contract is the path to the Good.

2092. Why is it that whenever an airliner crashes, the media announce that investigators are searching for the "black boxes" to help them determine the cause of the crash—this, when the "black boxes" have been painted orange for, what, maybe 50 years? Why don't the media simply say that investigators are searching for the "orange boxes" or better, the "data and voice recorders" to help them determine the cause of the crash?

Similarly, since the Richter scale was replaced by the Moment Magnitude scale in the 1970s, why do the media still refer to the Richter scale whenever we have an earthquake?

Someone opined that people are comfortable with familiar concepts. The logical conclusion to be drawn from that is that the news should tell people something they already know. That's an odd view of the news. Nevertheless, many journalists seem to write stories from templates, making the new details conform to the familiar script.

If a story is written as the accumulation of facts prescribes, rather than forced to grow on the trellis of stereotype, will the readers or viewers have to learn something new?

Is the news-consuming public really like junior high school students who stop reading something just because they came up on a word they don't know?

2093. Hollywood has a conundrum. Filmmakers want to show rebellion, opposition to authority, extreme individualism, the joy of breaking rules and throwing off moral constraints, yet at the same time make films that display the possibility and power of redemption, the second chance, the saving grace.

How do they do that? Christ showed the possibility and the power of redemption through obedience. Hollywood shows the possibility and the power of redemption through transgression. Whereas Christ was obedient to fulfill the law, to accede to the Father's will, and even to submit to Roman and Sanhedrin authority, Hollywood promotes characters who break laws, violate ethics, lie, cheat, steal, kill, seduce, trick—pretty much break all ten commandments—all for the higher good of saving the girl, the victim, or the world. Many times the character is an "ex" bad guy, given a chance to do something good to make amends for past crimes, which at the end of the movie are forgiven. "If you do wrong for the right reason, the wrongs you did for the wrong reason will be forgiven" (popular contemporary theology).

2094. Eat at Joe's Diner.

"Your order, sir?"

"Yes. I'd like scrambled eggs on toast and a cup of coffee with cream and sugar."

"Got it. [shouting to the kitchen] "Adam and Eve on a raft. Shipwreck 'em with a sandy blonde."

Classic American diner lingo shows us that any job can be made fun, creative, and entertaining. Being a waitress or short-order cook in a diner probably isn't the most rewarding employment most of us could think of, but the work is honest and honorable.

"What's your stomach telling you, Ma'am?"

"I'd like the toasted English muffins and three eggs."

"You've got it. [to the kitchen] Burn the Brits with a crowd of cackleberries."

The fact is, we love neologizing and creating metaphorical equivalents for ordinary things. The more creativity and novelty we can bring to our activities, the happier we are.

"Tell it like it is, honey."

"Gimme a well done burger with ketchup and onions."

"Of course. [to the kitchen] One hockey puck, paint it red and put a rose on it."

2095. Whatever state of life we are in, we have unfulfilled desires, leading to dissatisfaction. When we fulfill those desires, we might be briefly satisfied, but the very fulfillment moves us to a new state of life, in which we have new, unfulfilled desires.

2096. A major problem with the news media is that complex issues get compressed into little sound bites and short presentations, often framed in a script that the journalistic community has adopted.

When there is a multiple shooting somewhere, the media dusts off its gun control script. Not too long ago there was a mass stabbing, but the media, having no "knife-control script," couldn't advocate tighter laws for knife ownership.

To the point:

Discussion of global warming or its much more vague but newly popular alternate concept, climate change, seems too often to conflate, bypass, and ignore a number of questions relevant to the discussion. Here, then, are just a few:

1. Is global warming occurring? That is, Is the climate getting hotter permanently, not just on the rising part of a cyclical graph?

2. If the answer to 1 is Yes, then what is the base measurement? In other words, if the earth is getting warmer, since when? Since 2000? (It seems that global temps haven't changed since then.) Since 1950? Since 1850? Since 1500? Since 1000?

3. If the earth has warmed since the named baseline, is that an absolute rise or a rise on a larger cyclical pattern of rising and falling global temperatures? Do the Medieval Warm Period or the Little Ice Age suggest a cyclical pattern?

4. How can we know whether the earth is warming or not? This is a question about measurement reliability.

• How reliable are old data, such as the temperatures recorded a hundred, two hundred or more years ago?

• How reliable are new data? Was a parking lot installed around a measuring station that used to be surrounded by grass or trees?

• How representative are the data? Inductive leaps can be problematic.

5. If global warming is occurring indeed, is that bad? During the age of the dinosaurs, the planet must have been pretty lush to leave behind enough plant matter to give us all the oil we

now have. And anyone who has raised vegetables or fruit in a hot house knows what huge and delicious produce results.

6. How can we know if global warming will, on balance, be a negative? Sea levels could rise, but starvation might be almost eliminated because of a crop-friendly atmosphere.

7. If global warming is occurring and it is bad, what is causing it? It's popular to throw a dart at human activity such as burning fossil fuels, but is that really the cause? Sunspot activity has also been proposed. Is there a suite of causes and not just one?

8. If global warming is occurring and it's bad and humans are causing it, what can be done to ameliorate it? It's interesting here that some solutions are more popular among the chattering classes than others. Solar power? Got it! (But it doesn't work so well at night.) Nuclear power? Not so much. Wind power? Yay. (But those wind generators slice and dice endangered bird species. Guess you have to choose your eco-priorities.)

9. If you have developed a list of what can be done, then what should be done? Who's going to pay for it? Why them?

10. What if nations don't cooperate? Third world nations just now ramping up their energy needs and production are unlikely to shut down their power plants.

Whatever your position on global warming or climate change, I think it will be helpful to consider some of these questions as entry points for fresh thinking and analysis.

2097. Why do some people get so upset when you disagree with them?

Blaise Pascal references a question by Epictetus: "Why are we not angry if someone says that we have a headache and are angry if someone says that we are arguing badly or making a bad choice?" Pascal's answer is that we are certain that we don't have a headache, but we're not sure that we aren't arguing badly or making a bad choice. Indeed, it seems that the more some people fear that they might be wrong, the angrier they are.

It's been noted that disagreement and argument, rather than bringing about compromise or a search for common ground, actually polarizes the contestants further, making them argue in even more extreme terms.

To return to our initial question: Why do some people get angry when they face opposition or challenge to their assertions? Here are some possible reasons.

1. They are upset by what they view as error. Having perhaps arrived at their stated conclusion only after long and hard thought, or having adopted a position that seems to be the only one that corresponds to their other, deepest beliefs, to hear someone contradict them is a source of frustration, as if they are afraid that the long set of reasons and arguments must be revisited, to their distress.

People who invoke ideas such as "settled science" or "historical fact" are sometimes hoping to quash a rehash of what they consider long-ago-concluded arguments.

2. They feel threatened. Ideas and beliefs are deeply interconnected and interdependent, and to challenge one can imply a weakness — or even a failure — in the whole intellectual system or worldview of the person being challenged.

3. The introduction of a contrary fact or claim upsets some people because they believe it will result in confusion that would require a long discussion to clarify. Speakers (professors, presenters, etc.) who are attempting to present the basic ideas or arguments about a topic sometimes react with heat when one of their audience members raises a conflicting idea or an idea that shows the speaker's thesis to be oversimplified.

4. The disagreement is a misunderstanding, which, to the angry presenter's mind, shows a lack of understanding, knowledge, or expertise on the part of the objector. For example:

Presenter: "The circumstantial evidence convincingly points to the guilt of Frimpson."

Objector: "But Frimpson passed a lie detector test. He said he didn't do it and he passed the test. He therefore wasn't lying. He was telling the truth."

Here, the presenter gets upset because he perhaps was lecturing to an audience he assumed knew that passing a lie detector test is not an absolute guarantee of truthfulness. He is frustrated with the objector because a lengthy explanation would derail the presentation.

5. For people who are advancing a point close to their strongly held ideological framework, anyone who disagrees with their position is not just wrong, but is evil. Such people commonly see many political, social, and economic ideas in moral terms of good (their position) versus evil (their opponents' position).

All of these reasons should be considered in light of Pascal's Headache. Is the degree of anger commensurate with their degree of self-doubt?

2098. I had not eaten a Hostess Twinkie in at least 20 years. But recently, on an impulse, I bought a box, just to see what they tasted like, and to see how familiar they would be. In spite of intervening years and the change in ownership of the Hostess Bakeries, were they the same, familiar treat of my youth?

No. The Twinkies in the box of 10 seemed smaller and more carelessly made than the Twinkies of my childhood. They didn't taste the same, and even the texture seemed less fluffy. The cake was more dense than I remembered.

Now, it has often been remarked that things we revisit after many years of absence seem smaller than we remember simply because we were smaller as children and now that we are grown, the house or uncle Fred seem to have shrunk by comparison.

Similarly, as kids, our taste buds were working much better than they do today, as we enter or near our retirement years.

The counterargument, though, is that while brand names are created to provide a familiar, dependable, known-quantity product, behind the scenes is a lot more variability than many consumers understand. For example, I once looked up the formula for a very popular, national brand of laundry detergent. (This was in a poison-control book to aid doctors when a kid had eaten a mouthful or two.) The formula was like this:

"Depending on region, ingredient cost, and availability, X laundry detergent contains:
- [Name of one ingredient] 15% - 30%
- [Name of another ingredient] 20%-45%
- [Name of another ingredient] 8%-12%
- [Name of another ingredient] 13%-28%"

In other words, the next time you buy a box of the same detergent, you might not be buying a box of the same detergent.

Another issue is the brand name itself. Remember Polaroid? Established brand, good reputation, trusted, etc. But the Polaroid camera and film company went bankrupt. However, the Polaroid name was licensed to various manufacturers, resulting in Polaroid-branded batteries, light bulbs, DVD players, and so on.

Similarly, Ipana toothpaste was a popular brand in the 1960s, but lost market share and was stopped in the 1970s. Then a few years ago, the brand name was licensed by another company and Ipana came back on the market. But was it the same toothpaste or a modern formulation?

Also similarly, Emerson radio ceased manufacture of DVD players, TVs, and so on, but licensed its brand name to Funai.

Finally, many manufacturers have their products designed and actually made by third parties or operate plants in foreign countries. Check the labels: That quintessential Japanese manufacturer, Sony, now markets products made in China.

So are Twinkies really different, or am I just different? Food for thought; something to chew on.

2099. I just bought a new flashlight. The package says in a prominent, upper right corner, "Warning: Do Not Install Batteries Backwards." In the "Important Safety Instructions" inside the package, we read, "Warning: . . . 1. Do not install the batteries backwards. Follow the + and - symbols as shown in the instructions. . . . Save these instructions." Now, unless there is another instruction sheet missing from my package, there is no other set of instructions about battery installation.

So, I look all over the flashlight, including inside the cap and on the inside back, but can't see any. Then, as a last effort, I shine another flashlight into the battery chambers where there are some tiny + and - diagrams inside each tube.

It would be far better to put on the package and on the instruction sheet, "Be sure to install all the batteries with the + end toward the front of the flashlight."

The point then is, instead or scaring people by warning them about the (unspecified) dire consequences of doing something incorrectly, just tell them that it's important to do the task correctly — and tell them what that means.

2100. For a number of years now, pundits have remarked on the diminishing attention span of our culture, driven, it is averred, by the visual media: TV, film, MTV, TV commercials, TV news with its terse news bites, and so on. Now, however, some are also thinking about a diminishment in our ability to think long or deeply about anything.

Writers like Nicholas Carr, whose article, "Is Google Making Us Stupid?" suggests this phenomenon with concern, and David Weinberger, whose book, *Too Big to Know*, suggests that long, deep thinking provided by reading a book is pretty much a historical artifact, made me think that learning itself (such as the university experience) is tracking along these lines.

We used to be able to sit down with a lengthy book and read it carefully and thoughtfully. That last sentence probably lets you know how old I am, for many of today's college students won't know what I'm talking about. And that's the problem. Now, and this is true of me, too, if we attempt to engage a lengthy book or argument, a little voice (or at least, a sense of urgency) starts to irritate us with, "There are many other things to do today. You don't have time for this. Hurry and get the gist. Skim. Glance. Skip. Skirt. Read the summary."

The fact that we can surf from one place on the Web to another in just the blink of an eye (or if you have a crummy Internet connection, in just minutes), turns us into information channel-surfers. Get an answer fast and move on. But this is not good.

If we become mere information skimmers, knowledge hoppers, data browsers, staccato thinkers, who are unable to read, understand, and process an extended argument, we are likely to be much more open to the information con men and women, who know very well how to select details, slant the facts, omit what works against them and double up on what suits their case. We will be much, much more vulnerable to emotional appeals because the emotions can be engaged quickly and with fewer words that are required to engage the brain deeply.

And consider:

• Catching the gist of an idea is not the same as understanding it.

• Skimmers of gist are able to pay attention only to denotation — the obvious meaning of the words used. But those who create the message are able to exploit connotation — the emotional and sometimes judgmental meaning of words, thus manipulating the reader unaware.

• Deep thinking requires deep reading.

• Good decision making must be thoughtful and circumspect, and that cannot be accomplished by soda straw quick sipping off the Web.

2101. **An Analogy.**

Guy: "Look at that duck over there. I say 'duck' because it has webbed feet and waddles like a duck."

Observer 1: "It hasn't quacked like a duck, so I don't think it's a duck."

Observer 2: " Yeah, it hasn't quacked, so I don't think it's a duck, either. I think it's a chicken."

More observers arrive. Guy to new observers: "Look at that duck over there."

Observer 2 to Observers 3 and 4: "We don't think it's a duck. It doesn't quack like a duck."

Observers 3 and 4: "Yeah, we've looked at it and we haven't heard it quack either."

Guy, at the veterinarian's office, to the vet: "Can you take care of the duck?"

Vet: "I don't think it's a duck."

Guy: "But it has webbed feet and waddles like a duck and has a bill like a duck."

Vet: "Strange deformities for a chicken, huh?"

Next day.

Vet: "Oh, look. The animal jumped into the pond and started quacking as it paddled around. It's a duck."

Sometimes you need to get more than a second opinion. Sometimes you need a third or fourth opinion, especially if you have good reason to believe that the conclusions of others are just not right, because they are based on partial, incorrect, or distorted information. Quick, pigeonhole diagnoses should always be viewed with caution.

2102. What separates a really good stage or screen actor from those who come across as somehow wooden or fake is the simple fact that good actors don't act. The high school kid in the play acts the way he or she thinks (1) the character would act and (2) the way actors should act. The really good professional actor, instead of pretending to be like the assigned character, becomes that character, embodies that character. The wooden actor imitates another person while the good actor develops an imaginative identification with the assigned character and lives the role.

So, here's my Acting in One Lesson advice: Stop acting like the character, stop pretending to be the character, stop talking as the character would, and instead, let yourself become that character. And paradoxically enough, to do that you have to reference yourself. Don't ask, "How would this character say that?" but, "How would I say that if I were in that situation and had those values or options?" (For a bad character, for example, ask, "What would I say if I were a liar or confidence artist or thug?") If you want to be natural, you need to imitate the most natural person you know — yourself.

In a word then: Aspiring actors: You can become a good actor by becoming the character, by putting yourself into the character in the situation. Connect yourself to the dramatic situation, not just to the dialog. I hope that makes sense.

2103. Why Do We Brag? And What Do We Brag About?

Bragging or boasting is often done on the basis of mere association. That is, we have some peripheral connection with something that others admire, so we brag about it. "My team won! [therefore, I am great, too!]" Um, what, exactly, did you have to do with that performance? You assisted in that win and deserve credit how? You supported the team by watching them on TV and drinking beer? Or maybe you even bought a ticket? Wow, that is so amazing. Why, you practically won that game all by yourself.

"I drive a Mercedes! [therefore, I am impressive, just like M Benz!]" Um, the fact that you could buy or lease a Mercedes makes you impressive how? Shows that you have money? What year is the car? "Um, 1992. But I paid only $1700 for it! I got a super deal. So, I can brag about being shrewd!" Yeah, but save your money for that $4500 transmission repair coming up. Marketers say that the car you drive is a personal statement about who you are, an extension of your personality. I don't know. What if your lips say Lamborghini, but your wallet says Ford Fiesta?

"Well, my kid got kid of the month at school." And that reflects on your wonderfulness how? That you are a great parent somehow responsible for your kid's performance? Now, if you brag on behalf of your child rather than yourself, then you are on firmer ground.

"Well, the fact is, I'm [choose one: smart, rich, good looking, famous, influential]." This brings us to today's word of wisdom: "What do you have that you did not receive? And if you did receive it, why do you boast as if you had not received it?" (1 Corinthians 4:7b).

All of our talents, abilities, and personal attributes are a gift from God, so boasting about them is ridiculous. "I'm so great because I'm cute" doesn't cut the mustard of logic. You might boast about your parents' DNA that let you be cute, but that's a gift from the Lord via your parents.

Do we have so little genuine, humble self-esteem that we have to turn to loose associations with people and things that our short-attention-span peers find remarkable?

Let's see, what can I brag about? I once met a guy who knew the third cousin of a woman who shook hands with a guy who owned a store where a man shopped who had his hair cut by a barber who heard that the friend of a friend of a customer knew someone who once met Elvis Presley. I am soooo stoked!!! Me and Elvis! We're just like this!

Do you admire me now?

2104. It's not that we don't know the truth. We do, and we hate it. We hate the truth because it calls our rebellious hearts to obedience. And obedience implies submission to something (Someone) higher than ourselves. We "suppress the truth in un-righteousness" (Romans 1:18) in order to escape its implications, its claims on our lives.

2105. What's Wrong with Adolescents?

They are in the process of individuation, finding out who they are. They realize now that they are different from their parents. They want to be unique, powerful, and important — their own person. And, of course, they have no idea how to do that. So they take their individualism cues from peers (who also have no clue) and from popular culture, that teaches rebellion in whatever way is currently making money.

The reality is that, like most people, most adolescents are not really unique, can't be trusted with very much power, and aren't important to the world because they haven't served the world yet.

Nor do they see the irony in their conformist rebellion, where they dress and act alike as a statement of individualism.

Eventually, most adolescents grow up. But as adults, they still want to be unique, powerful, and important. Like adolescents, these adults have never gotten control of their ego.

2106. I wonder if the key to raising children through adolescence successfully is simply to help take the mundanity out of their existence. Give them a purpose and a goal that excites them.

2107. Pain is the stylus that writes meaning into our lives. Pain keeps us from loving this life too much. Pain, suffering and death remind us that life is serious and purposeful, not a place for endless self-indulgence or entertainment. Pain, suffering, and death remind us of the seriousness of sin. Sin implies guilt, and we run from guilt by denying sin — until we meet the consequences.

2108. God is not in a hurry. He is patient. God is a big picture person. He cares about specifics, each one of us as individuals, but he's more concerned with all of humanity.

2109. Why can't we see what's going on? The secularization of America was a deliberate process, and the process continues, intentionally, deliberately, and we sit back and say, "Well, times are changing."

2110. If evolution were true, we wouldn't need to search the fossil record for transitional forms. Transitional forms would be everywhere living around us, filling niches or simply in the process of gradually being filtered out of the gene pool. Instead of individually distinct animals, there would be a mass of half this and half that, one-quarter this and three-quarters that.

2111. The marketing of evolution. Part One, saturate the information environment promoting it. Desensitize people by proclaiming it everywhere. Note that most of the nonfiction books I read mention evolution favorably within the first 20 or 30 pages.

Part Two, jam the opposition. Object to every statement of criticism or doubt, every request for a hearing of contrary evidence. Label opponents as anti-science, pseudo-science, uneducated, extremists, religious fanatics. Part Three, conquer by showing that ordinary people just like them accept evolutionary theory as their origins model.

2112. We know that the genome of animals contains spectacular variant power. Hatch a bunch of Galapagos finches and you'll get several different beak sizes. The variation is limited, of course, and returns to a default once the environmental selectors disappear or change. DDT resistant flies die out and non-resistant flies take over again once the DDT is removed.

That is remarkable enough, but what about the dynamic environmental response that individual plants can show? From the seedling on up, plants produce a systematic response to temperature, humidity, soil moisture, nutrients, and sunlight. Plant a radish seed in the ground outdoors in the summer and get leaves an inch across and radishes an inch in diameter. Plant the same seeds instead in a hot house and get leaves five inches across and radishes two inches in diameter. This is a built-in response to environmental conditions. Explaining how that system could have arisen one accidental mutation at a time seems impossible to me.

2113. Love means respecting your wife's partnership; respect means loving your husband's leadership.

2114. We are not now who we were, nor who we will be.

2115. The road to sanctification is poorly paved.

2116. **Levels of Moral Integrity.**

Level 1. You avoid doing evil because you lack opportunity or lack the ability to do it.

Level 2. You avoid doing evil because you think you might get hurt or it will cost you too much.

Level 3. You avoid doing evil because it's illegal and you are afraid you will be caught and punished.

Level 4. You avoid doing evil because you don't want your friends to look down on you.

Level 5. You avoid doing evil because you don't want society to look down on you.

Level 6. You avoid doing evil because you believe it's wrong or immoral.

Level 7. You avoid doing evil because you don't want to do it.

2117. Second guessing God from a standpoint of limited human intelligence, knowledge, and understanding is quite presumptuous. (See Isaiah 55:9.) The question becomes, "Do you trust God or not?"

2118. What you have faith in determines the information sources you allow. Faith is a matter of trust in information sources (authority, senses, Scripture, etc.). If you have faith in reason, and know something about induction and syllogisms, then reason can be a source of information also. Reason is an information processing methodology that takes information from some source or sources and processes it in some manner. Reason can test information against one's knowledge base, against one's worldview, against the correspondence test of truth.

2119. Why Teaching Adults Is So Hard.
Wisdom from Samuel Johnson.

A. "What is new is opposed, because most are unwilling to be taught; and what is known is rejected, because it is not sufficiently considered, that men more frequently require to be reminded than informed. The learned are afraid to declare their opinion early, lest they should put their reputation at hazard; [and] the ignorant always imagine themselves giving some proof of delicacy, when they refuse to be pleased . . ." (*Rambler* 2).

B. "The task of an author is, either to teach what is not known, or to recommend known truths. . . . Either of these labours is very difficult, because, that they may not be fruitless, men must not only be persuaded of their errors, but reconciled to their guide: they must not only confess their ignorance, but, what is still less pleasing, must allow that he from whom they are to learn is more knowing than themselves" (*Rambler* 3).

2120. A quotation (wrongly, as it turns out) attributed to G. K. Chesterton is, "When a man stops believing in God, he doesn't believe in nothing. He believes in anything." Our current culture shows some evidence of this claim. We are disconnected from the basic truths of the Gospel, saturated by a secular worldview. Without absolute truth, we have novelty truth that changes according to those who have the cultural authority to declare truth. This includes the marketers. The marketers love relativism because it allows for the promotion of fads. The new, improved truth—or attitude—is available on a T-shirt for just $25.

Gotten rid of eternal truth and bored with the most recent new truth? Well, nature abhors a vacuum, so here's something to plug the gap. It might be tomorrow's whatever, but it's today's cool!

2121. Many people resist even the mildest challenges to their beliefs because of the perceived threat to their personal selves. Your worldview is not only what you believe; your worldview is who you are.

2122. **Principles of Hermeneutics.**

I've recently begun my fourth journey through the *Rambler* essays of Samuel Johnson, and it occurred to me that there is a great difference between simply reading something—such as a novel for enjoyment or a magazine for information or a textbook for an assignment—and reading for improvement.

It further occurred to me that reading for improvement tracks the three steps of hermeneutics (Biblical interpretation).

1. What does it say? This step is in common with ordinary reading. We want to comprehend the material, to grasp the writer's point. Understand the, the denotation and connotation of the vocabulary, the allusions and figurative language.

2. What does it mean? This step might be thought of as understanding in context, or as the larger significance of the work. As we read at this level, we always have the "so what?" in mind. What are the implications? This step shows we care about the ideas we are reading and are thinking about them and their role in the great conversation.

3. How does this apply to me? This last step takes the reading home to ourselves as we ask how it should affect, challenge, influence, or change the way we act, think, feel, and understand the world and our place in it.

Reading only for comprehension, so that you can do well on a test, limits the effect of the author-reader interaction to a simple, safe level. But if you want to grow wiser, better, happier, you must examine the ideas in the text at a higher step.

There is a saying, "We read because we find ourselves there, and we read because we don't find ourselves there." That is, we read in order to feel human, maybe normal, and to recognize our own feelings and thoughts, fears and hopes, ambitions and hesitations though those we read about (fiction or nonfiction). And we also read to escape from ourselves and our patterned lives, to move into the magical realms of story and interesting people, circumstances, challenges, and events.

To read well is to read through all three steps.

[October 21, 2014; age 64]

2123. Some people are afraid of making a decision because it means that every other choice will be unavailable. If you choose to take Highway 1, you can't take Highway 2. If you live in California and move to Chicago, the choice of going daily to a beach on the Pacific Ocean will no longer be available. However, making a decision also enables other decisions. If you do move to Chicago, the choice of going daily to Lake Michigan becomes available—a choice that was not available when you lived in California. Every decision takes place on a matrix or network, where every choice closes off and opens up other choices.

Now that I think of it, a look at electronic gates might help people to understand decision making a bit better. The gates of AND, OR, NOT, and NOR are useful, and for the more interested, XOR, XNOR, and NAND.

2124. How God works. Joseph is sold into slavery, and God blesses his master, Potiphar. Joseph is still a slave, but becomes a steward. Potiphar's wife lies about Joseph, and he ends up in jail. Genesis 39:21: "But the Lord was with Joseph and extended kindness to him, and gave him favor in the sight of the chief jailer." God doesn't interfere with the will of men and their cruelty and unfairness. But God can still bless the negative circumstances and soften the hearts of those around. The important thing to remember is that God can choose not to rescue us from negative circumstances or situations, but he can still bless us and use us in those circumstances or situations.

2125. Bookmarks help us keep track of where we are in the story. Without them, we would often repeat a chapter or two, having forgotten just where we left off. So it is with life. Without paying attention to where we are in our own story, we risk repeating ourselves, together with the painful lessons we have already worked through. Keep track so you won't have to live the same chapter over and over.

2126. ". . . let him judge for himself according to the sort of person he is at the time" (Pascal, *Pensees*, Lafuma 1). The judgments we make depend at least as much on who we are (at the time) as they do on the circumstances. How often do we hear a regretful, "Well, it seemed like a good idea at the time." Raw information or facts have to pass through our filters, processors, evaluators, and comparators before they get to our judgments.

"Just the facts, ma'am."

"Ha ha ha ha ha ha. Oh, detective, you're so funny."

[December 15, 2014; age 64]

2127. Whether sovereignly allowed or divinely appointed, every event passes through the hands of God to be shaped for a greater purpose.

2128. What is important today is what you will leave behind for tomorrow. You eat, you sleep, you sit idly in a chair. These things are not important. How you impact others in the future by helping or serving them today — that is everything.

2129. One of my favorite proverbs, from my own story, "The Strange Adventure," is, "Life is about meaning, not experience." But where does meaning come from? Experience is processed through a template of understanding to yield meaning.

2130. Knowing the truth sets you free. Knowing the opinions brings you insight and possibly conquest because opinion, not truth, rules the world.

[January 5, 2015; age 64]

2131. Politics is little more than a marketing campaign. The product is the politician, a platform, or a bill. To support it, slogans and buzzwords are created.

2132. **Lessons from the Consumer Electronics Show, 2015.**
    1. To get a long line of patient but eager people, offer a simple game with a pedestrian prize. You'd think the company had hired the Pied Piper.
    2. You can't unring a bell; but with a digital camera, you can untake a picture. However, you can't take a picture of something after you've left the area. So take lots of pictures and later on delete the ones you don't want.

3. How much are we willing to trust our own personal experiences over the opinion of the masses? For example, in my experience, those itty bity speakers sold to connect to laptops and smart phones all sound terrible. The treble is screechy, the midrange is muddy, and the bass is on vacation in another zip code. Yet these dinky ear assaults are everywhere, and the vendors act as it they are putting out fantastic sound.

4. Young women without a sturdy moral integrity or set of fixed values are most vulnerable to being exploited. (This comment was suggested by seeing a young woman wearing a T-shirt with the words, "Mount Something" promoting some product or other.)

5. "Like us or praise us on social media and we will give you a free T-shirt." (1) Isn't that bribery? You don't care whether the product is any good or not; you just want the shirt, so you Like the product. (2) Since all your connections on that social media network are soon informed that you have Liked the product, isn't that telling a mass lie to everyone? (3) Since the company doesn't seem to care whether or not you really like the product, but all they want is your Like, and they are willing to pay for your Like with a T-shirt or other item, doesn't that smack of prostitution?

6. Often the ostensible reason for something is not the real reason. Now some hotels are changing towels and sheets only on request for multi-day guests. The reason offered is that such a practice saves water and is therefore environmentally advantageous. However, the same hotels feature high-volume, water-wasting showerheads. These are the 15-gallon-per-minute type. The real reason not to change towels and sheets each day is to save the labor costs, both of making the beds and doing the laundry, and to save money on the washing and drying.

7. The way something works as described at a convention, expo, or even in a marketing meeting often differs from the way the item actually works. The obvious example that we encounter every day is the "easy open" package. This year, the hotel featured a tube of shower gel instead of a bar of soap. No doubt the marketers said something like, "It's so convenient; you just

squeeze out the amount you want into the palm of your hand." What they neglected to note is that, unless you are careful, when you release the pressure on the tube, it snaps back to its original shape, sucking the gel from your palm back into the tube.

8. When we are asked what seems to us to be an existential question about ourselves that seems to require that we justify our existence—or at least our presence—the temptation to exaggerate is nearly irresistible. We describe ourselves as a little bit better and more important than we actually are.

9. When sending someone to a convention from overseas or from several time zones away, it's a false economy not to allow an extra day for the attendee to recuperate and get over jet lag. This year, the Consumer Electronics Show boasted that 40,000 of the 180,000 attendees were from overseas. And we could easily believe that because there were Japanese, Chinese, and Koreans sleeping in every available place where they could relax. And those who couldn't sleep were likely much less alert than if they'd had an extra day to sleep to allow their minds and bodies to adjust to the new time zone.

10. When we see something that was previously outside our experience—that is, something new to us—its novelty helps us believe the claim of the promoter that it is unique. But herein lies the value of experience and research. The first vendor to present the pocket-sized recharger (mislabeled a jump starter) for an auto battery captures our attention and admiration. But then as we make our way through the 4 million square feet of exhibits, we encounter five or six more vendors hawking variants of the same item, all claiming uniqueness. That nifty, creative idea to make a rubber keyboard turns out to be an also-ran common item. It pays to do your research.

11. The new bait-and-switch.

"Here's a new amplified speaker. Isn't the sound great? Notice the bass coming from the unit. Solid performance."

"Well, the sound is good, all right, but it appears that you have 24 of those units connected together."

"Yes, but that's only because the expo hall is so big and filled with crowd noise."

So we look for a booth where we can hear only one playing. The exhibitor has two, which he keeps connecting together after a few seconds of playing only one.

12. Buzzwords have always been vague abstractions. Things used to be *relevant* or *viable* unless they were in need of *bifurcation* or *unpacking*. Now the golden words are *sustainable* and *supports*. This last weasel is used to describe "health" products that cannot claim any actual benefits, such as "cures a cold," "prevents heart attacks," and so on. You can't make such claims unless you have a product that (1) actually works and (2) has been proven to work to the satisfaction of the FDA. But you can always say that your product "supports heart health" or "supports kidney function."

2133. What is man? A pile of dirt containing the image of God.

2134. The goal of ambition should be to use the money and power acquired to serve others. Ambition for the sake of one's own indulgence, whether of consumption or ego, is folly and sin.

2135. The belief that our culture is getting worse has been attributed to the age of those who think so. Old folks are the ones who talk about the good old days. Sam, one of the people who seems wise in these things, says the following:

> Every old man complains of the growing depravity of the world, of the petulance and insolence of the rising generation. He recounts the decency and regularity of former times, and celebrates the discipline and sobriety of the age in which his youth was passed; a happy age which is now no more to be expected, since confusion has broken in upon the world, and thrown down all the boundaries of civility and reverence.

But those who complain of the worsening of the world are right, you say. I agree. But then, I'm getting old now, too.

So what, you ask? Well, Sam is Samuel Johnson, and the quotation above was written in 1750 (*Rambler* essay Number 50, published September 8, 1750). If every generation thinks (rightly?) that things are getting worse and the younger generation is spoiled and corrupt, and if we've had about 9 or 10 generations since then, why, we must be living in very confused times, where there is little civility and reverence. Hey, wait. That's right.

2136. God in general and Christianity in particular have been attacked by their despisers in many ways: persecution, denial, attempted refutation, ignoring them, diluting their message, reinterpreting the Bible, and so on. Among these attacks is the charge that God, by demanding worship and honor and praise, reveals himself as an egotistical being, thinking of himself above all else. This is incorrect.

I will not make the case that God deserves the praise and honor he demands because he has created a beautiful world (take a look at butterflies, flowers, tropical plants — and remember that the creation is under a curse because of the fall of mankind, so imagine what it was like before), or because he has given us existence and the free will that we so sadly misuse, or that he has given us a solution to the evils we create by misusing that free will (that solution is Jesus, in case you aren't clear).

In my view, the reason God demands that we worship, praise, and serve him is to get us out of ourselves. God does not need praise or anything else. As the creator of the universe, he's kind of set, having everything he could ever need. But he loves us and wants what's good for us. And since we, as a result of the fall, in which that Eden couple believed a shady stranger they had met for five minutes instead of their creator whom they had known for a while — since, we, as I say, have brought about calamity on the world by abusing our free will around those who promise paradise, God wants us to remove our focus on ourselves (wanna talk about me, I, mine, my) and shift it to something else. And since he picked himself, the fit is natural. Creator of wonders, giver of life, and savior from sin—that's right, worship him and realize that life is not all about you.

Yes, it turns out that many people have it backwards. They focus on themselves and act selfishly, and when they fail to find happiness, they think, "I need to think about myself more." God wants us to realize that happiness comes from giving to others, thinking about their needs instead of our own endless wants, and caring for those who live blindly and mistakenly in this hurting world.

The things that God demands—belief, trust, worship, service—are the things that will make us happy and stop the individual pursuit of our own earthly Utopia, a pursuit which has always resulted and always will result in failure, misery, and suffering. More than that, fulfilling God's demands heals our souls and brings us joy through the proper focus of life.

Ask yourself, of all the people you know, how many of the proud ones are genuinely happy? And now how many of the truly humble ones are genuinely happy? Like it or not, the road to happiness is paved with humility.

"Humble yourselves in the presence of the Lord, and He will exalt you" (James 4:10, NASB).

"You younger men, likewise, be subject to your elders; and all of you, clothe yourselves with humility toward one another, for GOD IS OPPOSED TO THE PROUD, BUT GIVES GRACE TO THE HUMBLE. Therefore humble yourselves under the mighty hand of God, that He may exalt you at the proper time" (1 Peter 5:5-6, NASB).

2137. I'm sure you're aware of the scarcity principle—how marketers make you think that unless you buy the item right now, you might not get it. Ever.

Examples are everywhere:
- Act now while supplies last!
- Limited time offer!
- Limited to stock on hand.
- Hurry! Sale ends soon!

- One day only!
- Quantities limited!

Then there is the ploy of the last chance ever. Some bookstores have a bin full of books labeled "Last Chance." Unless you buy now, you will never see these books again. Or, more dramatic is the "Going Out of Business" sale. Wow, better get in on the bargains before they are all gone. Related appeals to end-of-the-world scarcity:

- Closeout sale!
- Liquidation sale!
- Everything must go!
- Lost our lease! Must sell!

Related is the limit-per-customer ploy. If we see an ad for something with the restriction of "one per customer," we think the price must be so low that other dealers or resellers would be pounding at the door to get as many as they could, were it not for the limit put on it. (But then you see an ad for an angle grinder that includes the note, "Limit 8." That doesn't have quite the same power of threat that "Limit 1" has.)

So my question is, why are we such suckers to the scarcity principle? "Closeout? I'd better buy a few right now before they're gone forever." And no doubt most of us have had the experience where we bought a product on super sale, then returned to get several more, only to find them sold out. That seems to program us for succumbing to the scarcity principle even more strongly.

Experience teaches us that "Supplies Limited" really means "the supplies are limited to the number we can sell. Ever." And experience also teaches us that, when we don't get the sale item we wanted, something else becomes available that might even be better and cheaper.

The scarcity principle rushes some people into marriage. "If I don't marry him/her now, he/she will marry someone else and be gone forever." Read the slogans at the beginning of this

Glimmering and you'll see nearly every one of them could apply to the marriage situation.

Takeaways:

1. Just because someone says it's scarce doesn't mean it is really scarce.

2. If you are tempted by the scarcity marketing ploys, just think "alternatives," "substitutions," and "equivalents."

2138. There seems to be too much shallow thinking in modern life. When a problem occurs, we throw a law at it or cobble up a solution with some instant bandaid. The problem is that we don't think down the road, and consider what unexpected events might be caused by the solution. This knee-jerk failure to consider the consequences can bring about more harm than good.

Example: A building owner wanted to save money and water, so he removed all the old toilets and installed low flow toilets in every bathroom. Within days the sewers backed up and caused a mess. The owner neglected to think through the situation. Instead of thinking systematically — thinking of the waste system as a whole — he thought only of saving water. However, the sewer pipes were designed to handle high-flow toilets, making use of the water volume to move the waste along the pipes. When the flow was cut in half, there was insufficient volume to move the waste along.

Example: Feeling sorry for single mothers, the state set up payments to them, based on the number of children they had and on the fact that they were the sole support for the kids. Unexpectedly, the new welfare system both discouraged marriage and encouraged illegitimacy. If the single mother got married, her support would be reduced or eliminated, creating a disincentive to marriage. And the more children the single mother had, the larger the payment she would receive, thus incentivizing illegitimacy.

Economist Thomas Sowell reminds us to ask, "And then what?" after every proposal. Think beyond what you intend and think about what others might interpret or how they might respond in a way you wouldn't dream of.

Example: After an airplane accident where an infant was torn from its mother's arms and slammed against a bulkhead by the force of the crash, a law was proposed that would require a parent to buy a seat for the infant and strap the child in a carrier in the extra seat. But then some economists did some figuring. They argued that enough mothers and fathers would be unable or unwilling to afford an extra seat and would choose to drive instead. As a result, there would be nine infant deaths in automobile accidents for every infant life saved by the required seating in the aircraft.

And then what? What else would happen? How could the crafty take advantage of this? Where would this lead? What might be some unintended consequences?

Remember that each law, practice, behavior, and so on is an integral part of a system; this will remind you to ask how the proposed change will affect the entire system, both upstream and downstream.

Example:

A creative type was hired to improve the look of an old corporate web site. The designer moved a bunch of pages around, organizing them much more logically. However, the links from page to page were almost all rendered inoperative.

Think down the road. Think systematically.

2139. When two people present opposing arguments in a debate over politics, science, a court trial, or any other issue, the listeners or readers are most likely to pick the side that presents the clearest, most understandable arguments. You might have the truth on your side, but if you encumber and overlay it with incomprehensible statistics and a mountain of details, you are likely to lose the argument. People do not side with a position they cannot understand.

This fact explains two things: (1) It is why politicians and culture changers employ simple slogans and buzzwords to present their case. From "unconditional surrender," to "the right to choose," easy phrases that embody simply grasped concepts are more powerful than longer, more abstract ideas presented with qualifications. (2) It is why persuaders of all kinds use exemplary stories to argue their point. Instead of saying, "This proposal will help support disadvantaged [that is, poor] people by giving them reduced energy rates," the persuader says, "Martha G. a 79 year old widow in New Jersey, almost froze to death last winter because after she paid for the expired bread and cheese she got from the bargain shelf at the store, she didn't have enough money left over to pay her heating bill." And so on. The vivid, concrete story is much more appealing and understandable than abstract reasoning.

2140. If you have a lot of details to convey, write them down and give a copy to your audience. When presented orally, "Lots of details are lost of details."

2141. It is common knowledge that every choice involves a loss. Just call that fact to anyone's attention and they will agree. For example, tell someone, "It's obvious that whenever you make a choice, you lose the possibility of other options — if you choose a green car, you lose the choice of having it blue." The other person will say, "Of course, that's obvious."

The question, then, is, Why don't we have that "obvious" fact present when we make decisions? Why don't we think in terms of cost/benefit of the choice, or consider both what we are gaining and what we are losing or giving up or precluding in each case? The answer, I think, is that we are loss averse and we like the promises of making a choice, so we think only of the good and not the loss or downside. "Why be so negative?" our well-meaning friends will say. Because if they pointed out the downside, we'd think they were against our decision.

"I'm thinking about majoring in economics at the University of Chicago. It's a world famous program."

"Do you know how cold it is in Chicago in the winter?"

"Why are you against everything I want to do?"

A choice involves loss, of course. And a choice represents a change, even in small things. A minute ago you didn't have an ice cream cone. You made a choice that resulted in a change, so that now you do have an ice cream cone. And a change involves a loss, too, of your previous state. (Too many ice cream cones and the change, instead of a loss, will be a gain.)

2142. Quite perversely, our culture's answer to the problem of information overload is to create ways to produce even more information. Instead of developing information simplification techniques, we invent Twitter, blogs, self-publishing, "reply to all" email, cheap copy machines, and so forth. Anyway, here are a few ideas for moving in the opposite direction, toward getting a handle on the data smog that every day engulfs us. I'm not claiming originality for any of these.

Information Simplification Techniques.
1. *Stop thinking that you have to read, see, or know everything.* Reduce the quantity. Do you really need to subscribe to two or three newspapers, six magazines, and four newsletters? Develop a specific list of the kinds of information you need and want. Then use that list as a criteria filter to eliminate what doesn't match.

2. *Prioritize your information diet.* Try a technique such as sorting things into three priority levels. Level 1 gets 60 or 70 percent of your time and attention. Level 2 gets 20 or 30 percent, and Level 3 gets 10 to 20 percent. If you merely divide your tasks or information sources into three levels without assigning a definite time to each, you'll spend all your time on Level 1 items.

3. *Divide the incoming information by quality* and cut out the lesser quality stuff. Develop the habit of performing a rough triage of incoming information, and, per the above, divide it into Levels 1, 2, 3 and No. Put the No into the recycle bin. If you are fearful that you might lose out, create a level called "Later, Maybe" and put information items there that you can't force yourself to recycle immediately. Then, at regular intervals (a

few months or a year) go through what you've saved and toss most of it.

4. *Slow down your need to know instantly.* Forget Twitter, screen your phone calls, read your email only twice a day. The critical stuff will get through to you soon anyway. (If you are on a need-to-know-immediately job, do some cost-benefit thinking.)

5. *Skim.* Develop the ability to skim through your information sources. Pay attention to headings, subheads, the first sentence of each paragraph. If you discover that the information is really crucial, slow down and read carefully. Otherwise, stay on fast forward.

6. *Use curators.* Make use of information packagers and processors, of experts, summarizers, and reviewers. These sources have done a lot of legwork for you. Consult top ten reviews, experts, and dedicated sources.

7. *Summarize.* Follow the *Reader's Digest* model of efficient learning.

2143. The throne of your heart is not wide enough for both you and God to sit on.

2144. If you try, you might fail. But if you don't try, you will fail 100 percent of the time. A famous athlete once said, "You miss 100 percent of the shots you don't take."

2145. Forgiveness can't change the past, but it can change the future.

2146. Sometimes the hardest thing to see is what you are looking at.

2147. Waiting for the perfect time to act is called failing.

2148. If you don't make mistakes, you won't make much of anything else. A famous executive's advice to his new employees: "Make sure you make a reasonable number of mistakes."

2149. Look with your eyes; see with your mind. This proverb reminds us of Augustine's *credo ut intelligam*, "I believe in order to understand." What you understand or perceive is determined by what you believe.

2150. Of course we should avoid the Seven Deadly Sins (Pride, Greed, Anger, Lust, Envy, Gluttony, and Sloth) because we hurt others when we indulge them. But we also hurt ourselves when we commit them. And, what is often overlooked, the Seven Deadlies render us susceptible to harm at the hands of others. The proud, overconfident, arrogant, greedy people are exactly the targets of con artists. People who think they are too smart to be conned are the easiest targets, and those who are so greedy that they don't mind doing something illegal or underhanded at the expense of others are exactly the marks the fraudsters pick out. And how many people have been led into victimhood by lust? What did you say is the population of the earth now?

2151. **Lessons from *There's a Sucker Born Every Minute*:**
    1. "The true power of Madison Avenue lies in the fact that so many people are fast to claim that they cannot be influenced" (5).
    2. ". . . when greed takes over, it generates careless excitement and that leads to stupidity" (29).
    3. ". . . greed can exterminate common sense" (30).
    4. "Within one week of [hurricane Katrina] . . . the FBI reported more than four thousand websites had . . . gone live to help raise money for Katrina relief." But "the FBI says more than 60% were bogus" (39).
    5. Now add to greed, benevolence, and gullibility the button labeled "fear" (46).
    6. Fear generates a panic (47).
    7. You are what you throw away (56).

2152. Some people are fond of criticizing "book knowledge" while extolling experience, because book knowledge is a mediated form of reality while experience is the real thing. However, it could be argued that experience is much more limited than reading. We read to understand, and the author often relates an account of experience in a context of meaning, draws conclusions, analyzes, adds clarifying analogies, and gives us plenty of time to think through what we are reading. The immediacy of experience often means that it comes and goes before we know what to make of it. Thus, those who merely experience something understand less because their knowledge environment is smaller.

2153. Some people view marriage as a pie. The bigger the slice one spouse takes, the smaller the piece left for the other spouse. Hence, marriage becomes a competition in a zero-sum game, a tug of war, a conflict where both spouses think only of their share, their rights, their needs.

Other people view marriage as a fruit tree. By working together to water and fertilize the tree, both can enjoy abundant fruit. These spouses think of how they can benefit each other.

2154. Marriage is not about how well your spouse can meet your narcissistic fantasies. Marriage is a partnership for the accomplishment of external goods.

2155. **Which of the following do most people rely on to form their beliefs?**

A. *Evidence* (physical objects, photographs, documents, data, recordings)

B. *Reasons* (inductive and deductive arguments, applying to principles, laws, ideals, precedents, common sense)

C. *Stories* (analogies, parables, moral tales, clarifying examples)

D. *Familiarity* (common knowledge, examples from common life)

E. *Popularity* (what is popularly believed, what saturates the media space)

F. *Authority* (Professional testimony, official judgments and laws, expert witnesses, results of scientific analysis)

The true answer, for many people in many cases, is a combination of C, D, E, and F. We like to think that our beliefs are based on reason and evidence, but all too often we believe something simply because the idea or claim has been repeated over and over. We might assume that somewhere there is evidence for the claim, but we seldom bother to check. Similarly, we believe something if lots of other people express belief in it — especially people who are presented to us as authorities. And whatever is very familiar to us — we've heard that lots of times — we believe *because* of its familiarity. Hence the power of propaganda. And, we believe things that are presented to us in story form. Stories are much more persuasive than reasons, logic, data, evidence, or explanations because stories are narrative. This means they represent concrete, supposedly real-life experiences. We can relate to them. They seem real. They are interesting.

This leads to some unpleasant realizations.

1. Many people tend to adopt ideas that they hear frequently or that are popular with their peer group or with their professors at the university or with the information sources they prefer. They are unlikely to give up those ideas when offered reasons or evidence against them, since reason and evidence played no role in their adoption.

2. Many people don't understand that what is presented as the result of careful examination and analysis of facts is actually a predetermined conclusion.

3. Reason and evidence are often adduced later to support the predetermined conclusion.

4. Because reason and evidence are incapable of changing the predetermined conclusion, those who hold such conclusions become metaphysical ideologues trapped in a frozen paradigm.

2156. It has been noted by marriage counselors that most couples fight over nothing. One person makes a comment that the other finds offensive or that feels like an attack, so the other person replies with a counter attack. From there, both people simply blast each other with one emotional bomb after another from the arsenals of insult and criticism that they have built up during the marriage. And, of course, the argument typically escalates, with ever more hurtful bombs being thrown, with never a single concession to the other, because the pride in the hearts of each spouse makes them "talk for victory" as the saying is. Each one wants to win.

This fact explains why arguments quickly lose focus and range widely from topic to topic, growing ever more heated.

Here's a sample exchange:

"You charged $127 on the credit card for shoes? What were you thinking?"

"Well, you made me waste half that much when you didn't come home for dinner on time and didn't call me till the last minute. The meal was ruined."

"I came home late because my boss wanted to talk at the last minute and then I had to put gas in the car because you never remember to do it."

"Well, you're the one who uses all that gasoline — wastes all that gasoline — driving to those silly comic book expos, probably just to see the half-dressed girls."

Asking couples to focus on the issue is probably fruitless since there is no issue — at least not one named in the argument.

2157. Good works do not produce saving faith, but saving faith does produce good works.

2158. Not only is pride offensive to others, but it is harmful to the proud themselves. Have you noticed that proud, egotistical, arrogant people are almost invariably unhappy, while humble people are almost always cheerful? The proud see everything negatively, while the humble see life in positive terms. The proud are very difficult to please — nothing is good enough for them. The humble are content with human and circumstantial limitations.

2159. Proud people are never wrong (just ask them). But if you're never wrong, you can't learn from your mistakes. Thus, learning and wisdom and understanding require at least a degree of humility.

2160. One of the principal truths of relationships is that you must give what you want to get. This is especially true of what you expect to get. Before you become resentful over not receiving love, attention, adoration, affection, kindness, understanding, empathy, and forgiveness, do you give the other person these things? Remember the Golden Rule?

2161. Many people hate to receive advice because, first, it means they are deficient in some way — wrong or ignorant — because that's why they need advice; and second, it means that the advice giver knows something they don't and is therefore in some small way superior to the advice receiver. Who can endure this double humiliation?

2162. Worrying about what you don't have punches a double blow to happiness. First, it causes frustration, unhappiness, and even anger over your lack. Second, these negative feelings prevent you from enjoying — and being grateful for — what you do have.

2163. When your foot slips, you hurt yourself, but when your tongue slips, you hurt others.

2164. The more often a lie is repeated, the more true it appears.

2165. Sometimes the tongue can work all day and still not accomplish as much as the hands can do in five minutes. Other times the tongue can accomplish things in five minutes that the hands could never do.

2166. The more you get, the more you want. The more you want, the more you are discontent.

2167. The worst prison is a cold, lonely room with walls made of resentment.

2168. A dream by itself is an idle fantasy. But add a start date and the dream becomes a project. Add a deadline and your dream becomes a plan.

2169. So professor Stanley wrote a novel which, unfortunately for him, no one read, and worse, no one bought. He nevertheless adopted the demeanor of a novelist, permed his hair, and wore turtleneck sweaters. One or two of his curious students actually read the book, which they deemed unimpressive. The only parts they mentioned particularly were the passages of gratuitous sex that the publisher had insisted on including.

[Cue Rod Serling of the Twilight Zone] Witness another significant portion of a life of intelligence and creative effort, driven into nothingness. And his work destined soon to be pulped and made into egg cartons.

2170. A young man approached a wise man and said, "Oh, wise man. I want to become wise like you. What should I do?"

"To become wise," replied the wise man, "requires a thousand years of experience."

"But how can that be?" questioned the young man. "I will not likely live past a hundred. And besides, you are wise and not a thousand years old. So again I ask what to do."

"Gain a thousand years of experience from a thousand people."

"Now I'm more confused than ever," pouted the young man. "Tell me one thing I can do to gain even a little wisdom."

"Read," said the wise man.

2171. They cease to be virtuous because they want to belong. They are afraid of criticism, but mostly they are afraid of being laughed at. Mockery—even imagined, potential mockery—is a powerful influence on behavior.

2172. Samuel Johnson (*Rambler* 56) says that people feel a bitter resentment when another person demonstrates that they have been wrong.

2173. Kind words warm the coldest winter. — Chinese Proverb

[May 8, 2015; 64 years old]

2174. In "The Strange Adventure," one of my favorite stories from my book, *Seventy Stories and a Poem*, the story concludes by noting that "life is about meaning, not experience." In that context, the conclusion refers to the way we interpret what happens to us — that is, what meaning we give to an experience.

But I'd like to back up from there to note that finding meaning in an experience must be a deliberate act of thought. It is quite possible to have many experiences in life without ever finding meaning in any of them, simply because meaning was never sought. Experiences must be analyzed, processed, thought about, interpreted, before they will yield a meaning that can be added to our understanding about life and thereby added to our personal wisdom.

It's not simply by having lots of experiences that we grow wiser or increase our understanding about life or ourselves; it's by processing those experiences in light of moral contexts, analogous situations, and broader implications that we gain something solid and meaningful.

Next time you are sitting with a friend having a cup of coffee or a dish of ice cream, ask, "What does this mean?" and see what you can discover — about friendship, life, blessings, habits, will power, pleasure, pain, and so on. Don't live a meaningless life.

2175. I've come to the conclusion that people who hate the rich and want "wealth distribution" have a Scrooge McDuck view of the rich.

You'll remember that Scrooge McDuck was a Disney cartoon character, uncle to Donald Duck I think, who was known principally for his three cubic acres of money. Bills, coins, gold and so on filled a building which enclosed his dough. Since an acre is a bit more than 208 feet on a side, a cubic acre would be about nine million cubic feet and three would be 27 million cubic feet.

People who hate the rich are imagining all that cash and gold coins just sitting there. Scrooge McDuck used to swim in his money. No wonder these people dream of getting a beach bucketful or two for themselves. "Redistribute the cash so everyone can have some!"

The problem is, there is no bin with three cubic acres of money. Rich people don't accumulate warehouses of cash. Their money is invested, working for them. The money is in hospitals, schools, manufacturing plants, and homes. (Where do you think banks get the money to lend to people buying a house? It's not printed in the back room.)

So stop dreaming and put your own money to work for you, and eventually you'll have—more than you think.

2176. The contemporary political scene seems to be filled with terms that at once evoke strong feelings and yet do not produce clarity of meaning. In critical thinking, slinging around terms with negative connotations is labeled the fallacy of emotive language, as in, "He is a snake," "They are extremists," and "She is a lightweight." But now the political antagonists are using as emotional weapons words that ought to be useful and clearly defined.

For example, we hear everyday comments like these:

"I am for justice."

"You are a racist."

"I support human dignity."

"You are inhumane."

"These people are being exploited."

But what do these statements mean and how should we respond? I think that one way to help increase understanding is to ask the person making the comment to define the term:

"This is unjust."

"Please tell me what you mean by *unjust*."

"That's unfair."

"I'm not sure what you mean by *unfair* or in what sense you mean it."

My suspicion is that many people use these words merely as negative emoters, words intended as weapons of disrespect. There may not be a clear definition behind their use in a given context. If that's true, expect an angry reply rather than a definition.

2177. Our culture, including our educational system, has come to value subjectivity and personal opinion so highly—and has consequently come to reject fixed standards and even reason itself—that we now value every thought for its own sake, quite apart from any reason or evidence. We hear someone say, "I don't trust him," or "That movie was really great," or "That law is unjust," and then the speaker just drops a period at the end of the sentence. It used to be that we would hear a "because" after such assertions. "That law is unjust because it treats minor offenses and major ones the same way."

Not now, however. In fact, when high school or college students are asked to supply a reason for their opinions, many of them grow instantly angry. They are offended. They take umbrage. The conversation goes something like this:

Teacher: "What do you think about the main character's decision to leave town at the end?"

Student: "I think he's got another wife in another town and he's going to go to her."

Teacher: "And you think that because. . . ."

Student (growing angry): "That's my opinion. That's just what I feel."

Teacher: "But can you point to a passage in the story that supports your idea?"

Student: "I don't have to. That's my personal opinion."

Postmodernists and their fellow travelers have helped bring about this state of affairs by asserting that a given work can yield dozens of different but equally valid interpretations. It's a free-for-all with interpretations of literature, poetry, history, and of course political science. But the phenomenon goes way beyond textual interpretations right to the heart of interpersonal communication on any topic. No one is required to have evidence or a reason for what they assert. We're just supposed to accept it.

But accept it as true or merely as that person's personal belief? I think we are witnessing the derationalization of the modern world. People want to hold beliefs without any reason or evidence. Case in point are some of the conspiracy theories and urban legends that are so preposterous yet so firmly believed. Example:

"Did you know that TWA Flight 800 was really shot down by a US missile?"

"But an extensive reconstruction of the wreckage showed no such evidence."

"Oh, it was hushed up and the fake story about frayed wires in the fuel tank was spread."

"But that would require the cooperation and lying of hundreds of investigators."

Here would be a good time to ask, "And you believe the missile idea rather than the official reports because. . . ."

The answer to that leads to another discussion, about those who like to believe in the "true" explanations for our nation's disasters.

2178. How many goods in stores and activities in the world should be labeled, "Warning: This is a detour from your life's purpose." Not only do we spend too much of our lives waiting, goofing off, and pursuing phantom dreams, but we also do not need to museum-shop, as I call it. Museum shopping refers to spending lengthy periods of time in a store, comparing, examining features, and so on, looking around just to see what is available.

2179. A relationship without truth is a masquerade. Truth without a relationship is a book on a shelf. Truth embodied in a relationship is wisdom.

2180. Our ultimate goal is to become a thread in the tapestry of God.

2181. People are damaged to the extent they allow an experience to hurt them. Some are unharmed until they are told they have been hurt.

2182. At the very bottom of every human heart is the desire to matter. People want to matter. No compliment is greater than one that implies that the person matters. No insult is more offensive than one that implies that the person doesn't matter.

2183. Seduction is a slippery slope. One must be highly vigilant in order to discern the ever so slight movements in the direction of conquest. Otherwise, it will be too late to resist before one realizes what is going on. Sexual seducers, salesmen, confidence artists, thieves, and many others practice this subtle seduction.

2184. Evidence is the runway for the flight of faith. Once you are airborne, you no longer need the ground.

2185. If, as the writers on decision making are now telling us, reasons are generated ex post facto to support conclusions derived intuitively or based on predilections, where do the intuitions come from or how were the predilections formed?

2186. Re: Glimmering 2184. Evidence is the runway for the flight of faith. The purpose of the runway is to help you accelerate until the wind of the Spirit can get under your wings and loft you into the air.

2187. In order to take a powerful and effective leap of faith, begin with a firm foothold.

2188. Knowing the truth makes us free (John 8:32). Knowing opinion gives us understanding, for opinion, not truth, rules the world. To realize that the world is actually governed on the basis of wrong ideas gives us insight into human motivation and behavior.

2189. **Creation Note.**

A major problem with the creation-versus-evolution controversy is that the evolutionists (aka Neo-Darwinists) pretend that they all support a single theory, whereas the creation-intelligent design proponents cannot agree on a single description of their position. In fact, the various camps view each other with hostility. Can there be formulated a clear position that all can agree on? Christianity has many variations, but it is commonly attacked as a single entity because it has shared tenets in every variety.

2190. **Thoughts About Vacations, Suggested by a Cruise Trip, August, 2015.**

1. Most of the travel trips require that we keep moving, without time to pause and think. We need to pause and observe, to look around, analyze, and find the meaning in our experiences and in the places we visit.

"If you look out the right side of the bus, right, *now,* you would have seen the famous Denken Monument, erected in 1623, etc."

2. There is no time to stop and process the experience. Time is needed to think, to allow the experience to soak in.

"We saw a lot of famous places yesterday, which is why we didn't get to the hotel until almost midnight. And today, we are leaving at 5 AM so we can see many more sights."

3. Absorb the aura, feel the atmosphere, reflect on the past. Think about the meaning and the history of the narrow cobblestone streets.

"Back there we just passed the Street of World Armies, so named because soldiers from twelve conquering armies have marched down it over time. That building next to it is a museum with thousands of books, photographs, and video presentations. Too bad we don't have time to stop. But you can still say you were there."

4. There is no time to make choices. If you have to keep moving, you make random, abrupt choices—where to eat, where to stay, where to go next. Our choices are made in haste without consideration.

5. Enjoyment comes from thoughtful processing of experience both during the experience and afterward. Hence, there is limited enjoyment during a vacation, where we just go through the motions of engaging in experiences. A perfunctory experience produces a mediocre response.

"Maybe I'll remember this when I see the photos I took."

2191. "No" is only the first answer, from the first person. Ask again. One of the staff probably just didn't get the memo.

2192. The wall of rejection becomes the bridge of acceptance through the bulldozer of perseverance.

2193. Truth is in a bad way today. It used to be that people wanted truth. Truth was revealed and people accepted it eagerly. But gradually, the culture changed, along with the method of presenting the truth. The table here shows the changes and the new approaches. Originally, when the truth was presented, it needed only to be revealed and people accepted it eagerly. Truth was welcome.

Culture	Truth	Reaction
Open and honest	Revealed	Enthusiasm
Busy	Declared	Acceptance
Uninformed	Clarified	Curiosity
Complex	Offered	Confusion
Skeptical	Demonstrated	Caution
Unbelieving	Reasoned	Resistance
Disbelieving	Pleaded	Hostility

After a while, the pain of truth began to stoke a rebellion. Instead of, "Yes, we know that the truth hurts," many people began to reject "true truth" in favor of more palatable, interesting, and self-serving "truth."

2194. Acting in ignorance does not really mean acting without knowledge or information. Its real meaning is acting from false belief. People act on the basis of beliefs. Acting in ignorance means acting on the beliefs that were available, which, unfortunately were wrong or were not the beliefs that would have informed a better choice of action. As I've said before, choices are made from the available, identified alternatives. You can't choose an alternative you don't know about.

Acting in error: Rejecting a better alternative and instead choosing a poor one.

Acting in ignorance: Choosing a poor alternative in the absence of knowledge of a better one. The poor alternative might be the best one of those identified as available. Or as someone once said about the choice of TV programs, "Viewers choose the least worst program available."

2195. Dictators and ideologues both have the goal of gaining obedience by telling emotionally persuasive stories. But first, they must disarm their prey by causing them to stop thinking and reasoning. And what better way to do this than through the public education system? For example, stop teaching history for the moral and political lessons it can teach, or for the context of the past it provides. Teach history as an account of the oppression, genocide, imperialism, and exploitation of the weak by the strong. Don't forget to indict capitalism and especially America in the process.

2196. Why is it that some people are more hateful and angry than others? It's because they live their ideologies as religious struggles between good and evil, and they are always feeling indignation over their perception of life events.

Try this off-the-top-of-the-head thought. People who are less angry with the world think deductively, basing their conclusions on general principles (of justice, morality, etc.), while the angry think inductively, basing their conclusions on specific events or examples. Unfortunately, inductive thinking faces several challenges. The first problem is that forming generalizations from one or a few narratives of injustice can easily result in the fallacy of hasty generalization. Anecdotal thinking seldom produces fair or justifiable conclusions.

But this, it seems to me, is just what the angry folks do. They collect a set of useful narratives that support their (often predetermined) conclusions, and rest their worldview on them. For example, chew over the horrors of the BP oil spill (2010), the VW emissions fraud (2015), and the Spanish "cooking oil" scandal (1981), and you have all you need to conclude that corporations, or even capitalism, are evil, greedy, and untrustworthy. And once you have these examples and this mindset, confirmation bias keeps you solidly locked in—and angry about the injustice and unfairness of life, caused by those evil—choose one—capitalists, bureaucrats, lawyers, bankers, politicians.

Deductive thinker: "The Constitution prohibits the taking of personal property without due process. Therefore, the city has no right to take the Pelican restaurant and convert it into a homeless shelter."

Inductive thinker: "Eighty-six year old widow, Wilma Thorpe, has nowhere to go on an icy winter night because there is no shelter in her neighborhood. Last month she almost froze to death. We cannot allow corporate greed to condemn her to a terminal future of all-night wandering through the ice and snow in her threadbare clothes. The restaurant property is ideally suited for a shelter."

It also seems to be true that, because deductive thinkers appeal to specific standards and values (the major and minor premises in syllogisms), the success or failure of a plan or solution is important. Inductive thinkers, on the other hand, appeal to and are guided by feelings and good intentions, often based on a few examples. The success or failure of a plan or solution is therefore less important than the fact that those who supported the plan meant well.

"Do you realize that the welfare system, by effectively rewarding single-parent households over two-parent households, has severely harmed poor families and produced a culture of illegitimacy?

"Well, we had good intentions."

"Have you heard that banning DDT has resulted in the deaths by malaria of millions of people?"

"We meant well."

"Why did the inductive thinkers implement a policy of giving loans to those who could not afford to pay them back? It has caused an enormous financial disaster in the housing market, huge deficits, and uncountable foreclosures."

"Well, we felt compassion for those who couldn't share the American dream of home ownership."

2197. In my *Glimmerings II*, I mentioned this anecdote in #1737. But I have another response I'd like to share.

When I was an undergraduate at the University of California, Santa Barbara, I chose, from among the available requirements, a course in Introduction to the Theater. A major part of the course was to read and discuss various plays. One day early in the quarter, we were to discuss a Shakespeare play. The graduate student teaching the course put on his bright-eyed face and his hopeful tone, and asked, "Well, what do you think?"

After a bit of nonspecific interchange, ("I liked it," and "I couldn't understand it," etc.), a young woman, who had clearly already taken a course in race, class, and gender, announced in a deathly tone, "I can't relate to this. It's not about my people or about my experience." Now, since this was about 1970, it was probably the first time the teaching assistant had been confronted with this basis for rejection. He didn't have much of a response. But I have one.

I would tell her this. Fictional stories, including plays, novels, short stories, and even many poems, are read for two reasons. The first reason is, "We read because we find ourselves there." That is, we relate to a character or situation or problem or crisis that is handled by the work of fiction, and as a result we feel a sense of belonging, being human, since our problems are encountered by others. We lose a sense of aloneness and alienation. Now, you have specifically rejected this reason, because you say that you cannot relate to the plot, character, or any other part of the play. We can let that go for now, with just the reminder that we sometimes must use our imaginations to translate a character's circumstances, words, and actions into something we feel as relevant to our own lives.

But there is another reason to read fiction. It is also said, "We read because we do not find ourselves there." Now, taken with the first statement above, that might seem like a paradox, but it conveys another truth. We read about characters and circumstances that are very different from our lives because we gain insights into ourselves and into the possibilities for additional life choices that we might make. Like travel, reading broadens our outlook and gives us a better, more circumspect view of life. We find options, possibilities, choices we never might have thought about otherwise. And with a little imagination, we can translate even very different circumstances into some idea relevant to us. We might not have a personal tailor who presses us to wear larger epaulets, but we can use the incident to reflect on dress and how clothing symbolizes something about ourselves, our attitudes, our values, and who we are. We might not see 18th century fops anymore, but we do know that some clothing styles send negative messages.

Suppose you read about a character who lives in a mansion and employs forty servants. Not your life experience, huh? But can you put yourself imaginatively in his shoes and ask yourself how you would live? What kind of food would you eat? How would you treat your servants? How would you run the household? What do the answers tell you about yourself?

2198. No, the Secret to Happiness Is Not Complicated.
In fact, I can reveal the secret to you in two words. The

trouble is that, while the secret is not complicated, there are two obstacles. First, the secret is very difficult to implement because it conflicts with our feelings and assumptions and sometimes the defining characteristic of our personality. Second, most people are unwilling to attempt implementing the secret because it runs counter to their beliefs about how to be happy and their everyday habits for pursuing happiness.

So, yes, I am going to tell you how to be happy, how to have a successful marriage, how to develop and maintain solid friendships, how to succeed in business — whatever your current status in life. I'll tell you the secret, but you won't like it. In fact, you'll probably reject it out of hand and go on living your life as you have been, with perhaps less happiness and success than you might otherwise have had.

Now, if you are reading this the old fashioned way, in a printed book, please don't throw it across the room when I reveal the secret to you. You might accidentally hit someone and hurt him or her, causing a diminshment of happiness for that person.

So here it is. In two words, then, the secret to happiness is: Humble yourself.

You see, pride is the source of most of the misery we cause each other. More than that, it is an inhibitor, a preventer, even a destroyer of every kind of human progress.

Today's illustrative anecdote comes from the life of Ignaz Semmelweis, an obstetrician in 19th Century Vienna. He discovered, well before the germ theory of disease had been accepted, that his medical students were somehow transferring disease from the autopsy room to the women in the hospital. So he began the practice of hand washing before patient examination. The death rate among the women in the hospital dropped 90%, from about one in every five or six women to one or two in a hundred.

Did the medical establishment welcome this news, implement hand washing universally, and praise Semmelweis as a hero? Of course not. Many doctors were offended that anyone could suggest that persons of their exalted social status would have dirty hands. Hmmph. Pride sinks another good idea.

Oh, and besides, Semmelweis' solution ran counter to the "settled science" of the time. So instead of taking the humble road to hand washing, the disease problem was turned back on the women, where it was suggested that what the women needed was not a doctor's clean hands but a good laxative.

Arrogance, egotism, pride — these are enormously damaging to all of us and our social world. If you want to stop damaging others and bring yourself peace and joy, humble yourself.

2199. I Say, Down with a "Balanced" Approach.

The balance metaphor is responsible for untold irrational thinking and disastrous decision making simply because it presents the desirable or ideal solution or relationship between two ideas in tension as one of balance. "There should be a balance between head and heart," "Faith and reason must be in balance," "We can't have just unbridled freedom of speech or completely censoring speech codes — we need a balance."

The problems with this teeter-totter metaphor include:

1. It implies that the two ideas in conflict necessarily reduce each other. That is, when one increases, the other must decrease. Too much of one thing means less of another, when in fact often one can have an increase or decrease in both at the same time.

2. It allows the information manipulators to set up false tensions with "balances" that enhance or diminish an idea.

So what is the alternative? We need to choose a different default metaphor that represents how concepts can be joined. Instead of a balance, what about a blend, synthesis, symbiosis, interconnection, interaction, interinfluencing, mutual enhancement?

2200. I was thinking about criticizing the decline of intellectual content in religion: How, for example, the singing of hymns — which were filled with theology and thought — has given way to the singing of praise songs — which are almost devoid of thought and which instead focus on hyping the emotional state of the worshipper. Many of these praise songs have short, repetitive verses, and when sung over and over, appear to be intended to produce a mystical trance or a state not unlike hypnosis.

But then I thought, there has actually been a decline in the intellectual content of everything; the entire society and its culture have eschewed thinking and instead have embraced feeling. Who reads books these days? The Gutenberg experience is passé. Where once we might have read several books on a topic in order to form our own judgment about it, we now form our opinions from tiny snippets of information: sound bites, anecdotes, advertisements, blogs, and social media. How deep can an argument be when sent as a text message or a Twitter post?

2201. A life without regrets, eh? If you look at your past without regrets, then either

- you haven't been paying attention
- you haven't learned as much as you should have
- you haven't ever listened to what other people have been telling you
- you haven't taken notice of the better choices you could have made
- your ego is keeping you from learning from your mistakes

2202. Samuel Johnson has observed, (as have many others, no doubt) that philosophers talk better than they live. If, however, their philosophy has no effect on their own lives, then of what value is it? For posterity, you say. But who would desire to follow a womanizer's admonitions about the virtue of chastity? Or the embezzler's recommendations about the need for integrity in dealing with others? Or the liar's declaration that honesty is best policy? Doesn't Jesus say something about whitewashed tombs?

2203. Just as we speak of sins of omission as well as sins of commission, so we can speak of making a mistake by both doing something wrong and not doing something right. An obvious example of a mistake of neglect is not turning off the electricity before beginning to work on a light fixture. The same is true of forgetting to turn off the water before working on a sink faucet, failing to back up one's computer files, not installing antivirus software, and so on.

We tend to focus on negative acts that get us into trouble, when in fact it's what we don't do that causes us just as much grief.

2204. Is it the things that change that we like (novelty, variety, surprise), or is it the things that don't change that we like (tradition, familiarity, security)?

2205. **Why We Fear Change.**

Stuck in a lousy job, neighborhood, relationship (you're not really going to marry that person you're dating, are you?) or other unpleasant situation you just can't seem to leave? Still hoping that your sports team is going to start winning? That the bug-infested software package you have spent so much time and money on will finally be fixed "real soon now"?

Even when we're stuck in a rut, and making a change seems an obvious move, we often don't like change. Here are some reasons why change is often rejected.

1. The Status Quo is Comfortable. The familiar, even when substantially negative, gives us a feeling of security. We are used to this way of life. We can predict what Aunt Wilma will say. We know the dimensions of our current life and have learned to cope with our life situation as it is. Comfortable and familiar misery it might be, but comfortable and familiar it is.

2. Fear of the Unknown. All changes are uncertain in their benefits and outcome. For example, leaving an awful job for another job includes the possibility that the new job will be even more awful. Those who find change difficult or impossible are afraid of what the new situation might be. They are quite aware of "unintended consequences," "unexpected costs," and "unimagined downsides."

3. Fear of the Change Cascade. Making one change almost always involves changing a number of related things. Move to a new city and you've got to change friends, favorite stores, churches, schools. If you change climates, you might also have to change your entire wardrobe. To live a mature, coherent life, you must adjust your ideas to harmonize with the change you've just made or are planning to make.

4. Fear of Loss. We humans tend to be risk averse, and whenever we contemplate making a change, we look at whatever good we are giving up as well as the bad. This cognitive bias makes us favor the known positive (however little that may be) over the risk of not gaining a suitable positive replacement. We sometimes look at the choice of change as a guaranteed loss (giving up the current situation) trading for an uncertain gain (the unknown).

5. Habits are Easy. Do you ever drive down the street from your house only to wonder suddenly if you have closed the garage door? And when you drive back to check, you see that you did remember to close it? Habits, once established, allow us to run on automatic and not have to think about every movement. If it's Tuesday, it's time to read, watch, go bowling, or whatever. Habits take a load off our minds and allow us to think about something else while performing ordinary tasks. But if you change, your habits might cease to be relevant or even workable. New habits will need to be formed.

And yet, to live is to change, and to change is to live. Many changes are forced upon us and we must make new choices — choices that alter our lives significantly. Once we recognize that these reasons are often why we see change in a negative way, we can take steps to revise our outlook.

2206. The Downward Spiral.

When I taught writing (mostly freshman composition) long ago, I always crossed out the student's "I feel" and wrote in the margin, "I think." I wanted them to pass their ideas through a few neuronal pathways before putting them to paper. I was, of course, utterly unsuccessful, not any more successful than I was at curing vague pronoun references or the misuse of apostrophes.

But there's something about the use of "I feel" that reveals what a sorry state our culture is in.

1. You can't disagree with feelings. If I say, "I think the issue is so and so," you can point out my errors of logic, adduce contrary reasons or evidence, and so forth. You might even prove me wrong. But if I say simply, "I feel that the issue is so and so," what can you say? (If I say, "I feel happy," you can't very well respond, "No, you don't.") So feelings are the safe, lazy, thoughtless way to present your ideas, however unreasonable or poorly supported they are. Score one point for not needing to think.

2. Feelings are based on personal experience. No need for research or even taking a poll. All you need to support your opinion is your own example. External statistics, research, evidence, reasons, arguments, and the like are simply not necessary, not applicable.

3. Appealing to feelings makes you think it's about you. What this feelings-based philosophy amounts to is narcissism, worshiping your own (biased?) opinions. If you thought the conquest of objectivity by subjectivity was horrible, we're now faced with pure solipsism as king of the world. (The only question is who has the power to impose his solipsistic view of the world on everyone else?)

It seems that in the public schools the perfect storm that combined the self-esteem movement with the postmodernist view that any given text was subject to an infinite number of interpretations, resulted in celebrating the use of "I feel."

Example:

Teacher: "The question that is often asked by readers of the play is, Why did Hamlet fail to act sooner? What do you say?"

Jane: "I feel he was, like, so busy lusting after Ophelia that he, like, couldn't think straight."

Teacher: "Very good, Jane."

Tom: "I feel it's because he was gay and was, you know, oppressed by society."

Teacher: "Very good, Tom."

Sally: "Um, I feel he, um, secretly wished he had, um, killed his father so he could, um, marry his mother. You know, Oedipus and stuff."

Teacher: "Very good, Sally."

Bill: "I feel that he totally was busy thinking up ways to waste his uncle."

Teacher: "Very good, Bill. My, my, class. What bright and thoughtful readers all of you are."

[Friday, October 16, 2015; age 65

2207. It costs a worm to catch a fish. — Chinese proverb

2208. You may catch a few fish with your bare hands; more with a sharpened spear; still more with a baited hook; but the most with a well-placed net. — Suggested by a Chinese proverb

2209. All the boats felt the same wind, but the boat with the best captain sailed farther and faster.

2210. To be the best conversationalist, listen to seven words for every word you speak.

    1. People like to talk and have someone listen and sometimes sympathize. A good listener is a treasure.

    2. The listener needs details, context, a sense of the whole issue before a good response can be made.

    3. Good listeners ask questions to draw out their conversationalists, and questions require fewer words than answers.

2211. Our culture demands certainty from its experts — doctors, scientists, police detectives. There is the belief that authority equals certainty. And the authorities like it that way, because speaking with the certainty of an authority, an expert, reinforces the feeling of prestige, for both the audience and the authority.

Thus, we have the phenomenon of imposing exactitude on ambiguity. The fuzzy is made sharp, the nuanced is made simple and clear.

2212. *Experience* and *Expertise* Are Two Different Words.

Upon which I shall tell the reader a short tale.

Mike was a newly graduated technician in the mechanical field. He was partnered with Bruno, a long experienced technician. They arrived at a customer's site, where Bruno proceeded to install and hook up the wiring on a new fan motor.

"This is the third one of these motors I've put in this unit in a couple of years. They're just a bunch of junk," said Bruno in a tone of disgust. "They barely last a year, sometimes less."

Mike took a look at the hookup and noticed that some wires seemed to be out of place. "Doesn't the purple wire go to the capacitor COM terminal?" he asked.

"Naw," replied Bruno. "I've been installing these motors for twenty years. Trust me. I know what I'm doing."

"But," Mike protested, "the diagram that came with the motor shows that the purple wire should go to the cap."

"Nonsense. I've always wired them this way."

"But there's also a note on the diagram: 'Caution. Miswiring the motor can severely shorten its life.'"

"Look, son. If you want to continue to learn from an expert, you're going to have to listen to what I say. As I told you, I have twenty years of experience. Experience equals expert."

"But—."

"If you can't shut up and pay attention to me, you can just go and wait in the truck. And when we get back to the shop, I'll tell Dan that you can't learn this trade and need to find another job."

2213. We are such well-trained consumers that if we go to the store for just a single item, and if that item is not available, we will still buy half a dozen other things that we didn't have in mind the moment we entered the store. There must be such a thing as consumption hunger. Or perhaps it is possession hunger, a human foible that would explain expeditions to find sunken treasure or hidden riches.

2214. The first mistake of the intellect is in thinking that information is knowledge. The second mistake is in thinking that knowledge is wisdom. Information is aggregated and organized data, from which you can gain knowledge through the process of analyzing and understanding it. Neither of these processes is automatic or guaranteed. Wisdom is the application of knowledge in the proper time, place, and amount.

2215. Personal experience, however limited, trumps reams of statistics because experience is immediate and often emotional. Similarly, we believe anecdotes over data because we can relate to the anecdotes. Data leaves us cold and suspicious, while a story penetrates right to our heart and humanness (and may also touch our minds.)

As the authors of *The Invisible Gorilla* note, "It can be difficult to overcome a belief that is formed from compelling anecdotes" (177). So, the first to reach the audience with a bunch of stories fixes their beliefs so solidly that anyone later supplying refuting arguments, reasons, evidence, data, or logic can have little probability of changing that audience's belief.

2216. In *Thinking Fast and Slow*, Daniel Kahneman says that "rationality is generally served by broader and more comprehensive frames" (361). Reason needs context. In other words, the narrower your context, the less rational your conclusions or choices are likely to be. Thus, investigating a number of alternatives, circumstances, entailments, and consequences will provide a more reasonable environment for choice.

2217. In *Glimmering* #2198 I mentioned that the secret to happiness is "humble yourself." That this is true about happiness in marriage is shown by the fact that the main problem and source of arguments in marriage is the underlying thought in each spouse, "Why can't you be more like me?" Recall the comment by Professor Higgins in *My Fair Lady*, "Why can't a woman be more like a man?" Such proud egocentrism produces no end of conflict and hurt. Most people evaluate the behavior of others by using themselves as the gold standard. The more you behave and think like me, the better you are. The less you behave and think like me, the more pernicious and evil you are.

The question, "What's wrong with you?" often implies, "You are not like me. Therefore, there is something wrong with you."

2218. You'll never produce a successful, happy relationship by attacking people for who they are.

2219. Marital Discord.
In *Glimmering* #2205, the fear of change in general was discussed. A related question is, Why don't unhappily married people stop treating each other so badly? Why don't they change their behavior toward one another?

1. Pride. After long periods (sometimes many years) of mutual hostilities, the spouses' self-image or self-esteem has become closely connected with their positions of moral superiority. The "standard of me" has become entrenched. "I'm right and you're wrong. Why should I be the one to yield or change? It's unfair."

2. Habit. Again, after long periods of interaction, each spouse develops an automatic, habitual behavior toward the other. Sarcasm, bitterness, criticism, disagreement—all become automatic. The couple plays the same tapes in their minds and in their talk to each other. For example, let's play a typical tape from an ordinary couple:

"Good morning, darling. Did you sleep well?"

"As if you care."

"Fine. I hope you stayed awake all night."

"I'll bet you do. You snored loud enough to wake the dead."

"Well, you hogged all the covers—as usual. I almost froze to death."

"Oh, that's likely. I don't see how you can't have enough covers when you always hog the whole bed. I sleep on the edge of the mattress every night—listening to the chainsaw in my ear."

3. *The Wall of Separation*. Resentment, anger, frustration, and an unwillingness to give in or to repair the hurts that regularly occur gradually build a thick emotional wall that blocks the ordinary attempts at reconciliation or connection. Attempts to reestablish the relationship are met with boiling tar poured down from the parapet of the wall:

"Honey, what can we do to go back to the way things were when we were first married?"

"It's too late. Our relationship can never be what it was."

"But can we just try?"

"What part of *never* don't you understand?"

2220. **Some Thoughts from Nassim Taleb, in His Book,** *The Bed of Procrustes:*

"We humans, facing limits of knowledge, and things we do not observe, the unseen and the unknown, resolve the tension by squeezing life and the world into crisp commodified ideas, reductive categories, specific vocabularies, and prepackaged narratives . . ." (xii). Comment: There is the fear of unknown knowledge, that it will point to a truth that will point to Someone whose very existence will make them change their behavior. We must therefore control our perception and beliefs about the world, keep them safely fixed in the boxes Taleb outlines, to prevent their escape.

A paraphrase of an aphorism on page 4: Socrates was executed because he thought too clearly.

"It is a very recent disease to mistake the unobserved for the nonexistent; but some are plagued with the worse disease of mistaking the unobserved for the unobservable" (17). Comment: This "worse disease" has been around for a long time. Think of the germ theory of disease and how difficult it was to convince people that bacteria caused the illnesses that killed so many.

2221. We can tell a lot about contemporary civilization by the words it no longer (or seldom) uses: evil, sin, duty, sublime, grandeur, honor, virtue. When was the last time you heard one of these on the Six O'clock News or a talk show?

2222. When you eat in a coffee shop, the menu often contains photographs purported to represent the food you can order. When you eat in a fancy restaurant, there are no pictures on the menu: you must form a picture in your imagination. Unfortunately, whether the picture is on the menu or in your mind, neither represents very accurately what you will actually be served.

2223. Egotism: "If a knowledge claim does not fit my framework of reality, it does not exist. In fact, it cannot exist." Such a stance is driven by fear, fear that some fact outside the framework might point to One who has claims on your life.

2224. On the difference between information and knowledge. Information is aggregated, organized, and systematized data. Information presents a structure that the inexperienced are quick to act on. Knowledge is information understood in context. This deep understanding and contextual situating tells the expert the real meaning of the information.

For example, a car's "Maint Req" light might go on. The first level of understanding of this bit of information is that the light means, "Maintenance Required," which further means that the car is due for an oil change. But the person with knowledge of the car might know that the oil was just changed less than a thousand miles ago, so the light (connected to the odometer) can and should be ignored.

2225. It has been repeatedly remarked that those who say they are searching for truth are really searching for confirmation of what they already believe—the so-called confirmation bias. But the reality is that those who say they are searching for truth are really only searching for affirmation. Psychologist Paul Vitz says that in graduate school he became an atheist because he wanted to fit in and be accepted by his professors and his peers. (See *The Psychology of Atheism.*)

2226. Fatigued by the constant stream of postmodernist discourse, Darxul opened *The Book of One Hundred Lies* and read,

45. If I believed in such a thing as truth, I would be telling it to you.

46. A given statement has no single or best meaning.

47. It's settled science. There is no credible debate.

2227. There is a freely available popular drug, sold nearly everywhere you look, even though 2 grams can be fatal to a child. People take this drug to "feel better," but just look at the possible side effects: headache, nasal discharge, dizziness, nausea, vomiting, anemia, decreased kidney function, stomach ulceration, rectal bleeding, coma, and even pancreatic cancer. Yet worldwide, people who "just want the pain to go away" consume an estimated 40,000 tons each year. Talk about drug addicts. How much longer will we allow this drug, this aspirin, to be legal?

2228. It never ceases to amaze me how virulently ideas and their proponents are attacked when they oppose current dogma (economic, scientific, historical, philosophical, etc., etc.). And yet every discipline has a rich history of new or at least different ideas supplanting other ideas as new knowledge or experience shows that the new idea is better than the old. And yet the supplanting often occurs only after bitter and prolonged warfare. Is it for no better a reason than because egos are threatened? Or grants? Or is it because the new idea causes epistemic or ontological panic? ("If this new idea is true, not only has my life's work been for nothing, but my entire worldview is false.") Or is it the cosmic authority phobia? If the new idea is true, then God is true also.

2229. Failure to forgive is an example of the sunk cost fallacy. In both instances the injury, emotional or financial, is in the past forever and cannot be undone. To continue to spend emotional resources (resentment, anger) on unrecoverable past events just because of the hurt they have caused is the same thing as continuing to invest in a losing business (or in a Nigerian 419 con scheme) just because you've already spent so much money on it. The saying, "throwing good money after bad," is like "throwing new pain after old." Only forgiveness will release you from the ongoing, unproductive, wasteful investment in past history.

2230. A number of episodes of several crime-drama TV series include either criminal Christians (pastors, vicars, murderous self-righteous fanatics, tyrannical and abusive Scripture-quoting fathers) or Christians as murder victims—men of the cloth often spectacularly murdered in their church. It is said that we adopt many beliefs through anecdote and few beliefs through reason or evidence. I wonder whether these character roles from TV serve either as unbelief inducers or as food for confirmation bias. In other words, for those who are nominally Christian or those who are unsettled about religion and spiritual life in general, are they influenced against faith by these propagandistic ploys?

It's an old technique—associate something you want to make loathsome with something already thought to be loathsome. Are people so naïve that they fall for this?

"Fred is a lowdown, crooked snake."

"He is? Hey, Harry! Have you heard? Fred is a lowdown, crooked snake."

"Who knew? Tom, did you know that Fred is a snake and a crook?"

"Yeah, that's what everybody says."

2231. Just as rising meteors do not think back on their ascendant arc, so too do they neglect to think forward to their inevitable decline and fiery end.

2232. Just the facts, ma'am. Or, facts don't lie. Or, raw data is objective. But raw data fresh from the garden needs to be cleaned up and prepared before it can be used. And that makes it subject to experimenter bias, confirmation bias, political agenda bias, and so on. A given data set might be readied for analysis by first "fixing it up" thusly:

- Remove outliers that are "outside a reasonable set of data points."
- Interpolate to fill in missing data.
- Correct "obviously wrong" data.
- Adjust "anomalous" data.
- Recalibrate "measurement errors."
- Use proxies to substitute for actual measurements.

2233. How seriously do you take your faith, whatever it is? For Christians, we have some very sobering words from God about our living. Here are some of them:

1. "But I tell you that every careless word that people speak, they shall give an accounting for it in the day of judgment. For by your words you will be justified, and by your words you will be condemned." —Matthew 12:36-37

2. "If anyone builds on [the foundation of Jesus Christ] . . . each one's work . . . will be revealed by fire; the fire will test the quality of each one's work." —1 Corinthians 3:12-13

2234. As he looked upon the difference between what an inept service person had promised and what he had done, Darxul consulted *The Book of One Hundred Lies* and read aloud:

48. Oh, yes. I'm very experienced with this.

49. Don't worry. Everything is under control.

50. Relax. I know what I'm doing.

51. This completely unique new system guarantees results.

52. I'll always remember this. [or] I'll never forget you.

2235. What separates good problem solvers from less good problem solvers is the ability to avoid solution path fixation. If a given solution doesn't work, the good problem solver cheerfully goes on to try another solution. No regrets or angry determination to make the first solution work. As I've said before, the goal of problem solving is to solve the problem, not to implement a particular solution.

2236. Another thing that separates the good problem solver from the average problem solver is the ability to anthropomorphize the problem, especially when it involves mechanical, electrical, or electronic equipment. The average problem solver asks, "Why doesn't this work?" The better problem solver asks, "What is this thing thinking?" "What is it trying to do but can't?" "Where did the code get stuck?" By thinking about the problem situation as a living being with living systems, the good problem solver thinks about how the flow of operations works or doesn't work and then formulates analysis and solutions from there.

2237. "Weight Watchers meets at the Giant Buffet Wednesdays from 7:00 PM to 10:00 PM.

2238. "Yes, 2 PM is a good time to go to the gym because you can get a parking place near the door."

2239. "The last two items on the shopping list are seedless grapes at the grocery store and grape seed extract from the health food store."

2240. "I like this gym because you don't have to walk up to the second floor to get to the Stairmasters."

2241. "Focus? I'm so focused I can concentrate on ten things in five minutes."

2242. "Nobody goes there anymore. It's too crowded." — A comment attributed to Yogi Berra. Another Yogi attribution: "It was impossible to get a conversation going. Everybody was talking too much." These provide a perfect example of measur-

ing the world by oneself. Like the disputed and apparently ficti-
tious quotation, "I don't know how Nixon could have won. Nobody I know voted for him."

2243. When your arm hurts, your arm hurts. When your head
hurts, your head hurts. When your stomach hurts, your stomach hurts. But when your stomach is sick, *you* are sick.

2244. Why is there evil? This is an old problem. Human evil is
explained by the fall. Sin entered the world. Man was given free
will and he often chooses to do evil to his fellow man. But what
about earthquakes and tsunamis? The earth is under a curse
(Genesis 3:17-18). But what about cholera, the bubonic plague,
tapeworms, tuberculosis, measles, polio, cancer, malaria, Alzheimer's, and so on? The earth and life forms all became corrupt
(Genesis 6:11-12).

2245. To a mathematician, imaginary numbers expand the possibilities of doing calculations such as the square root of negative numbers. To one of my former bosses, imaginary numbers
are what he made up in order to fill out surveys, budgets, reports, award applications, and annual review ratings. I suppose
this demonstrates the gulf between academia and the business
world.

2246. **Source Evaluation and Critical Thinking.**
    There are lots of Web pages that tell you how to evaluate
sources—especially Internet sources. I even have such a page.
But there's something that you're not being told. Source evaluation is (1) a learned skill and (2) it's learned heuristically, not
algorithmically. Let me define for you. An algorithm is a step by
step procedure that yields a set result. A cake recipe is a good
example. Follow the recipe correctly, get a nice cake. Unfortunately, source evaluation is not algorithmic. And even more unfortunately, too many writers and teachers pretend that it is.
    Source evaluation cannot be learned by reading an article
that lists half a dozen factors (who is the publisher, who is the

author, how recent is the article, etc.) to take into account. Now, such articles are very good because those are important items to think about. But there are many nuances, variations, exceptions, and subtleties to include also.

A heuristic is a trial-and-error method of learning, where you gradually learn over time what the best answers are. Your knowledge—your skill—that you apply to evaluating sources must be refined so that you can sniff out that fake source that looks so reliable.

For example, suppose you are researching diet and you come across a Web site called the Investigative Institute for Human Health and Nutrition. There you find an article about the dangers of eating red meat. The article is by a couple of people with Doctor titles. Good source? Well, suppose further that you do a little digging and discover that the site is owned or sponsored by VeganMilitancy and that the doctors have honorary PhDs and not medical degrees. Bad source? Well, are there redeeming factors? Can you trust the statistics on the site?

Here is my advice for what to do:

- Triangulate the source. Are there other sources that support these arguments, data, reasons, evidence?
- Use the rest of the Internet to test the claims of the site.

2247. "Can you help me?"

"I can try. What's the problem?"

"This advertisement. It says, 'Your investment will earn 10 percent interest.'"

"What is your difficulty?"

"There's a little star-like symbol at the end, right after the word *interest*."

"Hmm. Let me see. Oh, that's an asterisk. It means, 'The previous statement is a lie. For an explanation of why it is a lie, see its brother asterisk at the bottom of the page.'"

"The asterisk—is that how you pronounce it?—at the bottom of the page says, 'Rate of return based on historical data from selected years. Actual rate of return on new investments will vary and is not guaranteed.' Does that mean I won't really get ten percent interest?"

"That about sums it up."

"But the headline says, 'Your investment will earn ten percent.' How can that be?"

"Excuse me, but what part of *lie* don't you understand?"

"But the headline — ."

"The lie is in the asterisk."

2248. Women evaluate themselves by comparison with other women. Men evaluate themselves by their accomplishments. And yet, aren't these largely the same? For men rate themselves by comparing their accomplishments to the accomplishments of other men. And women rate themselves by comparing their positions and relationships to those of other women. Would that both men and women would stop comparing themselves to other people and focus on pleasing the Lord.

2249. It's easier to dissolve the beliefs of others by using scorn and mockery than to produce new beliefs in them by reason and argument.

2250. The first time you see adultery depicted on TV or in a film, you are shocked. The hundredth time, you yawn, having been desensitized by repetition. The thousandth time you might feel yourself beginning to approve. And too many repetitions after that and who knows? Hollywood might have persuaded you to participate.

2251. Beliefs are created by anecdote, story, example, and personal experience. This makes them impervious to rebuttal by reasons and evidence. But not to countering anecdotes, stories, examples, and personal experiences.

2252. In 1 Corinthians 13:6, Paul tells us that love honors the truth. Those who don't believe in truth or who are chronic liars, therefore do not — cannot? — love anyone else.

2253. Another way to state #2248 is to say that women live by comparison (and therefore want to emulate other women), while men live by distinction (and therefore want to surpass other men).

2254. As he left the automobile dealership without having purchased a new car, Darxul was reminded of some entries in *The Book of One Hundred Lies*. These were so familiar that he recited them from memory:

53. I'm not telling you this as a way to influence your decision. I don't care which way you choose. I just want you to make a smart choice.

54. I'm not making any money on this deal. We hope you'll be satisfied enough to recommend us to your friends.

55. All the reviews are very positive. Everyone loves this.

56. We'll never offer a lower price, and you'll never find a lower price anywhere else.

57. No, these things never break down.

58. I really went to bat for you with my boss. He yelled at me and said I was offering too good a deal.

59. The owner of the business heard about my offer and is coming here to cancel it. The only way to save it is to sign the purchase agreement before he arrives.

60. I could lose my job over this offer. But I know how much you need this and I want to help you.

61. You don't need to worry about those numbers. Sales agreements are always confusing.[1]

2255. Why is it that so many people are discontented with their current state (life, relationships, job)? The reasons are apparent:

1. The need for novelty. People get bored, especially those who depend on externals for entertainment. Those who cannot stand their own company are the shallow ones who tell you, "I'm bored easily." (In other words, "Entertain me because I can't entertain myself.")

---

[1] See the note at the end of the book listing the lies covered so far.

2. The greed of imagination. Our present state is reality. We compare it to our imagined state and our present state always comes up short. Nothing we can ever attain can match our imagined life.

3. The pride of entitlement. We think we deserve better than what we have in our current state of life.

2256. We are conditioned to be waste generators. Outside the home, we use paper napkins, disposable straws, paper towels, paper cups, plastic forks and spoons and knives — not to mention those little unrecyclable packets of mustard and ketchup. And our burgers and tacos are wrapped in paper and put in bags. Many of the items we buy are wrapped in "tamper proof" packaging that adds to the stream of plastic and cardboard going to the dump. We generate an enormous amount of trash without even thinking about it, much less about where it goes.

At the grocery store last night, the checker put nearly every item into its own plastic bag. So I participated in the wasting culture, even without my explicit permission.

Nothing shows the waste stream quite like those 90-gallon recycling bins, which we not only use with enthusiasm but we fill them up to the brim almost every week.

2257. When we seek something (or someone) too ardently, we transform our perceptions of reality into the thing we seek, making ourselves believe we have found the object of our desire.

2258. Samuel Johnson says, in *Rambler* 64, that "he cannot be a useful counsellor, who will hear no opinion but his own." As our culture somehow encourages all of us to be more and more opinionated and fixed in our ideas, growing angry whenever someone has another opinion, it seems to me that we are losing the ability to counsel. A counsellor needs to listen with empathy and allow the one in need to express various alternatives. Then a discussion of those alternatives can produce an optimal choice. The would-be counsellor who allows only his own choice cannot rightly be called a counsellor.

2259. How Darkness Leads Us Astray.

I was recently asked to hang some picture frames in a family room at a relative's house. I packed my drill driver, some one-inch drywall screws, and a drill bit to make pilot holes in the "vinyl" walls. It turns out that the walls are vinyl-covered aluminum. Now, this family room is rather dark, but I thought I could see well enough, so I put the drill bit in the drill and started to make pilot holes. I couldn't believe how tough the aluminum was, because I could barely get a drill bit to stay in place on the wall. The bit kept skipping over the surface. With careful attention, I managed to settle it in one place, but then I had to lean in with a lot of weight to get anywhere. Finally, the bit broke through and I had a hole. I made about five holes, all with the same difficulty, and hung the pictures.

Then I moved to a place in the room where there was more light. In fact, there was enough light to notice that I had put the drill bit in backwards. I had been drilling holes with the butt end of the drill bit. A black drill bit in a dark room had fooled me. When I turned the bit around and started to drill with the business end, it cut through the aluminum like a needle through a sheet of paper.

So, having light lets you see what you're doing, lets you *know* what you're doing. And this applies to both the light of day and the light of truth.

2260. Many TV crime shows are clever only in the way they cleverly don't tell you all the facts (and motivations) until the moment they solve the crime. Many are so filled with red herrings that you can frequently guess who the murderer is by naming the person who has been on screen for less than two minutes and seems to be the most saintly. And if there is a church involved, the vicar did it.

2261. Why do so many people favor those with controlling personalities, those with absolute confidence, and those who are instantly decisive? Answer: We don't like ambiguity or uncertainty. We want definiteness so that we can fix reality and make our lives reasonable and comfortable.

2262. Just recently I installed backup cameras on my car and truck, and the result again reminded me of the difference between information and knowledge. The display showing the view from the camera is complete with green, yellow, and red lines, indicating how close you're getting to something behind you. That's information. However, it is not clear just what the distances are when, say, the object in back of you touches a yellow or red line. The meaning of the lines needs to be calibrated with actual objects, such as a car bumper. Once the display is calibrated so that you understand what the lines actually indicate, you'll have knowledge.

2263. When you try to sell your own book by yourself, you feel sorry for bookstores.

2264. If you want other people to help you, ask them to help you advance their own agenda.

2265. Truth and falsehood are both motivators to action because they both involve belief, and we act on the basis of belief. Unfortunately, falsehood is a better motivator than truth because the pimps of falsehood have tarted her up to gather attention and instill commitment, and make a few bucks. Poor truth is often rather plain looking, and not always good natured, either. Those motivated by her have to love her for what she is.

2266. Read too much; think too little.

2267. Gender Stereotype #72845. In a given situation, women tend to find problems when there are none, and men tend to overlook problems when there are some.

2268. Re: Glimmering 2265. Let's put a little makeup on truth and hope she fares better in the marketplace of ideas.

2269. Let's hope there is some psychic or spiritual benefit we confer when we attempt to help someone with a repair issue but fail. Today I visited a widow and attempted to repair her 40- or 50-year-old furnace. I spent a couple of hours trying to trouble-shoot it, but the information on the Web was all directed at newer furnaces. (This one, after all, still had a pilot light.) No amount of checking the wiring and resetting the gas flow had any effect. So I turned to another task.

Next, I attempted to reconnect the wiring from the house to a pond pump. Another couple of hours, circuit breaker installed, wiring connected, but no juice to the pump. The wires had been disconnected in four places and were all the same color (white), so it was difficult to ascertain which wire connected to which. Had to give up after limited amount of progress.

Lastly, I tried to figure out a way to reset a password on a Windows 8 laptop. After spending another hour or so trying to guess the password (After an incorrect entry, the screen shows *hint: church* but the widow had no idea what the hint meant). Researching the Web once again, I found some software that might work to expose and reset the password, but it needs more research.

So, basically, I failed at all three tasks. But again, let's hope that my efforts and personal interaction made a positive difference for the widow.

2270. The halo effect tells us that when we see a handsome man or a beautiful woman, we also tend to assume that the person is kind, intelligent, and capable, only because of the good looks. If we are wise, we recognize that this effect is very often a source of self-deception.

In a twisted or reverse form, the effect shows its perversity when we see someone homely and overweight, and consequently assume that the person is less kind, intelligent, and capable than the better looking counterpart.

At its worst, the reverse halo effect causes us to underestimate the capabilities of evil people and organizations. We are so convinced that intelligence, creativity, and ability are on the side of good that we can hardly attribute any such qualities to an enemy or the side of evil. For someone to say, for example, that "the Nazis were very clever in creating new weapons" or that "the Communists mastered the art of propaganda during the Cold War," would seem to be praising evil regimes.

But if we don't recognize the capabilities of the enemy in a frank and accurate manner, we are likely to ignore them or give too little credit to them. A current example is the way ISIS (the Islamic terrorist organization) is working to separate the loyalty of European Muslims from their non-Muslim fellow citizens. If non-Muslims make the Muslims in, say, France or Germany feel unwelcome, then those Muslims will be pushed into the arms of ISIS. And ISIS is very good at propaganda.

2271. **Deceived By Assumptions.**

A few days ago, I went to Home Depot to buy a Christmas tree. I saw a nice one in the bin labeled "7-8 foot Nordmann Fir." The one I chose was the tallest in the bin, so *I assumed* it was closer to 8 than 7 feet. I brought the tree to the net wrappers and went in to pay for it. On my return to the tree area, an employee asked, "How tall is your tree?" and on my reply he said, "Here's your tree," and grabbed a netted tree that *he assumed* was mine and carried it to my truck.

Just before I left, I looked at the tag and noticed that it said, "Douglas Fir." I returned to the tree area and soon located the tree I had paid for, not yet netted up. My name was on the tag. As the employee was about to go to my truck and get the wrong tree back, another customer said to him, "This isn't the tree I paid for." He pointed to a small Douglas Fir that *the employee had assumed* was his. In the end, I got my Nordmann tree home. However, it was in fact a 6-to-7 foot tree and not a 7-to-8 foot tree. I had *assumed* that it was in the correct bin.

2272. Before you can believe the truth about yourself, you must first reject the false. —Suggested by Meister Eckhart

2273. **The Ought of Pricing.**
Pricing is constrained for new items that are similar to existing items because, no matter how innovative, the new item exists in a pricing context. It would be difficult to sell a new radio-controlled car for $500 because "radio controlled cars shouldn't cost that much. Many cost between $20 and $50." But when a new item, such as a robot, is introduced, it produces a new paradigm. There is little pricing context.
"How much should a robot cost?"
"I don't know. I guess maybe $200 is the right price."

2274. When I am long gone, what will be the sum of awareness of my life? A biography? A story? An anecdote? An epigram? Perhaps not even an epigram.

2275. I have an aphorism somewhere that avers, "Pain is the chalk; laughter the eraser." Having the advantage of suffering sciatic pain much of the day, I'm willing now to say that "Pain is the eraser," because it makes me forgetful of everything but the pain. So today's witty maxim is, "Ache and forget."

2276. Just a simple example of the ruinous effects of pride: Think how many thousands—nay, millions—of delicious meals are missed every day because the Aunt Biddies of the world would never give their recipes for pot roast or turkey or fish to anyone. Oh, yes, they prided themselves on their famously delicious concoctions. Everyone loved them. But the cooks would never share their secrets. Instead, they all took those recipes to the grave.
It's a short-sighted vanity. By guaranteeing that only she will ever make her famous dumplings, Aunt Biddie ensures that she gets all the compliments. How jealous she would be if her niece Jane made her dish and was complimented for it. But what happens after Biddie goes to the great kitchen in the sky?

Generations that might otherwise enjoy "coq au vin the way Aunt Biddie used to make it" will never have a taste. Had she thought it through, Biddie would have eagerly shared her recipes with every cousin and friend, thereby ensuring her immortality as a great cook.

2277. On the meaning of "Urgent Care." This person developed a painful sciatic nerve condition. After bearing it a few days, he went to Urgent Care. He signed in and waited in the waiting room for three and a half hours. Then he was escorted into an examination room where he waited another forty-five minutes. So four hours and fifteen minutes after arriving, he finally saw a physician's assistant for five minutes. He was given a prescription that—he found out after filling it—has a very negative interaction with another medicine he is already taking. So six hours were wasted all told.

2278. We would all be better thinkers if we avoided making pronouncements about huge, categorical labels. Such labels are too encompassing to be accurate and therefore have little value. To say that "[Science, religion, politicians, ideology, history] has been responsible for much evil in the world, so it is bad" pounds on too much ambiguity. If, instead of *politics*, you say *Marxism*, instead of *religion* you say, *Islamic fundamentalism*, if instead of *science* you say *Neo-Darwinism*, then you're getting somewhere. Just remember that the bigger the abstraction under attack the more powerful the attacker feels, and therefore the less likely he is to reduce the scope of the attack.

2279. **Demystification.**

A man was driving on a mountain road one day and noticed how lovely the view was over across the valley. He pulled into a turnout and stopped the car. As he stood at the edge of the cliff, looking out over the beautiful expanse of green trees and grass, the brown rocks, the sky and the clouds, and the ocean in the distance, his emotions soared. Another man, who had also stopped his car to get a better look, stood nearby taking pictures. The first man said to the second, "Isn't this just amazing? So awe inspiring. It's almost a spiritual experience."

"It's pretty," said the second man, "but it's just nature."

"But aren't the mountains beautiful? The way they go up and down so artistically. It's almost as if you can trace the finger of God."

"Nonsense," said the second man. "Let me show you how plate tectonics produces mountains."

"Well, aren't you impressed by the great expanse of the ocean?" asked the first man.

"The chemistry of water is unexceptional," the other replied. "And the blue comes from a reflection of the sky."

"Well, I don't know about you, but I feel a real sense of beauty when I look at the forest. So well designed, so elegant. You must grant me that the forest produces a special feeling in you."

"Any emotions over nature come from a simple survival instinct, built in to our distant ancestors. And as for design, that's only an appearance manufactured by your brain responding to the products of fractal algebra and chaos theory."

2280. Vignettes from the Fantasy Life.

"Come to dinner, Wartle."

"What are we having, Mother?"

"Bacon wrapped, dry aged, prime filet mignon with truffles in lobster sauce."

"What?! Again?!"

"The main chef was out sick today."

"But we had that only two months ago. Why must we always eat the same thing over and over again?"

"I'm sorry. We'll just have to make do with what's available. Life won't always be this hard."

2281. Are there too many good ideas to allow them all to succeed, become known, be used? A pocket exerciser might be a great idea and an excellent product, but how will it ever stand out against the well-financed makers of, say, a fancy sports bottle? And how will a given new sports bottle become a success? There are already dozens on the market, and at the 2016 Consumer Electronics Show there were dozens more high-tech sports bottle makers, hawking bottles with speakers, bottles with room to store an iPhone, bottles with cameras, bottles with batteries, bottles that purify water, and so on. How will any of them make it in the already overhyped infospace against current and new competitors?

2282. Notable.

On the exhibit floor of a technology conference, a young woman was giving out bags with info and (it turned out) rechargeable batteries and a battery charger. I was the last person in line. Just when I got near the front of the now gone line, she gave the last bag to the guy in front of me. She looked at me and said, "I will get you a bag." She went off somewhere and returned with three or four more bags. She gave me one and I smiled and said, "Bless you!"

When I said that, she said, "Here, take another," and gave me a second bag.

Contrast this with my interaction with a drone salesman. I talked with him for several minutes about his product. There was no one else around, other than my colleague, Phil. Phil happened to see a sign saying, "Like us on Facebook and get a free T-shirt." Phil called that to the salesman's attention and he said that was right. Phil did the Facebook liking. I asked, "How can I get a free shirt since I don't do social media?" He said, "You can't." He then went to his supply and returned with Phil's T-shirt and with an expression on his face that seemed to indicate he was pleased that he had enforced the rules.

2283. Lessons From the Consumer Electronics Show, 2016, #1.

A maker of drones featured a sales presentation where attendees sat in "earthquake" chairs that vibrate and shake in sync with low bass rumbling sound effects. This experience was background to video of a young woman windsurfing, sometimes in slow motion. The sales idea was that the surfing was filmed by one of the company's drones. But rumbling audio and shaking seats seemed an illogical pairing with the video.

2284. Lessons From the Consumer Electronics Show, 2016, #2.
Quite a few companies offered something free (T-shirt, ear buds, water bottle, sample of product, etc.) if you Liked them on Facebook or Twitter. Hence the saying, "If you bribe them, they will come."

2285. Lessons From the Consumer Electronics Show, 2016, #3.
People will buy a product even though they don't understand how it works — if they can see what it does. But they won't buy something if they cannot understand what it does.

2286. Make a statement, get a yawn. Tell a story, get a convert.

2287. "Have you seen Kelley lately?"
"I saw most of her yesterday."
"Was she in her new dress?"
"Some of her was."
"What?"
"If she had anything less on, she could headline in her own show in Las Vegas."

2288. Life is a series of destinations.

2289. Uniqueness packaged as an upgrade to the familiar.

2290. "I don't believe in God because I don't believe in anything I can't see, and I've never seen God. Seeing is believing."
"So then, you don't believe in air because you can't see it, or gravity, or magnetism because you can't see them? And you don't believe in the aroma of perfume or the stench of a carcass because you have never seen a smell? Or for that matter, have you ever seen a sound?"[2]

---

[2] See also *Glimmerings* 2438 and 2463.

2291. **Powerful People.**

The characteristics of people who wield power include, in reverse order:

3. Those who use or threaten force to conquer, gain obedience, or maintain control.

2. Those who order others to use or threaten force to conquer, gain obedience, or maintain control.

1. Those who create, maintain, and promote the information that causes the enforcers to threaten force in ways that follow from the information they have been given.

Yes, the truly powerful are the propagandists, the spin meisters, and those who seed the social networks with their preferred narratives, causing others to see reality in a certain way. The so-called rulers make their decisions based on the stories the narratologists tell them, and the enforcers do what the rulers demand of them.

So, those who control the stories of a culture control the culture. Hence the battle for dominance of competing narratives.

2292. He was a kink in the garden hose of thought.

2293. Many universities brag about lifelong learning as one of the goals of their curriculum, as if the idea were a special gift. But lifelong learning is essential for everyone who wants to have more truth than falsehood in his brain. We read books and magazines and newspapers and Web sites, and we gain knowledge. In time, sometimes short, sometimes after a while, we discover that what we learned is wrong, false, partial, inaccurate, and was so even when we learned it. And we discover that much of what we learned that was true at the time is now no longer applicable, because it has been replaced, expanded, updated, or abandoned. If we don't learn about these changes, our minds will be filled with intellectual landfill rather than golden nuggets.

2294. To a mouse caught by the old "cheese in a mousetrap" ploy, the true cost of free is death.

2295. "I see two books on wisdom," the fool said. "I'll take the one with the prettier cover."

2296. When last we left civilization with the problem of too much information, growing by exabytes faster than they could be shoveled out of the way, one response was to invite everyone on earth to contribute even more information, in the form of 140-character chunks, er, I mean, tweets. Now, Twitter recommends that new users simply follow others and learn by reading—without necessarily becoming a contributor to the infoglut anarchy.

Most contributors seem to post links to longer articles elsewhere on the Web, because they long ago realized that few can contribute meaningful ideas (other than proverbs or short comments) in only 140 characters. That's not even a knowledge appetizer.

2297. She was as graceful as a cow, on roller skates, going down stairs, on icy steps, blindfolded, backwards.

2298. Expectation is hope on steroids.

2299. Why is it so much easier to point to people who are smart than to people who are wise? —Robert J. Sternberg

2300. One of the features confidence schemes often share is the difficulty investors face in joining them. The con men erect barriers to entry that make investing seem all the more attractive: Will I be good enough to be accepted? Will I qualify for this restricted deal? Being chosen makes the investors feel special and willing to be secretive because they are now on the inside with the elite few. Of course, the difficulty is a sham, with the only actual requirement that must be met is to have money.

It's all about ego. And when pride meets greed, you're doomed.

2301. Why do some wives and girlfriends seem to enjoy shaming their men? And often in public? Instead of sympathy, these women deliver guilt and shame.

"Harold, what's wrong?"

"My arthritis is acting up again."

"And how long did you exercise today?"

"About five or ten minutes."

"You know your joints aren't going to get any better if you don't exercise. And whose fault is it if you don't exercise?"

"Thanks for making me feel so much better."

2302. The saying is, "Happy wife, happy life." But the problem is that happiness is a natural disposition. A happy woman makes a happy wife. An unhappy woman makes an unhappy wife. And the husband of the unhappy wife doesn't know what to do to make her happy. So he withdraws. Which adds resentment to unhappiness. And so forth.

2303. **Musings on Ecclesiastes 4:13.**

1. You are not old until you stop learning.

2. The desire to know — which is curiosity — is the fountain of youth.

3. There is no connection between wealth and wisdom. In fact, there might often be a negative correlation. If you are rich, why waste your time in reading and thinking?

2304. **Musings on Romans 3:3.**

1. What we believe about someone or something does not change that person or thing. Our belief changes only our perceptions and attitudes. This thought also applies to what others think of us, and is summed up by my favorite quotation from Thomas à Kempis:

> Let not thy peace be in the hearts of men; for whatsoever they say of thee, good or bad, thou art not therefore another man: but as thou art, thou art.[3]

---

[3] The *Imitation of Christ*, translated by Richard Whitford, 3:28.

2. How many people really believe those things that they desperately want to believe are true or false? Are they truly convinced or only afraid? Atheists are a good example. Are they really that impervious to the book of creation—every flower, every butterfly, every drop of water?

2305. In a previous era, the young men called them rules, the experienced men called them guidelines, and the old men called them suggestions. In the new era, the young men call them suggestions, the experienced men call them guidelines, and the old men call them rules.

2306. Why don't students in their college writing classes learn to write better?

1. Students are economizers, and as with other classes, they want to do the least amount of work necessary.

2. Students are procrastinators, and put off writing papers until the day—or the night—before they are due.

3. Faculty are too easy on them, giving passing pity points to papers that should have failed.

4. Students want to get through and get by, not learn to write better. Witness the hastily written banalities they hand in. If they really wanted to learn to write better, they would put more effort into it.

What is the reality? They bring their paper to the professor for "help." Do they want suggestions about organizing or presenting an argument or structuring a good paragraph? No, they want "edits without understanding." They want you to correct their grammatical errors without learning why the errors were made (which would enable them to avoid them in the future).

And, of course, if the student doesn't get an A on the final paper, he will complain that he brought it in to you to help him, so the lesser grade must be your fault.

2307. Doesn't the idea of a wise man all alone on a mountain top contradict the idea of wisdom itself? Isn't the goal of wisdom to make good decisions? How quaint that modern education should be focused on learning massive piles of information—or knowledge, if you insist—without the prospect of ever using any of it to serve fellow human beings? As Dallas Willard notes in *The Divine Conspiracy,* in Jesus' day, the goal of a teacher was not simply to fill his students with lots of knowledge. The goal was to change lives, and to prepare others to change lives.

2308. **Yet Another Attempt to Categorize:**
- Observation produces data.
- Analysis of data produces information.
- Understanding information produces knowledge.
- Applying knowledge contextually is wisdom.

2309. The SQ3R reading method (Survey, Question, Read, Recite, Review) needs to be punched up a bit. For Survey, we should include not only gain an overview, but examine the source and the context. For Question, we should not just ask questions about the subject, but questions about the data and arguments and assumptions—and opposing views. Read should include both summarizing and paraphrasing, and perhaps outlining. Recite should include the development of disconfirming arguments and evidence, as appropriate. And Review should include further analysis and conclusions.

2310. Re: Glimmering 2308.
Wisdom is knowledge applied through insight.

[March 20, 2016; Age 65]

2311. **Romance.**
"I'm going to get a muffin."
"Want me to go with you?"
"No. You have stuff to do."
"I don't mind, really."
"That's okay, but I don't want to bother you."
"It would be no bother. I would enjoy it."
"Okay, great! I was hoping you would want to come."

2312. Patience is what you show on the outside, not necessarily what you feel on the inside.

2313. What is it about people you find it difficult to love? Difficulty loving someone stems from a wrong definition of love. If we expect to love only those who give us warm fuzzy feelings inside, then there are indeed people who are difficult to love. But if love consists not of emotion but of mercy and grace, then everyone can be loved.

2314. One of the books propping up my monitor is *The Natural History of Stupidity*. My only question is why the book isn't thicker or published in multiple volumes. Indeed, a volume a day could be written. And some of the tales could be about me.

2315. It has become quite common for someone to pick up a copy of one of my books, especially a Glimmerings book, read an entry, and say, "I disagree with this." Now, I am used to disagreement and criticism, so that's not what bothers me. The disappointment for me is that many of the entries here have been produced after quite a bit of thought, observation, and energy.

That aside, let me give my readers some ideas for making these books—and all books—more rewarding and less objectionable.

1. Don't be paralyzed by the negatives. Nearly every book contains errors, biases, outdated information, wrong thinking, and so on. Instead of jumping on such mistakes, seek what is true and useful for improving your life and the lives of those you love and care for.

2. Don't dismiss a statement because it is "a sweeping generalization." Of course it is. It's a proverb. Ask yourself, "Under what circumstances might this statement be true? When does it not apply? How does such a large generalization help me conceptualize the whole truth? Is the generalization (as a stand-in for a general truth) helpful or misleading?

2316. Wisdom unshared is wisdom impaired.

2317. The purpose of wisdom, like the purpose of knowledge, is to share it with others so they can benefit from the experience, thinking, or labors required to obtain it. Both the wisest man alive and the most foolish man walking the earth will eventually die. How sad if the wise did not share with the foolish the slightly easier way up the hill of life.

2318. We think that reason is a sharp, surgical knife that can cut through deception, irrelevance, fallacy, and falsehood. And yet we are capable of using reason to promote and defend the most irrational, idiotic, banal, crazy-on-the-face ideas and programs. Too often, it seems, reason is an after-prop, fabricated to support the emotional gauze of an idea that we want to be good or true. How else could some cosmologists, in order to account for the amazing fine tuning of our universe and yet still subscribe the universe's randomness, solve the conundrum by claiming that there are ten to the 500th invisible, parallel universes that weren't lucky enough to be fine-tuned like ours?

2319. Along the relationship path, there are many choices, many forks in the road where only one path may be taken. At first, the two are faced with the choice either to yield to the other or to resist—and insist on his or her own way. Then they are faced with whether to tolerate or condemn, to accept the other or criticize. And finally, there comes the choice of whether to enjoy or resent—decide to love the other as is or grow bitter over the differences.

2320. Opportunity knocks more often than most people think. But when Mr. Opportunity knocks, too many of us are asleep, not home, or out cruising for Miss Opportunity—pun intended.

2321. Darxul read the article with a pained expression and then quoted from *The Book of One Hundred Lies*:

62. This newspaper stands by its story of yesterday. In fact, we are more confident about it than ever.

2322. When a politician makes three promises during his campaign, he will fulfill none of them because the first is illegal, the second is unconstitutional, and the third is impossible.

2323. Recalling that *The Book of One Hundred Lies* was written by a con man, Darxul was not surprised to find these entries:

63. Most people never get the opportunity to become enormously wealthy overnight. But you are the lucky one, my friend. Your opportunity is right here. The money is as good as in the bank.

64. It's so wonderful that I could meet such a great and kind person online. I hope we can meet in person soon. Your picture reveals a generous heart. I'm glad to hear all is well with you. I'm fine, too. However, my sister's little girl (she's seven) needs an operation or she won't live more than six more months. But my sister doesn't have the money. I've given her all my savings ($2,200), but she needs another $800. Could you possibly help, my dear new friend? The money would go for a good cause.

2324. "You have turned a city into a pile of rubble, a fortified city into waste" (Isaiah 25:2a, Doax version).

Why are human beings so fascinated with destruction? We watch violent movies where cars and buildings are blown up; we slow down on the freeway to ogle accident scenes; we are mesmerized by forest fires; we like to break things up ourselves; and we fantasize about watching or doing violence and destruction to an enemy.

Why is destruction more spectacular than construction? Perhaps it's because construction requires more time and more effort. And if it's two things we don't want to do, it's take time for something (we're always in a hurry) and do more work.

2325. Many young people arrive at their wedding ceremony crammed with a pile of expectations — most of which are not going to be fulfilled by their spouse. The couple marries their own imagination during the dreamy ceremony and then wakes up later. At the awakening, first each partner feels surprise, then disappointment, and finally resentment. The spouse just doesn't measure up to those impossible (excuse me, very reasonable) expectations. And do notice that I'm using the word *expectations*, not *hopes* or *wishes*. The longer the courtship, the happier or more content the partners will be because they have gradually learned what they are going to get.

2326. **Found Among My Notes.**
      A tale that's amazing, but is it true?
      A little fact checking is what you can do.

2327. The answer to "What is life all about?" requires a long book in order to provide a significant and comprehensive answer. But hey, this is the age of Twitter and Instant Messaging. Our minds receive, broadcast, and think in short bursts of language. So, "What is life all about?" Meaning gleaning.

2328. The overall value of most things is a combination of utility value (actual usefulness) and constructed value (emotional connection).

2329. For every person who makes his own opportunity, there are probably three others who bump into it when they aren't looking.

2330. Every time you ask a personal question, you are taking a risk because the person you ask might tell you the truth, regardless of its cost to you.

2331. Multi-volume novel, novel, novella, short story, parable, maxim. This is called the progress of literature. Also known as the regress of attention span.

(Now that you have read this Glimmering, I hope you didn't lose attention, focus, concentration, or consciousness more than three or four times.)

2332. He was the founding editor and publisher of *Breaking News Quarterly*, circulation 17. It is not known why the publication never gained readership.

2333. Where Does Value Come From?
That is, why do we value certain things above other things?

1. Rarity or Distinctiveness. Things that only one or a few can possess are invested with value because of the competition for ownership. Those who have rare items feel special and often even proud or arrogant.

2. Social Evaluation. Those things that society values, for whatever reason — or for no discernible reason — we tend to value also. Modern art is an example. If the thought leaders in the art world tell us that a bunch of old coffee mugs in a pile called "Homage to Beethoven" is great art, we tend to go along and agree that it's worth the $16 million the museum paid for it.

3. Difficulty to Obtain. Things that require much effort to obtain are usually valued more than something we can get more easily. Examples would be a club membership that requires a lot of initiation activities, or a high cost to join. Climbing a difficult mountain gains value as an accomplishment simply because it's so hard. Danger adds even more value.

4. Personal Sentiment. We treasure things that have value only to us. An old postcard to us might be of much more value than an expensive sculpture.

5. Pleasure. We value things (and people) for the pleasure they give us.

2334. Why are great poets admired? Because they use language beautifully. For instance, the ordinary person quotes the maxim, "Actions speak louder than words." A cliché, familiar, wordy, somewhat wooden — even though true. But how does Shakespeare express the same thought? "Action is eloquence" (Coriolanus, III.ii).

2335. I once thought that being accused of having "a firm grasp of the obvious" was an insult. Now I believe it is a compliment because there are so many people without even a tenuous grasp of the obvious.

2336. **Thought Problem.**
   "What can I do to be happy?"
   "What have you tried so far?"
   "I took an assertiveness training course."
   "And what were the results?"
   "People call me a witch, with a B."
   "Have you tried humbling yourself?"
   "What do you mean?"
   "For example, have you tried being submissive to your husband?"
   "Oh, so I'm supposed to be a doormat and just lie down and let everyone walk all over me. No thanks."
   "In my experience, people who use the 'doormat' metaphor are too proud to learn the behaviors that lead to happiness."
   "You're saying that only wimps can be happy. You can just go to hell."
   "Yes, I am often told that. But why should I go there, a place filled with the unhappy proud, when there are enough of them here?"

2337. **A Wisdom Catechism.**
   Q. How do you know you are wise?
   A. When you act on knowledge appropriately, applying what you know.
   Q. How do you apply knowledge appropriately?
   A. By understanding context and human nature.
   Q. How do you understand context and human nature?
   A. By walking in the light.

2338. If you think, "I'm being humble about this," you're not.

2339. Impatience in the face of difficulty doubles it.

2340. Giving advice to someone after he makes a mistake is like offering painkillers to a corpse.

2341. No advice is given so earnestly as that which the advisor himself refuses to follow.

2342. Whenever the government promises some new benefit or service "free," the taxpayer is the asterisk at the end of the word.

2343. **Truths About Afflictions.**
    1. Most other people have worse afflictions, burdens, and sufferings than you.
    2. We should feel ashamed even to mention the "grievous suffering" we supposedly have because it is so minor compared with the real miseries of the rest of the world.
    3. If we look back on the times we felt so put upon by affliction, we usually see that the affliction and its suffering and its eventual outcome—and even lessons—were all good for us.
    4. The answer to, "Why me?" is, "Why not me? What makes me think I'm so special?"

2344. According to J. Frank Norfleet (in his book, *Norfleet*), all con artists have "a certain patronizing manner." I think that's because they can't hide their feelings of superiority—their pride—in knowing they are swindling someone. Their mark has fallen for the con; they know it; the mark doesn't.

2345. Once you give up the idea of eternal, objective truth—or even non-eternal, objective truth—you are left with subjective truth, situational truth, personal truth. "Was that true?" "It was for him."

But we can't live very long in a society where everyone has his own truth. "I know I signed a contract for ten years, but to me ten years is the same as a month." So the government must step in to keep order. The government declares what truth is. Of course, governments don't try to determine what the objective truth is. They impose their desired view of reality or even the wild and improbable narrative they wish to feed to the masses.

2346. Ideas Thrown Away on a Napkin.

041316. Are my books really teaching the world wisdom, or are they only killing trees?

032716. New grading scale (and who says we don't have standards?) from the realistic:

A. almost acceptable

B. basically bad

C. completely contemptible

D. disgustingly deplorable

F. flunky flopping failure

New grading scale from the self-esteemers:

A. amazingly articulate

B. blazingly brilliant

C. completely captivating

D. dynamically dazzling

F. fantastically fine

(And, of course, we remember that the definition of *fantastic* is "existing in the realm of fantasy.")

2347. Got humility? Instead of praying for a specific outcome (that is, telling God what to do), perhaps we should pray for God's will, since we don't know enough about his purposes to be specific in any situation.

2348. One of those restaurants where the food sounds better on the menu than it tastes on the palate.

2349. Is it that we didn't *have* or that we didn't *take* the opportunity?

2350. It suits the present system very well to have a secular society because those whose belief is only in this world are more likely to buy more and more stuff, beyond what they can afford. There is no heaven for them to store their treasures in.

2351. How is your value to society determined? Well, how much money do you make? Most people seem to view income as an accurate index into people's value. Maybe a more kind way to think of this is to say that your value to society is based directly upon your contribution to society in services or productivity—measured by how much you make in dollars. Society is very transactional, unfortunately. The person who really improves society by teaching good values or decision making is valued less than some rap star whose lyrics actually harm those who pay him. Part of the reason for this is that many don't realize that they vote with their dollars. Every time you buy something, you are approving of it.

So then, let's talk better valuation. What is your value to God? Remember, he doesn't need anything. Your value to God is based on

- your obedience to his commands ("If you love me, keep my commandments.")
- how well you use the talents he has given you
- how well you make or take the opportunities that arise

2352. Job Interview Questions.
- What interests you?
- What bores you?
- What motivates you?
- What offends you?
- Name ten things that don't describe you.
- Are you the roles you play or someone else?

2353. **Another Idea Thrown Away on a Napkin.**
041216. Old age: hello glasses, goodbye lasses.

2354. A French proverb tells us that as people grow older they become wiser—and more foolish. Knowing what is wise but doing what is foolish tells us a lot about the human heart.

2355. If, as is now frequently said, we can learn a lot by analyzing our failures, then why do we teach the young to have the attitude that "failure is not an option"?

2356. I just ate at a restaurant where the young woman serving us prided herself on taking the order by memory and not writing anything down. We ordered corned beef Reuben sandwiches (with sauerkraut), were served roast beef sandwiches (without sauerkraut), and were billed for pulled pork sandwiches.
    Is this what they mean by "delusions of adequacy"?

2357. Some people take long vacations to try to forget; others, to pretend to forget.

2358. Re: Glimmering 2344. Con men can't hide that "certain patronizing manner" because they are thinking, "I can't believe this guy is falling for such an obvious con! He must be really dumb and really greedy." Or, as in the case of a seduction, "I can't believe she's really falling for this line. She must be really naïve and clueless."

2359. "That most pitiful spectacle, the human being trying to get away from association with the secrets of his own soul" (*Norfleet*, 294).

2360. **Say It Again.**
    In order to learn from your mistakes, you must first admit that you make mistakes.
    If you don't admit to making mistakes, you won't learn from them.

2361. Life is cumulative.

2362. Selfishness can manifest itself in selective ways. We might call it circumstantial selfishness. The person who gladly gives us his seat on the bus and who spends Saturdays helping widows still wants to be one of the first in line at the Thanksgiving party potluck.

2363. I visited a market recently that had an eating area outside, where tables and chairs were shaded by umbrellas featuring beer advertisements. There was also a large, prominent sign reading, "No Drinking Beer or Alcohol Outside Market."

2364. For most people, experience is more important than truth. Experience is vivid and personal—they were there. But truth is second hand—they were told. And with truth being so abused and distorted, invented and mocked, no wonder it is given little value.

2365. The key to good decision making is the identification of a sufficient number of legitimate alternatives. Good decisions are less likely when the identified choices are few. "Buy this car, yes or no?" does not provide enough alternatives. Buy this car as equipped, another of the same model with different equipment, buy or lease, buy a different model or make with similar equipment—now you are beginning to get where a good decision can be made.

2366. And Satan said, "Behold, I will return to earth and problematize the narrative of God in order to decenter his hegemonic rule over his creatures. We will replace the privileged narrative with our own."

And so Satan entered the garden, where he was attracted to a naked woman. He approached her and said, "Did God say that you can't eat from any tree? Such a totalizing narrative reveals that you are a pathetic victim of the oppressor. Why, if you can't eat, you'll starve."

2367. "They were written for our instruction" (1 Corinthians 10:11). Much of what each of us says and does could be useful for the instruction of others. That's why I recommend that everyone create a legacy by keeping a written record of what he or she has learned. We learn by our mistakes, and our lives are filled with mistakes. So share them and let others grow wise.

2368. The old (that's me) find new technology to be unintuitive because we have learned certain patterns that we now assume still apply. Push a button and it does something. Maybe push it again and it's a toggle, turning the something off. But then the new arrives. Push a button, and it does something. Push a button and hold it down for a second and it does something entirely different. Push the button twice in quick succession and a third function is engaged. Push and hold and swipe across the screen and a fourth function operates. "It's the green and white button" doesn't really answer the question any more.

2369. Tell a lie once and it becomes the possible truth. Tell the lie twice and it becomes the probable truth. Tell the lie three times and it becomes the incontrovertible truth. (Or as someone said in the newspaper, "Tell a lie three times and it becomes evidence.")

2370. The longer I live, the wiser Pascal becomes. I used to object when he said, "All our reasoning comes down to surrendering to feeling." But as the author of *Black Box Thinking* says, people are much more ready to be persuaded by "the glitzy narrative," than by the "boring old data" that conflicts with the compelling story. Pascal says, "Reason can be manipulated any way you want," and the fact is, we locate or generate reasons (read, rationalizations) after the fact as a means of tarting up our conclusions based on stories we like, ideological bias, political correctness, and simple intellectual (or other) lust.

2371. Why is so much rancor involved when people disagree? Because they are defending their egos, their self-images, as well as (or even instead of) their ideas. Maybe better put: Their ideas become integral parts of themselves, so to attack their ideas is to attack who they are.

2372. Before he swallows that delicious-looking worm, the wise fish looks for a fish hook in it. The unwise fish sees only the worm.

2373. The wise fish can distinguish a meal worm from a bait worm. That is to say, he knows the difference between life and death.

2374. The unwise fish sees a free meal in a juicy worm; the wise fish sees the worm and asks, "Now who would offer me a free juicy worm without any strings — or fishing line — attached? What's the hook, or rather, What's the catch? or rather, Who's the catch?" And that superannuated old philosopher fish says, "Please to explain why earthworm floats in middle of pond."

2375. Not only are they sitting around idly, waiting for their ship to come in, but they expect the port to call them when it does and tell them that a stretch limo is on the way to pick them up.

2376. Why must we define ourselves by our disease? "Hello, I'm Joe and I have [fill in the blank] disease." Am I cancer? Am I Parkinson's? Am I schizophrenia? No, I'm me. Ravaged by disease, yes, but I'm not my disease.

2377. **Indignation Comes in Various Forms.**
We feel *righteous indignation* when we observe someone violating the moral order, behaving contrary to the rules and laws that bind society together. Even reading or hearing about flagrant violations can raise our ire.

Egotistical indignation results when we take personal offense to someone's action, which we believe was directed at or involves ourselves. Unlike the situation that provokes righteous indignation, the slight that produces egotistical indignation might be small or even nonexistent. And our anger stems not from the sense of wickedness at the violation, but at the affront to our pride. "How dare that person offend me in such a way! Who does he think he is? Does he know who I am?"

Ideological indignation arises from a violation of political correctness. Not only might the affront or violation be either real (that is, a true violation of PC decorum) or imagined or fabricated, but the indignation itself can be either real or pro forma, faked, unfelt. Violation of the PC ideology must be always identified and denounced, with full press emotional force. So, even though the accuser is not really offended, the offense must be punished per protocol. It must be publicized to shame the supposed offender and warn others of the consequences of violation.

2378. "I have learned more from my dogs than from all the great books I have read." —Gerry Spence

Is this a comment on
- the quality of the "great books" he has read?
- the number of the "great books" he has read or not?
- his ability to process and internalize the wisdom he reads?
- his choice of "great books"?
- the preternatural intelligence of his dogs?
- his definition of "great books"?

2379. **Narrative.**

An account of events, often in story form, that connects them together into a coherent relationship. The connections supplied by the narrator include cause and effect, linear sequence, thematic, or some other interpretive frame. Because there are usually several ways to describe events and to supply relationships, there are often multiple narratives covering the same collection of events.

Narratives are frequently tainted by bias or ideology. Commonly, differences occur when (1) only some events are selected, (2) some events are emphasized over others, (3) a spin or ideological meaning is imposed on the events.

2380. Alas, the name Robert Harris is as common as grass, as a stamp dealer once remarked about three-cent stamps. As a result, my novel, *The Million Dollar Girl*, is bought and read by fans of a British author of the same name. The fans don't like it. I put it all down to the result of unfulfilled expectations. Those who buy my novel, thinking that they will get more of the same style and plot that the other Robert Harris has offered, are greatly disappointed. As a result, the reviews of my book reflect the dissonance:

- "Rubbish. I was conned into buying this book. . . ."
- "Don't waste your time or money. . . ."
- "Awful writing by a hack. . . ."
- "Waste of money."
- "The book was almost painful to read. . . ."
- "Trash!"
- "A letdown."
- "Junk."

2381. Of course buffets are testimonies to the ease with which we all can succumb to gluttony. But I continue to be amazed at how a serving dish of crab legs makes so many people succumb to uncontrollable greed. How they pile up their plates, four, six, eight inches high. It's a buffet. There are 114 dishes to choose from, yet there are the plates filled to dropping with only crab legs.

2382. The reason we tune out those who speak without pausing is that our brains quickly tire of parsing one gigantic sentence that changes subjects every ten or twenty words.

2383. Even the most virtuous can be corrupted if given the right temptation. Hence, in the Lord's prayer, "Lead us not into temptation." And take the plank out of your own eye before you blame Eve.

2384. We are quick to pronounce others' weaknesses as foolish and our own as understandable, even when they are the same weaknesses.

2385. What we scorn in others, we praise in ourselves.

2386. The first rule of polite conversation is knowing when to stop talking.

2387. How many widows remember their husbands with fondness — and relief?

2388. **The Sociology of Mall Parking Lots.**
- *The Stalker.* He slowly follows shoppers walking from the mall through the parking lot to their car, eager to close in and take the shoppers' space.
- *The Waiter.* He spots a shopper putting packages in the trunk and stops in the aisle — regardless of how many cars are behind him — to wait for the shopper to get in and back out, leaving him the empty spot.
- *The Squatter.* This shopper gets back into the car after shopping — but doesn't leave. Instead, he or she will adjust the seat, listen to Beethoven's Ninth Symphony on the radio, eat a sandwich (with French fries and a dill pickle and a large drink), put on makeup, adjust the mirrors, change clothes, feed the fish, call a girlfriend, read *War and Peace* — all the while a "lucky" driver is waiting for the parking space to become available. See The Waiter, above.
- *The Reverser.* This driver backs up along the aisles, trying to find an open spot. Since driving forward didn't work, The Reverser thinks that maybe driving backwards will deliver better results.
- *The Pull-Througher.* This risk taker drives through one slot into the next slot in the other parking aisle. Sometimes he almost collides with another driver, who wanted to pull into the space, too.

- *The Cruiser.* This driver cruises slowly up and down every aisle in the parking lot, looking for the perfect parking space. Finding the right space may take hours. Chances are he will spend only five minutes at one store in the mall and then leave.
- *The Anti-Chipper.* This driver has a very well kept car, often new, and doesn't want anyone to slam a door open against it. So the driver parks in the lot boondocks, away from all the other cars in the lot. Anti-Chippers are also sometimes known as Marathoners since after parking they must walk 26 miles, 385 yards to get to the store entrance.
- *The Snatcher.* This driver pulls into a just-vacated slot that another driver was waiting patiently (and signaling) for. Before the other driver can get into the space, the Snatcher zooms in, often from the opposite direction.
- *The Exhibitionist.* This driver shows off the sound of his hot-rot car by roaring up and down the aisles, seemingly but not necessarily actually looking for a parking spot. The Exhibitionist is most frequently found in underground and multilevel parking structures where the roar of the engine and the squeal of his tires can be amplified by bounding off the concrete ceiling.

2389. First, people gave up thinking, reason, and evidence and turned to emotion, to follow their heart to find the truth they desired. Now, they have given up even emotion and form their beliefs on whatever stories they hear most often. Whatever is repeated often enough becomes truth.

2390. We don't want the same thing all the time; nor do we want something different all the time. We want novelty within structure. The predictable offers us comfort and security while the novel offers us interest and variety.

2391. People are not often corrupted suddenly and completely. They are corrupted by a slow erosion of integrity. The slippery slope of moral yielding.

2392. When some people are upset, they will take offense at the most innocuous comment and refuse to accept a neutral explanation. Moreover, the false, insulting meaning will remain encoded in their minds seemingly forever.

2393. One of our biggest human weaknesses is that we expect everything to be easy. We get upset over anything difficult. Why? We expect things to be easy because we fail to think through the process and the requirements and the problems that are likely to inhibit a quick resolution. We get upset over the difficulty because the difficulty injures our pride. We're so great that we can fix this in five minutes. Not.

2394. An example of the above would be the changing of a doorknob on an old house. How long will that require? Oh, ten minutes max. And then the problems arise.
- The screws are all plain end and they are covered with paint. Removing a few screws requires twenty minutes.
- The ornamental cover over the workings is held on in some mysterious way. Figuring out how to remove it requires another ten minutes.
- The screws holding the works together can barely be reached with a screwdriver because the doorknob is in the way. The screwdriver slips off continually. And the screws are incomprehensibly tight all the way out, many turns. Time to remove is another fifteen minutes.
- The old hardware is finally off, but now the new hardware doesn't fit. The hole for the latch is an eighth of an inch too small. Time to file it out (lacking the right tools), fifteen minutes.
- Finally ready to put in the new knob screws, and once again the knob itself is in the way, requiring some fin-

gerwork, manual screwdriver work, and finally the drill driver. Five more minutes at least.

So that quick job required more than an hour to do.

2395. Pride slows — and sometimes prevents — many simple solutions.

2396. The head forgives more easily than the heart.

2397. When pride governs the heart, there is little compassion, kindness, or forgiveness.

2398. I bought some large steel nails and some small washers recently. The nails, about the size of a ballpoint pen, were ten cents each. The washers, about the size of a quarter, were twelve cents each. Clearly, the hardware-pricing employee was more greedy than the nails-and-screws-pricing employee. Maybe it costs a lot to punch holes in metal discs.

2399. Why do some women wear deep, cleavage-revealing dresses and then expect men to look into their eyes?

2400. Mental models embody our understanding of how things work. Our mental models therefore determine how we attempt to use things. A wrong model means wrong use. For example, many people think that the farther they turn a thermostat up or down, the faster it will work. If you're hot, turn it down to 60 degrees so it will cool quickly. However, unless you are fortunate enough to have multistage cooling in your home, the thermostat simply turns the cooling on and the system runs the same whether it needs to cool from 90 to 70 or from 72 to 70.

A better example of a wrong mental model is the washerless faucet. Many people have the mental model of an old style faucet: If it drips after you turn it off, just tighten the handle. But washerless faucets do not work that way. Once they are off, they are off. Tightening the handle does nothing to stop a drip.

(If a washerless faucet drips after you turn if off, it needs a new set of parts.)

The last example is the touchpad button. We all know how to use a push button toggle switch. Push it once and it's on; push it again and it's off. But we older types do not intuitively figure out that if you tap it twice it does something else, and if you touch and hold it, you get a third option.

2401. Open the paper towel package and install the roll on the dispenser *before* you need a paper towel to wipe your greasy hands. —Just because it's the voice of experience doesn't mean it isn't wise or worthy.

2402. Wisdom is recognizing that you already knew what you should have done (or should not have done) right after you did the opposite.

2403. How can truth and virtue, which are already unpopular and have few genuine adherents, stand out in a world choked by information smog? How can any idea stand out in such an environment, where exabytes of competing political narratives, lies, advertisements, disinformation, and trivia bury everything?

2404. My Bible is 2,130 pages long. God creates humans on page three and they disobey him and fall on page four. Another 1,700 or so pages go by before the Messiah arrives, and the crowd kills him. He rises from the dead to meet his disciples, who don't know what's going on. He confronts Paul and sets him on a missionary tour where his reception is with whips and stones much of the time. The truth will set you free. But nobody said it would be painless.

2405. May you always park in the shade, under a tree with no birds in it.

2406. Perfection consists in doing God's will.

[July 10, 2016; age 66]

2407. **Ten Things Parkinson's Disease Has Taught Me.**

10. I'm on the way to becoming irresistible to women.

They say women are attracted to men who are tall, dark, handsome, and soft spoken. Everyone keeps asking me to speak louder. Even when I'm only three feet away. So, that must mean I am indeed soft spoken. And that's already one-fourth of irresistibility. All I need now is elevator shoes, hair dye, and a little plastic surgery. Then again, I guess I'll pass, because I'm already happily married.

9. Even with a blunted affect, I still can't play poker.

A blank facial expression might be good for poker, but for me, it makes people think I'm uninterested or bored, when the fact is, at best, I'm quite interested and at worst, I'm usually only thinking. And I don't even know how to play poker. I just have the same poker face all the time. Except when I laugh. I need to laugh more often.

8. I am not my body.

The person I'm talking about when I use the word *I* is not the same as my decrepitating body. I have to live inside it, and let me say it used to be a much more fun and comfortable home than it is today. Not only is the house showing wear from 65 plus years of weather and neglect, but Dr. Parkinson has come in and is in the process of smashing up the place. But I'm still sitting by a warm fire in spite of a drafty house.

To change metaphors, my body is a car and I am the driver. The car is an older model, so that today, the radiator leaks, the engine isn't running on all eight anymore, and the tires are going flat, but the driver is still fine. The driver just can't go as fast as he used to. Sometimes he can barely get out of the driveway.

7. Feeling frustrated doesn't make anything better.

You know, it's kind of aggravating when my mind tells my legs to lift me up and all they can say is, "That's above my pay grade. Let the arms do it." I tell my legs that they are very muscled, but they say, "What's it to ya?" And that chronic back pain; that gets old after a while. And then there's my diminishing ability to use my beloved tools. My right hand is getting increasingly uncooperative, so now I can't seem to make a pair of pliers do what I used to do with them. And the left hand has to help the right hand just to screw in a light bulb. But getting upset over all this doesn't make a difference, so why bother to get upset? Besides, not many people like a grump.

6. I don't take anything for granted.

My handwriting has been a joke since sixth grade, but now it's so bad even I can't parse it most of the time. Maybe I'm writing in secret code and I just don't know it. I dare you to try to decipher it. But how much longer will I be able to type, even with my clumsy, disobedient fingers that insist on leaving out some letters and doubling others—even in the same word. But I can still type, sort of. This is a blessing. And then there are those rebellious buttons that fight me every buttonhole. True, they no longer cooperate the way they did years ago, but, eventually, I can still button a shirt. This, too, is a blessing. In fact, I see every good thing as a distinct blessing, and not as an entitlement. Life is good—increasingly awkward, but good. Whether I eat a 99-cent taco or a prime steak, I'm content—no, make that happy. Grateful and happy. Some people take their health for granted. Big mistake.

5. I have a lot more compassion for the handicapped.

I've learned that we shouldn't judge others by using ourselves as the standard of measure. We can't fully understand what others are going through unless we ourselves have the same situation. I feel as if I've been put into a body that doesn't belong to me. I ask, "Why is my body stumbling around?" and "Why does my tongue stumble, too?" and "Why is my handwriting so small? Is there a paper shortage only my hand knows about?" Yes, I feel awkward and conspicuous when I walk around. Slight stoop; uneven, shuffling small steps. Now I know how other people feel who aren't young and agile and "normal." God bless them. So, less judgment, more empathy.

4. There's no "Why me?" here.

When something bad happens to some people, they ask, "Why me?" when the real question is, "Why not me?" We're told that in this world we will have tribulation. And while we're quick to ask, "Why me?" when we get sick or hurt ourselves, how come we never ask, "Why me?" when we're eating lobster on a vacation cruise or even licking an ice cream cone at home?

3. We can't predict the future.

Seems as if every time we expect a high fast ball, we get a low curve ball instead. Here we are, afraid of a future that probably will never come, and completely unaware of what is really going to happen. The fact is, only God can see around corners; we can barely see in a straight line. Maybe we should take the hint and trust God for our future instead of trying to outguess him.

2. I am now more aware of my mortality, and that's a good thing.

Yep, we're all gonna die. But we don't think about it that much until the Lord calls our attention to it in a quite personal way. Gonna die. Check. Got it. Getting ready.

1. I still have hope.

I have hope—not that I will be cured, but hope for the kingdom of God. And hope for strength during the remainder of my stay here. It is said that instead of asking God to remove the mountain in front of us, we should ask him to teach us to climb mountains. And in the meantime, put our hope in the peace and rest we'll find at the top. After all, we know that we will be given brand new bodies (no pot bellies, thin hair, joint pains, chronic diseases, broken fingernails, strawberry allergies, insomnia, poor vision, etc.).

The Bible is a good place to learn about hope. Isaiah says:

> Do not fear for I am with you;
> Do not be afraid, for I am your God.
> I will strengthen you; I will help you;
> I will hold onto you with My righteous right hand.
> —Isaiah 41:10 (HCSB)

2408. The Bible is a real page turner. Creation of the universe, page 1. Creation of mankind, page 2. God plunks Adam and Eve in the Garden of Eden and hints that they could eat from the Tree of Life, page 2 also. They don't. Instead, they eat from the one forbidden tree in the whole garden, destroying humanity's hopes and becoming the first two sinners, page 3. (This is going pretty fast, isn't it?) Then there's a curse, page 4; sex, also page 4; and murder, still on page 4. Oh, and lying to God, page 4 again. Page 5, more sex, twice on the page.

Then things get really serious. It doesn't take very long for God to get fed up with what his human creatures have done with their free will, so he destroys the earth and everyone on it (except for Noah and a few relatives) with a flood, pages 7 and 8. By page 11 the descendants of Noah are at work trying to build a tower to Heaven to pump up their pride and "make a name" for themselves.

At the end of the first dozen pages, we are caught thinking, "If this is the result of the creation of human beings, why doesn't God just blow off the Earth and start over in another universe? Why does he care? That's the question.

2409. For a solid and lasting relationship, your spouse or friend not only needs to be able to trust you, but must *believe* that you can be trusted.

2410. Becoming bitter at God because he hasn't answered your prayers means that you view God as your butler whose duty it is to bring you what you want on demand. When he doesn't deliver, you scold him.

2411. The most encouraging thought I've heard in 50 years: *Light floods into darkness, but darkness does not flood into light.* Darkness cannot overtake light. Darkness can only hang around, pervasively perhaps, but it cannot conquer light. It can obscure and even hide things, but those things — good and bad — await exposing by the inevitable light. Darkness may fill the universe, and even the heart of man; but light is swift and penetrating and it will flood the darkness, which has no resistance or remedy.

2412. Jesus the teacher. In John 1:38, Jesus notices the two disciples following him, and he asks, "What are you looking for?" Jesus isn't asking an informational question, as in, "How may I help you?" Instead, he knows what they are interested in. He wants to find out if they really know what they are seeking. "Are you looking for a rabbi (teacher), a prophet, a messiah, *the* messiah?" It's as if Jesus had asked, "What are you looking for in life?"

2413. A patina of faith. In John 1:49, Nathaniel declares to Jesus, "You are the Son of God!" In John 2:11, after Jesus turns more than a hundred gallons of water into a nice, fine wine, "his disciples believed in him." Yeah, but even after three years of this, they all still ran away and wandered around confused for a while.

2414. **Observations About the Gym.**
    1. Every gym member's primary goal is to find a parking space near the door.
    2. The typical male gym attendee spends twenty minutes fiddling with some complex apparatus or other, while looking around the gym for attractive young women. Then, the male attendees gather in the locker room and spend forty-five minutes talking about the attractive young women they saw.
    3. In a multi-story gym, the attendees all use the elevator rather than the stairs.
    4. At work or a party, whenever the discussion turns to exercise, half the people will say, "Yeah, I've got a gym," even though they hardly ever go.

2415. What is the most effective way we learn knowledge and humility at the same time? What is it that teaches us so pointedly that we never forget? What produces better judgment, even wisdom, all at once? Failure. Yes, call it a mistake, an error, or "a learning experience"; if we analyze our failures, we can improve our lives substantially.
    So, don't be ashamed to admit an error; learn from it.

2416. Why do people want absolute guarantees, when virtually all of life is contingent? Can't we accept that our behavior might void the contract?

2417. In a movie, the visual elements form the action track, the spoken words form the thinking track, and the music forms the emotional track. Movie music tells you what to feel about the scene you are viewing.

2418. "The dogma of the group is promoted as scientifically in-contestable—in fact, truer than anything any human being has ever experienced. Resistance is not just immoral; it is illogical and unscientific. In order to support this notion, language is constricted by what Lifton calls the 'thought-terminating cli-ché'" (Lawrence Wright, *Going Clear*).

Is this comment about (a) climate change, (b) evolution, or (c) Scientology? Answer: Yes.

Thought-terminating clichés? "Settled science," "deniers," "survival of the fittest," "science versus religion."

2419. Admit it. We live in a theocracy. We live in the theocracy of Darwinism. Just take a look at ordinary non-fiction books. It appears that no matter what the subject, every author must praise Darwin or mention evolutionary theory approvingly—and that by page 30 or 40.

2420. We read (or hear) but do we understand? Aren't we all too often trapped by our interpretive assumptions? Case in point: "No one comes to the father except through me" (John 14:6b). Many people seem to assume that this means only those who have had the Gospel presented to them and have accepted it will be saved. But Jesus himself implies that Abraham was saved (see Luke 16). Doesn't that appear to imply that, while we can be saved only by Jesus' blood (he died for all), someone who lived in 1000 BC in South America could be saved through Jesus' sacrifice without knowing the Gospel during his lifetime?

2421. Another provocative Scripture that we overlook often is in John 10:16: "I have other sheep, which are not of this fold; I must bring them also, and they will hear My voice; and they will become one flock with one shepherd." Where are these sheep? We can only speculate, but our thoughts can range to other people in the Middle East, to other countries, continents, even planets, for all we know.

2422. I would like to quibble with those who assign research papers and require that all sources be less than five years old. Here at my elbow is an eloquent analysis of the deception of believing that change is progress, that change in society is inevitably moving in a progressive direction. However, the article was written in 1999. Does that mean that I or Joe Student cannot cite it in a research paper? Or do the rules for science writing not apply to philosophy, literature, religion, history, or economics? It would be unfortunate — no, tragic — if they do, because the most valuable record of thought in all these areas would thereby be put off limits.

2423. Few people relish ambiguity. It irritates them when they are unable to fix on "the answer" or "the outcome." So their minds fill in a few details, add some inductive leaps, season the brew with a handful of assumptions, sneak in a few hidden prejudices, and, presto changeo, end up with a tasty, satisfying conclusion that no subsequent argument or pile of facts will change.

2424. Inconsistency is evidence of truth. Some people criticize the four Gospels because they have slight discrepancies. But as every cop knows, if four people told exactly the same story, it would be evidence of collusion, not truth. I read somewhere that one of the 20th century's con artists, when he was repeating the story to the police about how he had obtained a manuscript, deliberately put little variations into his narrative, which made his story all the more credible. If he had told it exactly the same way each time, it would have appeared rehearsed, and therefore less credible. The writers of the four Gospels wrote at different times to different audiences, so they were unable to get together and make their stories perfectly in agreement. All Scripture is "God breathed" — which is to say, inspired but not dictated.

2425. Most "historical" dramas are pervaded by presentism. That's the practice of attributing present ideas and concerns to historical characters of long ago.

"Og, why you not build fire to cook wooly mammoth? Besides, it cold in here."

"Og no want to affect climate change in harmful way."

2426. Thinking about conspiracy theories, I have a question. For a given event complexed by one or more conspiracy theories, why do you believe the evidence that supports the conspiracy theory you believe, instead of the evidence that supports the official explanation? How is the quality of the evidence different? What is your standard for crediting knowledge claims as facts?

The point is, the official explanation and the conspiracy theory both offer facts and evidence and eye witnesses and photographs (with interpretations), and reasoning. So, why do you find the conspiracy theory sources more believable than the sources supporting the official explanation?

Another question is, why do you find the debunkers of the official explanation credible and the debunkers of the conspiracy theory incredible?

A final question: Because most of the controversial events have multiple conspiracy theories, what caused you to choose one over all the others? Who killed JFK? Oswald, the Mafia, the Soviets, Castro, right wingers, left wingers? What was your process for choosing one over the others?

2427. **Postmodernism: The Ttriumph of Solipsism and Laziness.**

Postmodernist literary theory suits the young academics very well because it allows infinite interpretations, context-free analysis, and a rejection of all those strictures that in the past required so much time and effort to learn: previous scholarship, methodology, criteria, logic, and historical context. Now just gaze at your navel, make something up, get tenure.

2428. Knowledge interprets experience. So, the more you know, the better you can see. If you drive up to an untouched tribe in some remote area of the world, the chief isn't going to look at the instrument panel and remark, "I see you are low on gasoline."

And, of course, experience interprets knowledge. If you grew up on a farm where the only roses were red ones, you would gain the knowledge that all roses are red. Later, when you saw a bouquet of white, yellow, and pink roses from a farm out of town, your experience would shape your knowledge.

2429. Kids often ask their teacher, "Why do we have to learn this? In real life, we're never going to need to know who won what battle or how to solve a quadratic equation, or what the metaphors are in an old poem."

The answer is: In order to function well, your brain needs a large stock of metaphors, analogies, models, and examples, together with an understanding of what worked and what didn't and why. Your brain needs good thinking habits, strong analytic skills, and a knowledge of fallacies.

2430. Before you decide that you want to go beyond the edge of the map, be sure you understand what the map is.

2431. Understanding is the ability to discern an underlying principle and to use that principle to predict or at least expect a future event. Understanding is the act of finding order where others see only randomness or chaos. If you can predict the next number in a series of numbers, you understand the principle behind the series. Others see only a string of random numbers.

Number series: 2, 6, 4, 12, 10, 30, 28. By analysis you discern the pattern of multiply by three and then subtract two.

2432. Kids can have fun pretty much anywhere you take them. That's because they still have creative imaginations and can place a layer of make believe over reality. (Three and four-year-old kids call this "just betend," while grownups call it "augmented reality.") Adults have long ago jettisoned all that foolish imaginary thinking stuff in order to present the sophisticated, urbane, man of the world persona they think will get them praise or at least acknowledgement. As a result, adults are easily bored. They can't very well turn to office stuff to work on and domestic issues to address when it's that stuff that has created the boredom.

2433. Politics is essentially a marketing business. And the soul of marketing is fear: Present a problem or something to fear — dandruff, high utility bills, a political opponent in the coming election — and then present the solution — the shampoo, home solar, the right candidate. Then everything will be happiness and sunshine again.

2434. **Basic Principles of Salesmanship.**
    1. The foundational principle is to move the prospective customer's thinking from rational to emotional. Emotional thinking will produce an emotional response. Emotions are much more easily manipulated than rational thoughts. To move the customer to emotional thinking, use words with emotional effect: *feel, love, proud, power, powerful, enjoy, excitement, thrill, satisfy,* etc. etc. Then,
    1. Make the prospective customer believe that he has an unmet need.
    2. Increase the prospect's sense of need through fear (or envy, or greed, or pride).
    3. Offer a solution to the need.
    4. Explain away the prospect's objections to accepting the solution.
    5. Close the deal by using the scarcity principle (Act now! Limited time offer! Only while supplies last! And, you know, we have another buyer coming in shortly.)

2435. Darxul, reaching for *The Book of One Hundred Lies*, accidentally took out *The Book of Asterisks*, and read from the section, "The Big Print Giveth, and the Small Print Taketh Away":

1. *Your mileage may vary.

2. *Terms and conditions subject to change without notice.

3. *For example only. See your dealer for actual terms.

4. *Plus tax, processing, handling, and delivery fees.

5. *Not available in all states.

6. *Void where prohibited, licensed, taxed, or restricted by law.

7. *Some assembly required.

8. *Batteries not included.

9. *This price is for the first month of service only. After that, regular rates apply.

10. *Picture shows item larger than it actually is.

11. *Item pictured is for example only. Actual item may vary.

12. *Results shown are not typical.

2436. Darxul took out *The Book of One Hundred Lies*, removed the rubber band holding the well-worn book together, and read.

65. This has been thoroughly tested, so you can know that it is reliable.

66. Don't worry; you'll always have the choice.

2437. "You shall know reality, and knowing the way things really are will set you free." —John 8:32 (DOAX)

2438. "I don't believe in God."

"Why not?"

"Because there's no evidence for him."

"Well, since you must be ruling out the enormous amount of evidence from design in the natural world, what exactly do you consider 'evidence'?"

"Well, I can't see him. I believe only in what I can see."

"So then, you don't believe in air, or gravity, or subatomic particles?"

"Of course I do."

"But you can't see them."

"Well, we know they are real by their effects."

"And again, the design of the world doesn't give you a hint?"

"But how can I know he's real? No one can prove it."

"How do you know I'm real?"

"I can see you. Seeing is believing."

"But you could see what isn't really there for any number of reasons. I could be a dream of yours. Or a hallucination. Or an avatar in an augmented reality game, or a piece of a virtual reality setup, or a hologram, or a robot, or a particularly vivid memory."

"But I can talk to you and touch you."

"Doesn't change any of the options I just named, except maybe the hologram. You can think you're touching something real when in fact, you aren't."

"But seeing is believing."

"So when a stick put into a jar of water looks bent, it really is, and when the moon appears larger when near the horizon than when it is up in the sky, it actually changes size?"

"Well, no. Those are illusions."

"So then, reality tests appearances as well as the other way around."[4]

2439. Just as the natural world reveals God's creativity, so too does the world of human invention. God is in the creativity that produced the water fountain, alarm clock, rocket, cell phone, computer, automobile, jet plane, television, and all those ridiculously complex microprocessors. It is God's image in man that has made all these things.

2440. The tap water in Portland, Oregon is the most delicious snowmelt I've ever tasted. Portland is, in fact, noted for the quality of its from-the-spigot drinking water. And yet, the stores

---

[4] See also *Glimmerings* 2290 and 2463.

and vending machines in the city are full of the various brands of commercial bottled water, just as they are in cities where the tap water is essentially undrinkable.

2441. Having attended yet another convention where the producers supplied attendees with free coffee and tea, I yet again notice the long lines at the nearby Starbucks. Once again, the free coffee is quite good. But, you know, sipping "quite good" coffee while you listen to a speaker describe the horrific state of someone suffering from a degenerative, painful, and debilitating disease just isn't as enjoyable as slurping your Starbucks coffee while you listen.

2442. Thought on eating biscuits with country gravy. This delicious but remarkably high calorie dish seems to beg for justification. Then you think, country recipes are often packed with calories — from fat or from sugar. And then you wonder, Why aren't all country folks overweight? Finally you realize that the country farmer's day often includes digging postholes, plowing his field, carrying rocks from the field to the side, carrying hay bales from barn to horses, pulling an animal out of the mud, and on and on. I mean, this guy needs 5,000 calories a day just to stay alive. And then, during the winter months. . . .

2443. **Why People Get Cranky in Their Old Age.**
    1. They are unhappy that they are losing their autonomy.
    2. They are frustrated that they cannot do simple things they have done all their lives: button a shirt, drive to the market, see well enough to sew or put a fresh battery in a watch.
    3. Anger is sometimes the redirected manifestation of grief. As we age, we can grow grief-stricken and angry over the impairment of so many of our physical attributes: Our eyesight becomes poorer, we might lose our sense of smell, we get weaker and our sense of balance declines. We find ourselves putting ever more salt and pepper on our eggs. When someone tries to help us, the offer reminds us of our diminishment and our dependency and we are upset by the thoughts. So we get cranky.

4. They were cranky when they were young.

2444. We want to hear the opinions of experts, but we want those opinions to agree with what we already believe. Pursuing confirmation bias is the great American pastime.

2445. We fiercely defend a belief in the face of facts and arguments to the contrary, marshalling our own logic and proofs and examples. We are resolute. And then someone tells a story that makes us change our mind completely. "I don't believe the experts or their statistics, but that story. . . ."

2446. It's bad enough when people lie to you—that's in their nature and their interest. But when a product lies to you, that's really offensive. I have here a nylon faucet washer that has stamped on it, 1/2 as clear as can be. Now, do you suppose this washer has a diameter of half an inch? Its actual diameter is three quarters of an inch. Is this a vicious conspiracy by the plumbing industry to confuse ordinary homeowners and prevent them from changing their own faucet washers?

2447. **Do the Math.**
"Mrs. Smith, I assure you that this KerPlunk vacuum cleaner is unequalled in the world."
"But it's so expensive. After all, $4,000 is so much money."
"With this vacuum's performance and features, $4,000 is a bargain."
"But I can get a vacuum cleaner for $50 at the discount store."
"Those vacuums are junk. How long will they last? Six months? This KerPlunk will last you a lifetime."
"Hmm. At $50 each, I could use that $4,000 to buy a brand new vacuum cleaner every six months for 40 years. And I'll always have a relatively new one, not a 10-, 20- or 30-year-old model."
"Ooh, why, just look at the time. I'm late for another appointment. Nice talking to you. Bye."

2448. If you believe only what your eyes see, then people get larger as they approach you.

2449. Revolutionaries constantly scream about what they are against. They are often less clear about what they are for. When asked, they reply with clichés of the most abstract kind: justice, equality, fairness. Truth is mentioned rarely. And in the process of revolutionary change, they are not at all clear about what they want to preserve out of the wreckage of the present system. Nothing? Throw everything out? No rule of law? No freedom of speech?

2450. When ideology finally turns the brain to mush: "The prisons are not filled because people commit crimes. The prisons are filled because of the need for mass incarceration by the prison-industrial complex, which needs the free forced labor of prison manufacturing to increase profits."

[October 25, 2016; age 66]

2451. **Is the Concept Difficult or Only the Explanation?**
    Student: "Professor, what is a plurality?"
    Professor: "Given set A, composed of subsets B, C, D, and E, the subset that, when compared to the other subsets is larger than any of the other individual subsets taken by themselves, but not more than 50.0% of set A itself is designated the plurality subset."
    Joe Laborer: "Hey, Tom, what the heck is a plurality?"
    Tom Laborer: "That's when you've got three or more folks running for the same office and one gets more votes than either of the other two, but no one gets more than half of the total votes."

2452. **Critical Thinking Quiz.**
    Label on a box of laundry detergent: "One scoop cleans a whole washload."
    Question: What is your response?

C answer: How many scoops in a box?

B answer: How much does a scoop cost and how does that compare to competitors' cost per washload?

A answer: How big is the scoop? What is the cost per scoop? What is a "washload?"

A plus answer: "Define *cleans*. And how does the detergent's cleaning performance compare to the performance of the competitor's detergent?"

2453. Why is misinformation — or disinformation, for that matter — so popular and so wildly spread through social media? Because the standard for determining which information to spread through social media is not truth, but juiciness. "Who cares if the rumor is true? This is too good not to share." Hmm. Let's see a list of criteria for valuing and re-transmitting "news" via social media:

- hyperbolic, unbelievable "fact"
- scandal, very negative gossip
- humiliating and ridiculing societal and religious values
- anything that violates common sense
- supposed fact that supports or opposes a particular political ideology

2454. In former times, conflicts and disagreements over policy were argued on the basis of facts and ideas and choices. Of course, disagreements still arose over what the facts were and over what the consequences of different choices would be. And sometimes these disagreements remained unresolvable. But at least there was the belief that the conflict could be reasoned about. Now, however, those who disagree with us pretend to take offense at our position, thereby moving the conflict from the realm of reason to the realm of emotions.

This movement of the argument from thinking to feeling creates several problems.

- Because we are generally sympathetic to the feelings of others, this shift exploits our humanity and our emotions.

- It stops argument because feelings can't be refuted.
- It implies a presumption toward the emotionally injured (the offended), putting pressure on the alleged offender to apologize or feel ashamed of his position.
- It moves the dispute from a choice between one solution or another based on merit (efficiency, benefit, cost, logistics, effectiveness, etc.) to a choice between a moral solution and an immoral solution.

2455. Opening sentence of my next novel: "He spoke slowly, like a man whose wife had never interrupted him."

2456. Knowledge rides on the train of words.

2457. Re: Glimmering 2456. But what if some of the boxcars with the most freight in them have been hijacked and filled with low quality substitutes? In other words, how can we communicate when our most important words have been given new, often politicized, meanings?

2458. Their resentment and loathing are almost palpable. The angry disgust on their faces well matches the contempt in their voices.

2459. Some people seem to have a natural tendency to be rational, while others tend to be emotional. Unfortunately, fewer people attend to rational arguments than are influenced by emotional appeals. Consider:

Rational appealing candidate: "Vote for me and I'll support a bill that increases personal freedom."

Emotional appealing candidate Liberal: "Vote for me because if you vote for my opponent, sick children will die."

2460. Interestingly, those who are all about feelings call people names when they get angry, evidently hoping to hurt their feelings and shame them and ostracize them from the public forum.

2461. A premier piece of advice for everyone, including parents: Share your mistakes. A story about a mistake has ten times the learning power of a story about a success.

2462. Another piece of advice to everyone: Remember that God is God and you're not.

2463. "Maybe we should pray about this."
      "I don't believe in God."
      "You don't? Why not?"
      "I never met the man."
      "So, you don't believe in the existence of anyone you haven't met? You believe that only a few hundred people live on the earth?"
      "Well, I don't believe in anything I can't see."
      "So, then, you don't believe in air, or gravity, or magnetism?"[5]

2464. So you've kind of been expecting a special blessing from God because you've done something to please or serve him? Whatever gave you that idea? God didn't give Mary and Joseph a villa to reward them for birthing and raising his incarnate Son. Nor did he make Joseph independently wealthy. Joseph worked for a living all his life as a *tekton*, a carpenter or possibly more likely, a stone mason or both. He apparently died before Jesus was crucified, leaving Mary with less emotional and financial support. She did, however, apparently have about ten children (five sons according to Matthew 13:55, with probably an equal number of daughters, odds are).

"Joseph! You need to carve those stone blocks faster. We need the money. Jesus is okay, because he can make bread whenever he wants, but those other four sons are eating us out of house and home. And those daughters of yours — they're al-

---

[5] See also Glimmerings 2290 and 2438.

ways inviting their latest boyfriends over for dinner and to meet the parents."

"But that's good, Mary. We get to meet those rascals who probably have evil intentions toward our daughters."

"Evil intent or no, they are always famished when they arrive."

2465. One of the sorrows of modernity and postmodernity is the replacement of action with feelings. Love used to be action—active protection, support, security, provision. Now it's an emotion, sometimes conflated with lust. Faith used to be an action, too—active following of Jesus' commands, our actions and service to God. Now it's just a feeling. That's why few people seem to understand James when he says,

> What use is it, my brethren, if someone says he has faith but he has no works? Can that faith save him? If a brother or sister is without clothing and in need of daily food, and one of you says to them, "Go in peace, be warmed and be filled," and yet you do not give them what is necessary for their body, what use is that? Even so faith, if it has no works, is dead, being by itself. But someone may well say, "You have faith and I have works; show me your faith without the works, and I will show you my faith by my works."
> —James 2:14-18 (NASB)

2466. Disagreement over politics, behavior, even philosophy and facts, has moved from the intellectual arena to that of feelings. Now when someone disagrees, instead of marshalling rebutting evidence, reasons, and examples, they pretend to be hurt or offended. Since feelings can't be argued with or refuted, the "offender" feels that the only polite response is an apology and a feeling of shame. Thus, the politically incorrect position is removed from consideration, especially after the pretendedly offended has pronounced the idea, and probably its exponent, as racist, sexist, homophobic, classist, a denier, and so forth.

2467. Darxul pulled a yellowed sheet from *The File of Old Notes* and announced, "Here are Ten Attitudes Necessary for Good Thinking. The source is unknown."
1. Intellectual curiosity
2. Intellectual honesty
3. Objectivity
4. Intelligent skepticism
5. Open-mindedness
6. Belief in cause and effect
7. Systematic thinking
8. Flexibility
9. Persistence
10. Decisiveness

2468. The promotion of rebellion, anti-authority, irrationality, subjectivity, relativism, a denial of standards — did advertising, TV sitcoms, Hollywood films, the university professoriate, or some other force support the rise of postmodernism?

2469. We have counted and measured the petals but are completely ignorant about the meaning of the rose.

2470. We have memorized the answers but do not understand them.

2471. A book is seen, not as a wise friend or provocative opponent, but as a source of thought bites that can be recited on demand to prove how knowledgeable we are.

2472. Fancy words can be very valuable. Here at my elbow is an article, "Games Con Men Play." Titled as such, it could be a feature in the Sunday supplement or the Features page of the local newspaper. But this article has a subhead: "The Semiosis of Deceptive Interaction." Presto, it's a scholarly article suitable for publication in a peer-reviewed journal.

2473. The next big careers will be in information simplification: info conservation, info efficiency, info filtration, info curation, info packaging, info summarizing.

2474. Why do some people so deeply enjoy hating those who don't share their ideology? Hatred involves rejection; rejection involves judgment; judgment involves standards; standards involve a moral foundation; judging others negatively from a moral foundation produces a feeling of moral superiority — an ego rush and a sense of being better than others. The problem is that for many judgment involves special pleading, scapegoating, and hypocrisy; the standards are subjective, shifting, situational, and sometimes self-serving; and the moral foundation is forged from trendy political correctness and identity politics — in other words ad hoc, expedient, and made of shifting sand.

2475. Self-righteousness is a function of pride.

2476. Someone gave Darxul a copy of *Excuses for Rejecting an Idea*. Darxul began to read.
    1. It's never been tried before.
    2. It's already been tried.
    3. It might not work.
    4. It's against company policy.
    5. It's too futuristic.
    6. It's too old fashioned.
    7. We don't have time.
    8. That would mean changing the way we do things.
    9. People just don't do that.
    10. It's too little, too late.
    11. It's too much, too soon.
    12. None of our competitors are doing it.
    13. It's not practical.
    13. It's too simple.
    14. It's too complex.
    15. It's too pie-in-the-sky.
    16. It's too obvious.

17. It's too expensive.
18. We don't really need it.
19. We've never done it that way.
20. The current system works fine.
21. It would be too much trouble.
22. Management would never approve it.
23. It wasn't invented here.
24. I don't like the sound of it.
25. It just doesn't feel right.

2477. Most people come to an understanding of the world and develop their beliefs and values not through reason or logic or evidence, but through stories. For one thing, many people view reason as too linear and too abstract to comprehend reality. Our lives and their pursuits grow organically in ways that are difficult even for matrix representation to make sense of. Lots of people seem to live in that postmodern world where logical contradictions do not apply.

More than that, however, is that people perceive their own lives as stories rather than logical sequences. Their experience of the world is felt as a series of narrative plots: X happened; then Y happened, and this is what it means. Life experience can be seen as a standard plot type: man against man, man against nature, man against fate, and so forth. The logic of cause and effect and the moral implications derived from matching standards to particulars requires thinking, while narrative meaning involves simply imposing understanding on experience, while values float subjectively and situationally in the ether of feeling.

2478. Why do we endeavor to reason people into faith when their objections, rather than genuine issues, amount only to protective barriers that keep considerations of faith safely away?

2479. Playing every note in the piece is important, of course, but the space between the notes is also important.

2480. A good chef watches the plates of food as they go out to the diners. He wants to see what is popular. A great chef watches the plates as they come back into the kitchen from the dining room. He wants to see what the diners didn't eat.

[February 12, 2017; age 66]

2481. Faith is trusting God when you don't understand.

2482. Seconds toward eternity, inches toward infinity.

2483. The sad thing about the fall of mankind is that it has distorted reality by reversing so much truth. In too many cases an opposite falsehood is so deeply ingrained that the truth seems obviously counterintuitive. For example:
Operative Myth: To be happy, think of yourself first.
Actual Truth: To be happy, stop living for yourself.

2484. On the last day of our lives, each of us is thinking about tomorrow.

2485. We observe, we generalize, and the generalization thereafter controls our perception. We observe, we filter the observation through our biases. We accept the explanation that most closely fits our biases and preconceived ideas.

2486. We can't understand what we choose not to see.

2487. Here is a toast and an appreciation to those who pick up after us: God bless the back enders, the janitors, the street sweepers, the trash collectors, the sewage plant workers, the stadium cleaners, the hotel maids—all those in the Sweep, Mop, and Dust Society. May we never take them for granted.

2488. **Boomers Versus Millennials.**
Given a new electronic product, boomers will read the manual to see how to work it. Millennials will push the buttons

to see what happens. Boomers are great on knowledge; millennials are great on immediate experience.

2489. The wise carpenter never says, "This piece of wood is useless because it is too short to be a rafter." Instead he says, "This piece of wood will serve very well as part of a door frame."

2490. The policeman, so well trained, carefully states, "Just the facts, please." But the problem is not the facts, but what *are* the facts, are they still the facts, do they apply here, are they all the facts, are they slanted facts, are the facts mixed with error?

2491. An eager young man once asked Darxul, "What is the best way to win an argument?"

"There is a saying," said Darxul, "'Before you disagree, ask a question.'"

"I don't understand," said the young man.

"That is exactly the point," replied Darxul. "Before you can disagree properly, you must be sure you understand what the true point really is, not what you think it might be. For we all very often push the statements of others into our preconceived boxes."

"But what do you mean by asking a question?"

"Ask a question that tests your assumption about the other person's statement," Darxul answered. "For example, 'Does your statement apply to everyone or only certain people?' or 'Can you be more specific?' or 'What is your definition of the word you are using?'"

2492. The wise man discusses his mistakes. The foolish man tries to rationalize them or blame them on others. The wise man learns how to avoid the mistake in the future. The foolish man knows how to avoid the blame the next time he makes the same mistake.

2493. Before you answer, think about the effect your words will have.

2494. You know the proverb, "Think before you speak." Too many of us are ready to jump in with a reaction to some statement made by another person before we understand the person's point. "A fool does not delight in understanding, but only in revealing his own mind" (Proverbs 18:2), and "He who gives an answer before he hears, It is folly and shame to him" (Proverbs 18:13). (18:13 is from the NASB, but compare the CEV: "It's stupid and embarrassing to give an answer before you listen."

2495. "He who gets wisdom loves his own soul." —Proverbs 19:8. By reversal, we might say that those who don't care to study or learn wisdom don't care about their souls or even their lives.

2496. The more insistent they are that the idea "can't lose," the more likely it will.

2497. Let's not forget that the "con" in "con man" is short for "confidence." Of course he is confident that he's offering you a sure thing, can't lose, guaranteed proposal. And of course he makes you feel confident about him and his idea. After all, *he is a con man.*

2498. Why is it that some customer service people can say, "Have a nice day," in a tone of voice that says, "I hope you're hit by a truck"?

2499. There is so much more to communication than the literal presentation. Someone can say, "I love you," in a way that conveys the opposite of the words. And there is probably no harsher criticism of a concert pianist than to say, "He played every note."

2500. Are bigoted intellectuals any less reprehensible because they are selectively bigoted? Or because they condemn only those bigotries that they don't indulge?

2501. Clarify Before You Vilify.

"If women did not exist," declared the professor emphatically, "no one would care." The students' surprise was almost palpable. In a few clicks, half a dozen of the women students had brought up a form with the title, "Report of a Hostile or Unsafe Learning Event" and began to fill it out. Their faces clearly reflected the vitriolic sentences they were typing.

A male student said in a whisper to those around him, "I guess the prof doesn't know where babies come from. Without girls, there wouldn't be any guys."

"How can you think that?" one of the young women finally blurted out, glaring at the professor but not speaking the words "you evil, slimy, sexist pig," clearly written on her face.

"How can I think that?" echoed the professor. "It is easy. Women are the caregivers of the world. While men are self-absorbed, women are caring for others. Hence, if women didn't exist, there would be no one to care for others."

2502. Wise Crackering.

"How do you like the new crackers we just bought?"

"They would seem to be very wise."

"Wise crackers? Oh, I get it. Too bad that scores so low on the Funny scale."

"But my intent was not to provoke laughter. My comment expressed a conclusion derived from an investigation of said crackers, together with the common observation that wisdom normally comes with age."

"And your point is?"

"These crackers have been crackers for a long time."

"So they're old and stale, like you? No longer fresh?"

"No young woman has ever accused me of being fresh. By the time I pronounce the "O" in "hello" they have already turned away and started chatting with someone else."

"I guess that's the way the cracker crunches."

2503. Thoughts on a River Cruise Down the Rhine.

1. The one thought that really stands out from this trip to

Europe is how deeply religious the people were a thousand years ago. They built enormous stone churches on nearly every block, churches that still stand today.

2. Coming from a country where every five or ten years we tear down our buildings and put something else in their place, seeing the typical neighborhoods that were built in, say, 1543, fills me with quiet awe.

3. How happy we are the day we leave for vacation, and how happy we are the day we return. Happy to go, happier to get home.

4. On the flight over and on the flight back, KLM airlines offered two meals and three snacks for the 10-plus hour flight. Generous, I'd say, compared to some of the American airlines practices of selling you food. KLM also served almonds as a snack, unlike the peanuts—or worse, pretzels—other airlines offer. But it wasn't all joy. My medication and constitution dehydrate me, as does the low humidity air on the plane. So I was thirsty. An hour or so after I finished the 8-ounce bottle of cold water served with the meal on the way over, I asked the steward if he had an extra bottle of water. He said, "I might have. I'll check." That was the last I heard from him.

Then on the way back, we were served a four-ounce packet of filtered, ice cold water. I asked for more and was told, "Certainly, sir." He then gave me a cup of room temperature tap water.

2504. **Luxury on Steroids.**

Having had the opportunity recently to stay in a five-star hotel, I can now pronounce, using the common practice of creating a sweeping generalization from a single example, that five-star hotels have the following qualities:

1. The bath towels are larger than the towels at lower class hotels. We had towels that measured about 37 inches by 64 inches, meaning that they were (a) awkward and heavy and (b) too big to use comfortably. Unfolding the towel caused one end to drop to the floor every time, regardless of how I tried to prevent it.

2. The bathtubs are huge. Our tub was about one and a half times as deep as our home tub, and perhaps 20% longer, almost enough to fit my legs in straightened out.

3. The toilet paper (!) is four-ply, much stronger than our domestic two-ply. In fact, it seemed that all the TP in European restrooms was 4-ply.

4. Having the suite appear elegantly functional and abundant in luxury, the tiny bathroom features a set of twin sinks set into a vanity that left only six inches on each side.

2505. The purpose of education is not to shelter you from ideas that you don't already agree with. The purpose of education is to help you learn how to think, to evaluate new — and old — ideas, to separate truth from error, to grow in understanding, to learn what is worth knowing, and to develop a moral and spiritual center.

In the process of becoming an educated person, you will encounter some really bad ideas, ideas that offend many people.

Thinking that you should be protected from every belief or idea that you disagree with or that you find offensive harbors the assumption that you have already encountered every idea there is, analyzed each carefully, and chosen only the "correct" ones, and that your collection will never change.

2506. If men who can't see God in nature are fools, what are we to say of men who can see God in nature but deny it?

2507. We've been in a secular culture for quite a while now. But recently this culture has become arrogantly secular, evangelistically secular, and discriminatorily secular.

2508. There is a progression in both labeling and treatment. Once the formerly mainstream Christians are deemed fanatics or extremists, it won't be long before they are also known as prisoners.

2509. What causes me, someone who thinks of himself as a cynical realist, to write 2500 Glimmerings for the benefit of posterity? It is my hope—it is my prayer—that, perhaps somewhere, 100 years from now, they will fall into the hands of a ten-year-old girl or eleven-year-old boy who will be genuinely interested in finding whatever insights, truths, or wisdom they can. For they, unlike their friends and parents, will still believe in truth and wisdom.

Even now they will be curious, teaching themselves how to think by asking questions such as, "Why did he say a ten-year-old girl and an eleven-year-old boy?" (The answer is, partly for the sake of art and partly in acknowledgment of differing speeds of maturity and verbal fluency.)

Unlike their peers, who treat texts as found objects, the readers who appreciate my little effort at enjoyable thoughts will be asking questions, such as, "Why does he say that?" "What does he mean?" And especially, "Is that true?" "When?" "Under what circumstances?" "Why?"

2510. Readers who are tempted to throw this book across the room or into the fire should note that these Glimmerings are twigs—insubstantial kindling perhaps, but useful to light the fire of ideas in the heart and imagination of the reader.

2511. Many people still draw their conclusions by constructing a generalization from a short, chance observation applied to their limited stock of experience. One summer I entered a takeout restaurant when my Parkinson's medication was at a low point, compromising my ability to balance. A customer in the restaurant saw me take two small steps backward and said, "He's drunk." What can we conclude from this short tale?

1. We often draw erroneous conclusions because of our limited knowledge and experience. Had the patron known about Parkinson's and off times, he would have been able to use that information in a differential diagnosis, leading him perhaps to a more accurate analysis.

2. Availability bias is always ready to jump in and suggest a conclusion at hand. (See Thinking Fast and Slow.)

3. The fundamental truth here is what has been said many times. We select an answer or solution or choice from among the alternatives we believe are possible, that fit within our plausibility structure (as the early postmodernists used to say).

2512. If you call the pack of cheese crackers "my friend" when you get hungry at 2:00 AM, is that a reasonable expression or an indication of incipient madness? I mean, when do you eat your friends?

2513. Travel is valuable in the cause of wisdom because it supplies context for one's knowledge, lending itself to a greater understanding of the whole of life. Circumspection is always a benefit and a defense from gullibility. Further, travel supplies us with the material for analogies, and analogies are among the foundation stones for understanding.

2514. Having knowledge is insufficient for best practices. You must also know when and how to apply it. Otherwise, you will be known as the foolish guru.

2515. **The Evil Trinity of the Nineteenth Century.**
Darwin denies the Creator, God the Father, by substituting evolution.

Marx denies God the Son by substituting corrupt social structures for fallen man in personal need of a redeemer.

Freud denies God the Holy Spirit by substituting a psychosexual mythology for the spiritual needs of human beings.

2516. Those who don't suffer from a problem usually see the solution as easy. Insomnia? Drink a cup of warm milk. Constipation? Eat more fiber. Relationship issues? Talk it out.

2517. What's funny? Humor is frequently caused by a reversal of expectations. The punch line presents a conclusion or idea seemingly in conflict with the set up. The unexpected reversal of the story's rational progress makes us laugh.

"The food here is terrible."
"And the portions are so small."

"How could you have spent your entire six months' wages on a three-day shore leave?"
"Well, some of it I spent on cheap booze and fast women. And the rest of it I wasted."

"Let's not eat there. No one goes there anymore."
"Why don't they?"
"It's too crowded."

2518. Smervitz is the author of "Truth? Hah!" and "Fifty-seven Meanings of the Word, 'No.'"

[May 16, 2017; age 66]

2519. How many kind and generous acts are really propelled by vanity? "Here's a truckload of money. Oh, you're putting my name on the building? Why, thanks." In my case, it's, "Here's a book I wrote, filled with my wisdom. You can have it free." But doesn't that show how actions that are rooted in vanity can produce good fruit?

2520. What's the difference between, "'Every work should have a beginning, a middle, and an end,' says Aristotle," and, "Every work should have a beginning, a middle, and an end"? The first is much more impressive. We pay attention.

2521. Our love for action-adventure movies would seem to make a negative comment on modern Western civilization. Filled with cars crashing, helicopters and buildings exploding, people being killed wholesale, and all manner of blood and guts and graphic cruelty, what are we to think of ourselves who exhibit such an appetite for violence as entertainment? And then we think of the practices of premodern civilization — the gladiator fights of ancient Rome, for example—and we see that it is human beings who are spiritually damaged, not simply the current culture.

2522. "The hot dogs made by this plant are so inexpensive. How do you suppose they make them so cheap?"

"I don't know, but I do know I've never seen a cat or a dog within five miles of the factory."

[May 25, 2017; age 66]

2523. Faith involves belief, which involves trust, which involves obedience, which involves action.

2524. Aristotle says that virtue is an activity of the soul. Christ says that faith is an activity of the soul. In both cases, the soul needs to get busy and do good deeds.

2525. Where did the idea come from that once we accept Jesus as our savior, our bodies (and souls) can lie around in a hammock all day?

2526. Any sort of inner transformation should show some outer evidence. Most of all the transformation into faith.

2527. Woman to doorbell ringer: "I can't talk now. My husband is upstairs cleaning his tools." When they make the movie, the character based on the woman will say, "I can't talk now. My husband is upstairs cleaning his guns."

2528. **Hollywood.**

"*A True Story.*" Almost half of the events in the movie actually happened, though not in that way or in that sequence or to those people, or with that degree of exaggeration.

"*Based on a True Story.*" Maybe ten percent of the events depicted sort of happened, and the rest we turned upside down and backwards or just made up.

"Inspired by a True Story." None of this really happened, but we heard a story that gave us an idea. Basically, we just bought the rights to the story so we could do our own film but still get the box office pull that saying, "Inspired by a True Story" would give us. And frankly, if we didn't use the phrase "true story," people would say the film was ridiculously impossible and boring, too.

2529. To a wise man, everything is unexpected, but nothing is a surprise.

2530. The fact that young boys, who have high-pitched voices, can sing beautifully in a choir, until their voices crack and they begin to speak like men, shows that every stage of life has its own value.

2531. One of the advantages of Biblical Christianity is that the believer does not need to pray to saints or angels or Jesus' mother — there is a direct line to God, open all the time. If praying to God the Father is too daunting, Jesus is there to listen.

2532. Con men put lifts in their shoes because they are telling tall tales.

2533. Why is it that greed and lust can so easily conquer reason, so easily force reason to be on their side?

2534. The con man makes his scheme sound probable, but greed makes it sound like a sure thing.

2535. Whatever is of high value will be counterfeited: money (in coin and bill), jewelry, designer everything, watches, works of art, virginity, and especially, information. Counterfeit information (disinformation) is common, and yet most of us are not cautious enough about the information or "facts" aimed at us daily.

2536. Lots of people promise to love each other until they die. Then something happens and they break up or get a divorce. The problem is that these people think that love is a feeling. You can't promise a feeling, because feelings can change. That's why in some modern weddings the couple promises not "until death us do part," but "as long as we both shall love." When, by this definition, love goes out the door, so does the spouse.

Suppose, on the other hand, that love is not a feeling but an action. You can promise an action, and you can remain faithful to perform an action. Your feelings are irrelevant to your promise. What is important is your character, your trustworthiness, your integrity.

2537. He told me that when he was young and selfish, he thought that life was all about him and that others existed to raise him up. Now that he was old, he said he thought that life was really about others and that he existed to raise them up.

2538. We often spend time trying to figure out other people, but we seldom spend time trying to figure out ourselves.

2539. It appears that the government is going to take over healthcare in the future, with the promise of excellent care for everybody under a New Plan. You can enjoy that same healthcare now. Simply take a sheet of paper and write, "Diagnosis: idiopathic malaise," together with your name. Add a scribble in imitation of a doctor's signature. Then take a bottle of vitamins — or, if you really feel sick, of aspirin — and tear off the label. Instead, write the name, "Ceboflaxotrate XR-L" on it, together with the instructions, "Take one tablet each day."

Next Lesson: How you can have the same hospital benefits now that you will be getting under the New Plan. Bring a razor blade and a Band-Aid to the next meeting.

2540. **Questionable Questions.**
"Do you think I need the operation?" he asked the surgeon.

"Does my car really need that repair?" she asked the auto mechanic.

"Are these new washing machines better than the old ones?" she asked the appliance salesman.

"Are the Brandex TVs better than the competitor's?" he asked the Brandex dealer.

2541. If you approach a stranger on the street and say, "I heard about your problem," the stranger will say either, "Who told you?" or, "Which one?" Why is it that everyone seems to have several serious problems—health, relationships, finances, jobs? Wouldn't the statisticians tell us that such a distribution violates the expectation of statistical probability? The answer, of course, is that those who lack real problems either create problems for themselves or elevate minor problems to major ones. "The only parking space I could find was a hundred yards from the gym's door. What a terrible day."

2542. Ecclesiastes 6:11 in the NASB reads: "For there are many words which increase futility. What then is the advantage to a man?" Kind of abstract and hard to process, huh? Well, let's turn to the CEV: "The more we talk, the less sense we make, so what good does it do to talk?" Now, *that's* a translation I can relate to.

2543. People become like their enemies—and sometimes like their friends.

2544. Truth is a steel ruler; we've got to stop treating it like a rubber band. Truth measures our beliefs; we shouldn't stretch truth to match our beliefs.

2545. The purpose of integrating faith and learning is to reascend to the holism of knowledge that originally existed.

2546. No expectations, no disappointments. So to prevent or limit disappointment. . . .

2547. The questions we are most afraid to ask are not those whose answer we fear. The questions we are most afraid to ask are those whose answer we already know.

2548. Stop working so hard on your job and start working harder on your life.

2549. Anyone who rushes you doesn't have your interests in mind.

2550. Haste is the father of bad decisions.

2551. If you are waiting for your ship to come in, be sure you are at the right port.

2552. The gift that Freedom gives you is decision fatigue.

2553. They flip through the pages of the Bible and ask, "What else is forbidden that we can go and do?"

2554. Why do we always think that God should feel our pain, but we never think we should feel God's pain? What about a little empathy for God? Do you think he's pleased with his creatures and the way we turned out?

2555. Life is a dynamic where we must constantly decide between acceptance and resistance. Accepting everything makes us exploited doormats while resisting everything or fighting everything makes us destructive reactionaries.

2556. Sometimes the best part of the conversation is found within the silence between words.

2557. Why do we tolerate the crudity constantly pushed on us by the entertainment business? Constant profanity, sick themes, the promotion of adultery and whoremongering. And why are we so attracted to violence—ever more graphic and gory—as entertainment?

2558. Considering what boring covers most textbooks have, I have been surprised at how accommodating my publishers have been to use my more colorful ideas. Does this mean that most publishers aren't as open to ideas or that most textbook authors have no esthetic imagination?

2559. I am constantly reminded of the perpetual conflict between artistic design and practical utility. Whether it is the award-winning tiny, gray type you can't read or the celebrated tall, narrow sandwich that you can't fit into your mouth and that tips over and falls apart on its own, or the architectural award-winning bathroom with the open shower where you are likely to freeze without any trapped warmth—the more design awards something gets, the less useful it is.

2560. By saying, "I could comment on your deficiencies, too," you already have.

2561. He liked sky diving, cliff jumping, motorcycle racing, and white water kayaking. She liked reading, museums, classical music, and philosophy. So, of course, they were attracted to each other.

2562. Yes, alas, she's your second choice. But cheer up. You are her third choice.

2563. Many people keep diaries to remind them of what they did. I recommend keeping a spiritual diary. Each day talk to God and record your conversation. When you look back, you will see your growth in knowing God and growing in spiritual maturity.

2564. Are humble people happier than proud people? The humble are able to appreciate things they know they could never accomplish themselves. The proud must believe that they could accomplish the same thing better than what they saw, or else denigrate the whole activity.

2565. Those who attack lies have always been punished more severely than those who attack truth. Those who promote lies have always been more cruel and intolerant than those who promote truth.

2566. Every benefit comes with a cost.

2567. The realist's definition of *free* is "paid for by someone else."

2568. The pessimist's definition of *free* is "something you think was paid for by someone else, but if you trace it back far enough, the ultimate payer is you."

2569. We arrogantly assume that if something happens to us that we deem bad or that we don't understand, then there's something wrong with God. We never blame our own weakness, inadequacy, incapacity, sin, lack of context, inability to see beyond ourselves and our immediate circumstances. But if you calm down a minute, and sit back and think, the idea of judging God seems pretty stupid.

2570. I have said somewhere in these pages that the expectation of gratitude is the first mistake of the human heart. The second mistake is the expectation of sympathy when something goes wrong. In both of these instances, if you reverse your expectations, you will be right, though not necessarily happy. Instead of gratitude, expect resentment (or silence if you are lucky). Instead of sympathy, expect blame.

2571. Victory in war is international, because so many people love a winner; defeat in war is national, because those on the losing side are subject to oppression; but grief in war is personal, the quiet despair of those whose loved ones will never return.

2572. Intellectuals, especially those in academia, live lives of ideas, not of actions and their consequences. Therefore, a nice-sounding idea gets promoted in spite of the evils it might entail.

2573. Some people with a problem create obstacles in front of every solution. Then they complain that they are stuck without options. Any suggestion of a solution is immediately rejected as impossible. It's almost as if they enjoy feeling trapped.

2574. Ask not what God can do for you; ask what you can do for God.

2575. "We have kitchen cabinets for $100."
    "Okay. I need ten. That's $1,000, right?"
    "Yes, but you'll want these upgraded doors for $30 each, and the stain is $40, and all plywood instead of that nasty particleboard is $50. Trim is $30, remaking from 24 inches to 18 inches deep is $140. And installation for all ten is $2,000."
    "Is that it?"
    "Countertop for those cabinets is $1,400, plus a rounded edge for $400, sealer for $350, sink cutout for $200."
    "So the total is?
    "$8,250."

2576. Some things simply cannot be comprehended in any complete way. We can try to get a tentative handle on them, but a full understanding is just not available to human brains, no matter how smart. Whether you're thinking of theology (Do you really think you can understand God?), science (Do you really understand the physical nature of the universe, or even quantum entanglement?), or a blend of theology and science (What was occupying space before space and before the Big Bang?), all we can do is get a bit of an idea and pretend we understand more than we do. In all three cases, however, we can know even though we cannot understand.

2577. Have you ever noticed that most people refuse to admit to personal inadequacy or failure? Instead of, "I can't do that," they say, "That can't be done," or "You don't want that," or "People who have that don't like it." And instead of, "I broke it," they say, "It was defective," or "It broke," or, as in the case of a college friend who was working on my brand new radio, "It killed itself."

It is rather sad that we've come to such a point of disclaiming personal responsibility that we must allege the suicide of our electronic products when they suddenly cease to work while we hold them in our hands and apply a screwdriver.

2578. **The Law of Unintended Consequences.**

Also known as Failure to Think Things Through. Example:

"Let's require ethanol as a gasoline additive to reduce dependence on oil from other countries. We will subsidize it to make it competitive."

"Done."

"What happened?"

"The price of corn went up a lot because of the huge increase in demand."

"And then what?"

"Many poor people in the third world could no longer afford to buy enough corn to keep themselves and their children alive."

"And then what?"

"The high price of corn caused farmers to plant more of it and to abandon other food crops such as soy, wheat, and rice, which drove up the prices of those crops also, causing even more malnourishment and starvation in the third world."

"Oops. Well, anyway, we had good intentions."

2579. We read those words, *grace, mercy, holy, eternal*, but do we — can we — know what they really mean?

2580. Advice to the Young About Happiness.

1. Happiness is not an entitlement. Even the Declaration of Independence says that people "are endowed by their Creator with certain unalienable Rights, that among these are Life, Liberty and the pursuit of Happiness." That's the right to *pursue*, not to *have* happiness.

2. It is no one's job to make you happy. Stop thinking and acting as if it's everyone else's job to do whatever you want. (Besides, if everyone else did what you want, that wouldn't make you happy; that would only increase your wants and corrupt your character.)

3. No one will make you happy. If you seek friends or a spouse who will make you happy, you will be frustrated and disappointed. And with the attitude you'll develop, you certainly won't make others happy, either.

4. Being happy is your own responsibility. If you are not happy, it's your fault and your concern. Don't blame others. and don't blame your circumstances. (When life hands you a lemon, mix it with the sweetness of your response to make lemonade.)

5. You can't buy happiness. Happiness does not consist in the abundance of possessions. The more stuff you own, the more time you have to spend maintaining it. The joy of that new gizmo vanishes quickly as you soon take it for granted. So stop maxing out your credit cards.

6. Pretending to be happy when you're not is your duty. Do not show off your grumpy, bored, angry, or unhappy feelings. There is no good reason to drag others down emotionally just because you are sad or in a snit. Pretending to be happy will produce a powerful influence on your mental state and you will become less unhappy.

7. Life really isn't about happiness, your happiness, or you. As Westley says in *The Princess Bride*, "Get used to disappointment." Moments of happiness are often rare and most lives experience emotional trauma.

8. Life is about what you can do, not how you feel. Possibly with the exception of a few close friends, no one cares how you feel, anyway.

9. The more you think about yourself and how to be happy, the less happy you will be. Ever notice that egotistical people are not very happy? Selfishness leads away from joy.

10. You will discover your own happiness by serving others. Happiness is a byproduct of other activities. There is a saying, "Life is what happens while you're making other plans." Similarly, happiness is what happens while you're doing other things.

11. Expect less, live more. Life cannot deliver the degree of happiness most people demand from it, and so they inevitably end up frustrated and miserable. To many people, life is the supreme disappointment because they expect from it more than it can give.

2581. From the very first notes, you realize that you are in for two hours of bad acoustics.

2582. His life was bad music in high definition.

2583. A trickle meets a trickle and becomes a rivulet. Rivulets embrace and become a stream. Thus are mighty rivers born and boundless oceans filled.

2584. How vain we are when we hunt eagerly through a list of 500 "People in the Parade" in the newspaper, breathlessly looking for our own name. And if it's not there, we are upset — though we will deny it.

2585. I personally have no recollection of being upset when my name was not in the paper, but I've been guilty of perhaps even worse. When I was a faculty member and some sort of award or other recognition was announced, I always thought it might be me they were describing. You know how it goes: "This award goes to an outstanding colleague who has always gone way beyond what is required, has been a great resource to the other faculty and is so loved by students, blah, blah, blah." And then,

"Yes, this recognition celebrates our fine friend—Doctor Sam Smervitz." Oops.

2586. On a given day, forty three trillion and fourteen words are spoken on earth, of which two hundred million and three are heard.

2587. The most loving, supportive, positive, esteem-building three words in the English language are not, "I love you," but, "I agree completely."

2588. We are never so angry at others as when we are at fault.

2589. The truth isn't always the story that makes the most sense.

2590. Your past might explain your present, but cannot excuse it.

2591. "Most Studies Have Wrong Conclusions, Study Says."

2592. "Expert Testimony Is Unreliable, Expert Testifies."

2593. "Professor Proves That Truth Does Not Exist."

2594. "Researcher Demonstrates Conclusively That Nothing Can Be Known With Certainty."

2595. If you want to gain some perspective on current events, read the front page of any newspaper from twenty years ago.

2596. Ego looks bad on anyone.

2597. Don't wish for many more possessions than you already have. The more possessions you have, the more time, effort, and money you need to expend just to take care of them. And if they are all in working order, you won't have time to use them all.

2598. Before artificial intelligence can truly replace humans, the software will have to be programmed or learn how to be imperfect. This thought occurred to me while watching a dance performance preceded by spotlights roaming around the stage. The lights moved around all right, but then they stopped with such precision that it was obvious they were operated by computer-controlled stepper motors rather than by human hands. If humans were moving the lights, they would not have stopped so precisely. Instead, they would have moved a bit after reaching their target locations. Humans can't hold lights as steadily as stepper motors. Imprecision and variability are what make us human.

2599. Looking at a lithograph copy of an Old Master painting on the wall of an art museum rather than the original Old Master itself is analogous to listening to a soundtrack behind a live show rather than having a live orchestra play the music. Where is the diminishment? If you are not told you are looking at a copy or hearing a recorded performance, would you notice? Would your experience be any different?

[August 24, 2017; age 66]

2600. If a woman were given a necklace, or earrings, or an engagement ring made of cubic zirconia rather than diamonds, would she be any less satisfied? Most of the women I've talked to say, Yes, they would be less—much less—satisfied. But few can tell the difference, and from two or three feet away, only a jeweler can tell. So, why insist on real diamonds?

2601. Formula for an "accident": Drive way too fast. Add a bad road. Add rain or snow. Add night. Add while drunk. Mix and crash.

2602. When you think, "I want to pursue wisdom," stay put for a moment to reflect that there is wisdom all around you, in your every experience. Most of the time we're too busy to think about the meaning of our experiences. Oh, and when you think you want to pursue wisdom, make a commitment to act on it when you find it.

2603. When the only choices are blaming yourself or denying reality, well, after all, "reality" is only an intersubjective construct, whose narrative is easily decentered.

2604. To be blunt about it, some people are just too proud to have a happy marriage.

2605. **Roughing It.**
"Let's get away from it all, just take off and be completely by ourselves."
"Great idea. Let's go right now."
"Okay. Got your mobile phone, your tablet, your laptop, your GPS, your portable Blu-ray player, and your TV?"
"Check. And you have your books, magazines, and today's paper?"
"Check."
"So let's go."

2606. Many lies are made plausible by adding another lie after the word *because*.

2607. In the *Pensees*, Pascal says (Lafuma 1) that in the act of asking someone's opinion, we invariably influence it by the way we ask: "Isn't that a great poem?" He says that we should not say anything and let the other person decide for himself. But this would be to abandon the field and let everyone else have the freedom to influence the other person by employing their own focus, elucidations, distortions, and manipulations.

2608. Every society, culture, and era is ultimately conformist. Each applies pressure for its members to dress, speak, and act in certain ways. In the 1800s, proper beach wear for young women was a neck-to-ankle "bathing costume." Today, it's a bikini.

Wearing a bikini in 1850 would have resulted in an arrest for indecent exposure. Wearing a bathing costume today would result in ridicule.

Clearly, those things to which the members of a culture must conform change over time and vary by place. The questions that arise are these:

1. Who makes or influences the changes? Is it art (such as movies), marketing (advertisers), the news media, academia, or a group of social innovators propagandizing for what is important to them? Is it in part what technology makes possible?

2. Why do people gradually go with the flow and accept whatever changes are pressed upon them?

3. What affects the speed of change?

2609. Does our thinking proceed from reasons that lead to a conclusion or from a conclusion to the reasons that support it? Are reasons identified or even created ex post facto to support an idea or conclusion that popped into our mind—therefore making them rationalizations—or are the reasons the genuine precursors and arguments that led us subconsciously to the conclusion—therefore making them the belatedly verbalized sources? Do we conclude from pre-verbal thought?

2610. Anyone who is honest—whether scientist, philosopher, theologian, professor or layman—sooner or later realizes that when he says, "I know," he means, "I believe." For knowledge is a type of belief—sturdily held and rationally backed, to be sure—but still a type of belief. Only God really knows.

2611. A true religion must explain the confusing nature of reality: There is heart-stopping beauty, artistic design, soul-filling wonders, human kindness and human wisdom; and there is also grotesque ugliness, chaos, banality, human cruelty and human folly. Only the explanation that we were created in the image of God and then fell into evil can account for it all.

2612. Why is it that certain ideologues reject vociferously those values and standards and truths that promote happiness in individuals, relationships, and entire cultures? It is because standards imply authority, and our culture (K-12 education, universities, publishing, Hollywood, news media) has for many years been hostile toward authority. The ideologues equate authority with authoritarianism. Standards are rules and rules inhibit their "freedom" to do whatever they want.

This revulsion toward rules and authority explains why modern heroes in action movies have to break all the rules, reject the constraints of the policing organization, and disobey the constraints imposed by their superiors — all, of course, in order to succeed at catching or killing the bad guys.

2613. A ten-cent ballpoint pen in the right hands can change the world.

2614. In the intellectual battle against evil, too many Christians are fighting with squirt guns.

2615. In youth, there is boldness and folly; in middle years, caution and wisdom; in later years, caution and folly.

2616. **Literature Class.**[6]

"Okay, class. How many of you read the Shakespeare play for today? Hmm. That's all? Just Alice?"

"I didn't read the dead white man's play because I couldn't relate to it."

"You couldn't relate to it? Tell me, John, what do you mean by that? In what way were you unable to relate to the play?"

"I couldn't relate to it in any way. It's not about my people. It's about a bunch of long dead, high class nobles in a white European hegemonic culture hundreds of years ago. I feel nothing in common with any of these people."

---

[6] This version of the anecdote is the third rendering (see Glimmerings 1737 and 2197).

"Well, let me respond to that by saying that you can relate to these people, beyond their historical periods and cultures. These plays are not really about kings and courts and England at the end of the sixteenth century. The plays are about the human nature that we all share—hopes, dreams, frustrations, ideals—and about the problems we all face—loyalty, honesty, integrity, and faith—all set in tension with betrayal, cheating, selfishness, and greed. Contests between the proud and the humble, the giving and the self-serving—these tell us about ourselves, regardless of where we are placed in time or culture."

2617. Evil people are given false things to believe:

> Then that lawless one will be revealed . . . whose coming is in accord with the activity of Satan, . . . with all the deception of wickedness for those who perish, because they did not receive the love of the truth so as to be saved. For this reason God will send upon them a deluding influence so that they will believe what is false, in order that they all may be judged who did not believe the truth, but took pleasure in wickedness.
> —2 Thessalonians 2:8-12 (NASB)

This is because truth is a reward for virtue:

> David sent messengers to the men of Jabesh-gilead, and said to them, "May you be blessed of the LORD because you have shown this kindness to Saul your lord, and have buried him. Now may the LORD show lovingkindness and truth to you; and I also will show this goodness to you, because you have done this thing." —2 Samuel 2:5-6 (NASB)

Those who are not virtuous do not have or deserve the truth.

2618. If life is a tree, many women see themselves as roots and men as trunks. Unfortunately, many men see themselves as birds and women as fruit.

2619. Men and women will never really understand each other because they are so fundamentally different emotionally and psychologically. This problem is exacerbated by the methods men and women use to try to understand each other. When a man or woman sees some strange behavior, value, attitude, or comment coming from a member of the other sex, he or she first evaluates it by his or her own standards and self. "I would never say that unless I meant. . ." or "I don't understand that, because if I said it, it would mean. . . ." Total confusion and inaccuracy. Worse, when a man or woman is completely confused by a member of the other sex, the woman asks another woman what the man's words or behavior means, and the man, if he asks anyone at all, asks another man. Total chaos. Women think men are more complex than they really are, while men think women are as simple as men.

2620. You feel proud of that accomplishment? Think how many people in the world don't even know you exist.

2621. No matter how famous, rich, and powerful a person is, compared to the whole planet, he is still a dinky fish in a great big pond. And compared to the number of galaxies. . . .

2622. Why do we get so upset over the tiniest of things? If a shark takes off your arm, or your house burns to the ground, it's okay to be upset. Those are life-altering events. But if you yell and complain and sob and curse when you break a fingernail, see a small blemish on your new chair, discover that your dog has had an accident on the floor, or if your waiter forgets to bring the toast, take some time to think about what's wrong with you.

2623. Did you ever notice how the Jewish authorities in Jesus' day were so absorbed in themselves and their legal system that they missed the main event? John 5:1-12. Jesus heals a man who had been sick for 38 years. Do the authorities marvel and praise God for a miracle? Of course not. They don't even ask, "Who performed this wondrous healing?" Instead, they demand to know who told him to carry his pallet unlawfully on the Sabbath.

[October 14, 2017; Age 67]

2624. Why do we continue to reread the Bible even though we have read it so many times? There are several reasons.

1. There is something we have missed in past readings. Perhaps we have read inattentively or presumptively and have passed through that chapter or passage many times before without getting the meaning.

2. We have neglected the truth of the passage. We need to be reminded more often than informed, Samuel Johnson says. It's not that we don't know the lesson, rule, law, or behavior—it's just that in our overly busy lives we have neglected to implement the teaching.

3. We learn a lot in our information-driven era. And that means we also forget a lot, with Scriptural truths included. So we must continue to read to be informed.

4. The Holy Spirit brings the Scripture to life and points out specific passages that apply to our lives today in a special appointment that didn't apply yesterday. In other words, read to find God's will for you today.

2625. Until wisdom is lived, it's not wisdom.

2626. Looking over the remainders at the bookstore today, I noticed how many titles there were about Hitler and the Nazis. And I was once again moved to reflect on the power of hatred—the need so many people have to hate someone or something. Even though he is long gone, Hitler is hatred's poster child because he is perhaps the only villain everyone can agree upon.

2627. The news media have long ago ceased to pretend to be objective or even dispassionate. Now just about every media person is dripping with unreserved and uninhibited loathing for people and ideas they don't agree with. If you disagree, you're not just wrong — you're evil.

2628. When you look back on your life, if you don't regret more than half of it, you haven't learned much: You haven't been paying attention.

2629. In the industrial age, the big devoured the small; in the information age, the fast devour the slow.

2630. If you write a book supporting a dominant theory, you will be given tenure, a promotion, and grant money. If you write a book attacking a dominant theory, you will be fired, persecuted, and smeared. These facts we call the scientific method.

2631. "Progress, far from consisting in change, depends on retentiveness." — George Santayana.

Cultural advancement depends not on throwing away the "old" ideas in order to adopt "new" ideas, but on preserving, and where needed modifying, the best solutions to the problems of living. The better cultures have enjoyed a better range of potential solutions and these better options have enabled better choices. A genuine progressive, therefore, should always be testing new, proposed ideas against the current best practices.

Revolution is usually the breakfast of villains. Revolutionaries like to throw over the old system because that includes rejecting the moral foundation of the society. However weak and often neglected in practice, that foundation provided for many years a standard, or an anchor, that held people together and offered at least the hope, and often the opportunity, for safe and orderly living and for personal advancement.

2632. No civilization should be content to use its own practices as the standard of measure for new possibilities. Cultures, in order to grow and improve, must seek out, adopt, and preserve those values, habits, practices, and solutions that best make life less difficult. Every culture should feel free to take the best ideas from every other culture. This practice has propelled Western civilization.

2633. "Is it progress if a cannibal uses a knife and fork?"
—Stanislaus Lec.

Technological progress is not moral progress. The refinement of harmful, immoral, or evil practices is not progress. Adopting the most popular practices from other cultures is not progress. Societies must use a moral standard — in the West, this has been ultimately derived from Biblical principles.

2634. **Sensitivity Training.**

Prejudice, whether racism or sexism or misogyny or some other kind, cannot be cured by education, especially not by sensitivity training, mandatory multicultural sessions, or punitive re-education meetings. Participants see such events as shaming, humiliating, browbeating, and offensive. They quickly perceive the ominous atmosphere of threat, feeling as if they are being treated like wayward children. Instead of remedying the problem, such sessions are met with bitterness and hostility.

The result of this resistance is resentment and rejection of the message. Any existing prejudices are driven deeper and made stronger because highly moralistic, often hectoring, attitude adjustment training comes across as brainwashing with propaganda. Trying to legislate or install attitudes by fiat just doesn't work. In fact, it backfires, often increasing distrust, suspicion, and hostility among the groups supposedly being reconciled.

If the real goal of the company, school, or organization is to improve trust and harmony among its diverse members, then the processes of familiarity, friendship, and focus will work better than classroom training.

Familiarity. A major source of prejudice is ignorance. To cure ignorance, get people working together. Teams of two to seven. Sponsor picnics for everyone, with activities designed to randomly get folks together.

Friendship. Pay for pairs to have lunch together. Sponsor lunch clubs on many topics. Send diverse teams to conferences, expos, meetings, and the like.

Focus. Create small diverse work teams of limited duration. The best sensitivity training involves teaming, partnering, or eating together.

2635. When you see a problem, adjust your glasses and you'll see an opportunity.

2636. God offers us salvation of our souls, not necessarily deliverance from our physical existence. Jesus didn't give wealth or power or even a good end to his disciples. Many of his precious servants down through history lived in hardship and suffered from disease, not to mention persecution.

2637. When it comes down to either blaming oneself or denying cause and effect, guess which option most people choose?

2638. The mind is enormously powerful, even in the most modestly gifted, for in an instant it can cross billions of light years of space or scale from thinking about a quark to thinking about the entire universe.

2639. Every highly successful person has been self-taught. Whether it was a high-school dropout who developed an automobile customizing business or a Harvard PhD in physics, the key to their success was a keen interest and a powerful self-motivation. In other words, successful people do not rely on others to train them, educate them, or motivate them. Many successful people are smart, and that often helps. But the real key is that hunger—the desire to know, to solve, to create, to understand.

2640. Even Christians have to go to the dentist.

2641. Everything of a high value will be counterfeited. Hundred-dollar bills, Old Master oil paintings, jewelry, concert tickets, driver's licenses, prescription medications, aircraft parts, designer handbags, watches. Take any one of the previous items and add *counterfeit* to a Web search and you'll see what I mean.

2642. "This watch includes a *Proof of Authenticity* certificate."
"But this watch is obviously a counterfeit."
"Of course. And so is the certificate."

2643. What is the solution to the counterfeiting problem? There are several.
1. If it's too good to be true, it probably is. Don't expect a genuine $17,000 watch to be offered at a swap meet or online for $60.
2. Know the product. Even the makers of superfakes (extremely well-made fakes) make mistakes.
3. Attend to provenance. Is the item from the factory or an authorized dealer? Or is it from some guy who seems to have plenty of very expensive items at bargain prices?

2644. The fierceness of opposition to a new idea is often in direct proportion to what those who oppose it have to lose.

2645. Show me a man who still believes in free will and I'll show you a bachelor.

2646. I can understand many kinds of sin — lust, greed, envy — but I am at a loss to fathom cruelty. That is especially true of cruelty for its own sake, against the helpless, weak, and innocent.

2647. How foolish yet how common it is for people to measure their behavior and attitudes by those of others.

2648. You can be taught what it means to be honest (ethics), but you still must choose to be honest (character).

2649. The major part of the value of most things lies in their utility. As objects, their value is limited by their replacement cost. Sometimes, even people are thought of this way. In the "people-as-furniture" model, just as chairs can be replaced, so can employees. Hence also the exaggeration, "He was irreplaceable." As the saying is, the cemeteries are filled with irreplaceable people. Nevertheless, people are unique, with knowledge and skills aggregated and improved over time, so they are not chairs after all.

2650. Why not simply rely on personal observation and experience for knowledge and forget external sources? Personal observation and experience can be misled by a mirage, a misperception, a misinterpretation, an anomaly leading to a hasty generalization, a misremembrance, a con artist.

2651. **Some Definitions From My Scattered Notes.**
Faith. Trust in authority as a source of knowledge, a belief in knowledge claims that you cannot personally verify.
Religious Faith. A subcategory of faith, where the trusted source of knowledge is God.
Truth. A statement that corresponds to (that is, correctly describes) reality. Some truths are eternal ("God created the universe") and some truths change ("It's raining outside now").
Proposition. An assertion of truth. A truth claim.
Belief. Adherence to the truth of a proposition.
Knowledge. A form of belief. Properly justified true belief.

2652. Statements that reveal a proud culture, where ego has run away from reality.
"We're modern."
"We're in the now."
"This is completely new."
"We're sophisticated."
"We believe in progress, not tradition."
"Change is good."
"We have really arrived."

"We scorn the old, the traditional, the yesterday."

2653. "Just the facts, please." The mere need for facts barely opens the problem. What are the facts and how can they be discovered amid disinformation, opinion, rumor, prejudice, error? And are they still the facts? Do they apply here? Are they relevant?

2654. **All in a Name.**
"Well, congratulations on your purchase of this new sofa. It will give you many years of good service, God willing and the creek don't rise, as they say. Now what is your street address for delivery?"

"We're in the new Pristine Forest development, at 38773 Creekside Lane."

"I know that area very well. It's amazing how planting some trees can turn the desert into a seeming oasis."

"Uh, yes it is."

"Creekside Lane? That's right next to Ratbone Gulch, isn't it? The rubble bed that drains the muddy water when it rains?"

"No, we're next to a stream bed called Shy Brook."

"Oh, yeah. That's its new name. Before the developers came, it was known as Drainage Ditch RS-471. Not too romantic a name, eh?"

"Are you sure?"

"But that was just its most recent name. Before that it was called Flash Flood Wash Ravine 681.2 or was it 681.1? I forget."

"Huh?"

"Its first name was Dry Gully R232. But that name was changed after the flood of '42."

2655. **The New Book.**
"Hey, look, my new book just came out. Here is the first sample copy, sent to me. Isn't it wonderful? It looks so good. I'm so happy. I want to celebrate."

"Oh, that's nice. By the way, have you seen that new TV show, *The Wonders of Sand*? It's just amazing."

Most of our accomplishments have to be celebrated privately, or with one or two admiring friends. If we expect or even hope that others will fuss over us and respond with enthusiasm, we will meet disappointment.

[January 29, 2018; age 67]

2656. While we were waiting for our flight at the Long Beach airport, every five minutes an announcement came from the TSA security checkpoint, where travelers and their carry-on luggage are screened for weapons and explosives. (I've had two of my tiny Swiss Army knives confiscated. Who knows what havoc I could wreak with a two-inch blade?) After a while I started to write the announcements down:

1. Someone left their luggage at the TSA checkpoint. If you are missing your luggage, please return to the checkpoint and claim it. (Did they put it in the scanner and then walk off to the gate?)

2. Someone left a large amount of cash at the TSA checkpoint. If this is yours, please return to the checkpoint. (Yes, you have to empty your pockets before walking through the metal detector, but you're allowed to put the stuff back in once you're through the detector. That stack of cash wasn't a bribe, was it?)

3. Someone left their tablet at the TSA checkpoint. If this is yours, please return to the checkpoint. (Now, what did I do with my tablet, with all my business PowerPoints, travel info, and music on it? Hmm. I should pay attention to my surroundings. Maybe I should ask the TSA police if someone stole it.)

4. Someone left their jacket at the TSA checkpoint. If this is yours, please return to the checkpoint to claim it. (I came for the jacket. Very nice one. Oh wait. That's too small. Never mind. Say, do you still have that large amount of cash? I think that's mine.)

I thought this was comical and nearly implausible — until we arrived at the Fort Lauderdale airport. While we were waiting at baggage claim, the PA system announced:

1. Someone left their backpack at the TSA checkpoint. If this is yours, please return to the checkpoint to claim it. (You mean they didn't automatically know whose it is and where it's going and check it through to Dallas? What's wrong with these people?)

2. Someone left a very valuable item at the TSA checkpoint. If this is yours, please return to the checkpoint to identify it. (Is it a Rolex watch? A diamond pendant? A new cell phone? Laptop? How many guesses do I get?)

2657. Truth will always be suppressed and those who tell it will always be punished because wherever truth is told it will expose error and lies, and the truth will be believed. "You shall know the truth and the truth will make you free." The truth is often inconvenient and seldom the narrative that most people want to promote.

2658. Regarding those "Duh" warnings on products. Why do manufacturers put them on?

"Here's your fresh, hot coffee, sir. Please note the warning label on the side."

"What? Oh, 'Warning: Contents are very hot.' Really? Oh, OK."

And then there are:

"Remove product from package before using."

"Suffocation hazard. This bag is not a toy. A child can suffocate and die if you let him play with it."

"Do not use this hair dryer while bathing."

"Keep hands away from saw blade."

"Do not smoke when refueling. Gasoline vapors are flammable."

One of my favorites is:

"Electrocution hazard! Do not use this ladder around power lines. You could be killed!"

2659. Why put obvious warnings on products? Here's why:

"If the court please, the plaintiff next calls Mr. Hiram Bot-mouth to the stand. Mr. Botmouth, what is your job?"

"I am a professional expert witness, the vice president of Testimony R Us, LLC."

"And what is your expert opinion of this case?"

"Clearly, there should have been a warning label on the desiccant that said 'Warning: Do Not Eat.'"

"There you have it, ladies and gentlemen of the jury. Little Joey had to suffer trauma, sickness, and terror, barfing his little guts out, fearing imminent death because MegaCorp was too cheap, careless, and lazy to print a few words on the desiccant bag included with the toy. MegaCorp clearly has no conscience. They are interested only in exploiting the consumer and increasing their obscene profits, even at the risk of poisoning helpless little children. It's up to you to send MegaCorp a message they won't forget."

2660. Modern society lacks
Intentionality → purpose → rationality → respect → integrity → context
Commitment → loyalty → clarity → reverence → decorum→ deference

2661. You say the ocean is big by looking at a map. Another person says the ocean is big by looking from the shore to the horizon. I say the ocean is huge by being in a boat in the middle of the ocean where all you can see is the ocean in every direction—north, south, east, and west—all the way to the horizon.

2662. They are so blinded with hatred that they seize on every little twig of support for their case. They talk and talk about it, opinionate over it, expand on it, speculate about it, until it appears that they are really discussing not a twig but a log—no, make that a large branch, well, actually, a whole, massive tree—only to miss the real forest fire blazing around them.

2663. Don't be like the driver who hits a small pothole in the road and becomes so upset with the failings of the highway department that he calls them up to give them a tongue lashing. He gets so wound up and obsessed with the imaginary affront that he speeds unseen past the sign saying, "Bridge Out."

2664. **Facing the Information Firehose.**
Using tools, techniques, and technology to improve the use of information.

1. Filtering. Restricting the flow of information in order to make the resulting volume more manageable. Eliminating unwanted results or hits. Example, Boolean operator NOT. Downside: Some valuable or desired information is inadvertently eliminated by the filter.

2. Attenuation. Allowing only popular or respected sources to be considered. Example: Peer Reviewed. Boolean operator AND. Downside: Popularity is subject to fads and valuation by entertainment criteria. Respected can be distorted by elite ideology control, keeping out dissent and alternatives.

3. Squelch. Selecting a cutoff point for delivering hits. Example: "After 1985." Downside: Cutting off historical development can distort perspective and cause the repetition of errors made in the past.

4. Curation. Relying on area experts to digest and recommend sources. Example: Top 10 Reviews. Downside: Curation is the most susceptible to control and manipulation. If the GizmoPro is the number one choice in the top ten tonsil vibrator category, does the maker of the GizmoPro own that Top 10 website? Or pay to have the product reviewed by the website?

5. Summarizing. Reducing and focusing content. Example: Business book summaries. Downside: The process of summarizing involves generalizing and selecting details. Both activities require skill and are open to bias.

6. Contextualizing. Increase understanding by adding context. Downside: Contexts need to be specified: economic, historical, political, social, global, ideological, etc.

[February 7, 2018; age 67]

2665. You want to be Number One? At what? There are many hierarchies in life: economic, talent, skill, power, authority, intelligence, strength. No matter which hierarchy you consider, there will always be people above you and people below you. Learn from those above you and help those below you.

2666. Huge, tall trees are actually well balanced in most cases, and they have an excess of wood holding them up. If you watch some trees being cut down, you'll see that the woodcutter must cut through 90% or more of the trunk before the tree will fall.

2667. Cicero says, "Trust is basic to justice. By trust I mean stability and truth in promises and in agreements" (*On Duties* 1.23). But we need to take this a bit further. To trust someone means that (1) you believe they are genuinely the person they present to you (honest, reliable, dependable), and (2) when they are away from you, they maintain the same character and integrity.

Con artists are neither the person they seem when you are with them, nor are they the same person when away from you. Getting you to trust them is one of their most powerful weapons against you.

2668. Of the crimes of robbery, theft, and a confidence scheme, the last one is the worst crime because it breaks down the trust between people that is necessary to keep society together.

2669. "Let's see whether Elijah will come to take him down" (Mark 15:36b). Many people prefer to be spectators rather than actors or initiators. Let's just sit around and see what happens.

2670. "Additionally, the documents he used to authenticate the Gospel of Jesus' Wife showed signs of forgery themselves."
    — *Bible History Daily* 6/30/2016.

When the standard is corrupted or faked, nothing can be known.

2671. "The lesson that can be learned from this saga, however, is that scrutinizing where an antiquity came from can be just as revealing as assessing and conducting scientific tests on the object itself." —Robin Ngo, *Bible History Daily* 6/30/2016.

The first question, especially for artifacts that possess dramatic implications, is, "Where did you get this?" Provenance is one of the most important and least refined assessment tools. At the least, we should ask:

- Where did this come from?
- Who owns, sells, benefits from, profits by it?
- What is the chain of custody and how far back (how close to its origin) can its existence be traced?
- Why this? Why just now?

Unfortunately, we must consider personal motivation and cultural impact of "just discovered" artifacts because of the historical attempts to foist fakes upon the world.

2672. When you look back on your life from the standpoint of old age, the principal feeling that strikes you is what a waste you have experienced. Wasted time, wasted money, wasted effort. You could have accomplished ten times as much.

2673. The history of civilization is the history of confused people, encumbered by bias, superstition, libido, and idolatry, attempting to understand themselves—their desires, fears, and hopes—and the meaning and purpose of their lives. That's why revealed truth is the essential Rosetta Stone.

2674. Sorrow is often a type of grieving. Much of grief is for ourselves—sadness over the loss to ourselves of a loved one's presence. Similarly, sorrow can be involved with grieving for our own losses or missed opportunities. We grieve over how our lives have turned out, the poor decisions we have made, "the bad hand that life has dealt us." We all feel at least some remorse over what we have done that we shouldn't have done and what we have not done that we should have. When our actions diminished the happiness of others, we feel guilty for the unhappiness we have caused or the happiness we have prevented. If we dwell on these failures long enough, if we obsess helplessly over them, then hopelessness can begin.

The grieving dwell on the finality of their interactions with the lost loved one, realizing that there will never be an opportunity to love, help, serve, benefit, care for, talk to, ask forgiveness from, or even listen to the one who has transitioned from this life to the next. Procrastination is at an end. There is no more, "Someday, I'll visit mom more often," or "I really should get around to fixing grandma's kitchen," or "I need to look into helping my sister."

Regret over what we did or didn't do, now that we understand that we can never do it or make up for not doing it, can eat away at our hearts until the grief becomes a permanent melancholy. "I should have had my dog's teeth worked on when the vet first suggested it, but I was too cheap to pay for the operation. Now, I can never remedy that or give him the two years of lost life it probably cost him."

If there is a treatment for melancholy, it might come from the remedy for grief. Since grief involves a focus on oneself and one's past deeds and omissions, a common remedy is to stop the self-obsession. Get out of yourself and get busy ministering to the needs of others. Serve, help, support, care for other people. While you're soaking in self-pity and regret, there are millions of people in desperate need of even a kind word.

2675. Yes, They Are Trying to Control Your Brain: Brain Railing.

Sometime close to twenty years ago, I was in the market for a Chihuahua puppy. I visited a few pet stores and searched the classified ads in the newspaper (I did say this was nearly twenty years ago), and located some possibilities. At one pet store, I was shown a loving, mocha-colored short-haired dog that impressed me so much I even named him, "Latte," for his coat color. The downside, which I mentioned to the owner of the pet store, was the price — $1,000. I wondered aloud whether or not such a dog could be obtained for a lower price (hoping the owner might make a substantial adjustment). The owner scoffed, and said, "These pets are certified purebreeds. We get them from legitimate breeders, not from some Arkansas puppy mill."

This declaration caused my mind to wander off the present issue and to focus on what kind of sinister locus of animal cruelty and exploitation an "Arkansas puppy mill" could be. This was one of my first exposures to brain railing, a common technique for controlling the focus of a discussion. Brain railing introduces a compelling idea, embodied in a compelling phrase, that immediately becomes the center of the conversation. It puts your brain on rails that can move your thinking along in only one direction, the one that responds to the phrase.

Students of logic will recognize brain railing as somewhat related to red herring, where the discussion is led off topic by the introduction of a new subject that demands attention. Commonly, in the past, the red herring was an entire sentence or more:

"I think the shortage of electricity could be addressed by building more nuclear electric generating plants."
"But nuclear power is dangerous."
"Actually, it has a great safety record."
"But what about Hiroshima and Nagasaki?"

Suddenly, the subject changes from the desirability of nuclear power to the use of nuclear weapons.

In the past, a red herring was often only an off-the-cuff statement intended to derail the argument and move it in a direction that benefited its introducer. Now, though, the brain rail is more often carefully constructed as a memorable short phrase that obtrudes itself into the entire communication dynamic, changing the subject and forcing the focus of the discussion onto the new topic, as framed by the brain rail.

Brain rails can become part of the linguistic structure of our culture, serving as automatic, knee-jerk thoughts. As an example, a few years ago I was watching a quiz show where the object was for the contestant to guess a word based on a verbal clue given by a teammate. Thus, the word "waste" is a clue for the word "basket," because "waste" and "basket" form a common pairing, so common, in fact, that "wastebasket" is now a single word.

But imagine my surprise when on the show the clue given was "religious," and the teammate's immediate guess, without a second's hesitation, was "fanatic." Not "religious service," not "religious worship," not "religious experience, " not "religious book," not "religious monastery," but "religious fanatic," now functioning as one of our culture's habitual, preprogrammed brain rails.

Current brain rails sometimes have built into them the implication that the subject has been debunked, refuted, or otherwise discredited, so that it can be safely ignored. There is often an element of ridicule built into the phrase. In her book, *The Smear*, journalist Sharyl Attkisson says that the term "conspiracy theory" was created to allow easy dismissal of any explanation of events that conflicts with the official version. Referring to an explanation as "just a conspiracy theory" seems to imply that only toothless hicks and leftover hippies still smoking nontobacco products believe it. Other examples are "nuts and sluts" from the Bill Clinton era, "pseudoscience," and, of course, "fake news."

Many brain rails are constructed to force the discussion down a certain track, while ignoring or preventing an alternative discussion. A common example is "hate speech," attached to any statement that the accuser disagrees with. Rather than a possibly fruitful discussion about a controversial idea, what follows is an attack on the character and motives of the accused, who must defend himself. Argument over terms ensues and the original topic remains unexplored.

Other examples of brain rails include "war on the poor," "war on women," "white privilege," and "fair share." In all of these cases, a controlling concept has been introduced that demands discussion under its own, biased terms.

We should strive to avoid adopting automatic response, fixed boxes to which we compulsively turn for our terms of discussion and our understanding of controversy. Concepts expressed in a phrase or a slogan are often contained in such boxes, unable to incorporate objective reality or measurable data into their ideological mass. While it is unlikely, in my experience, to move the discussion on to something profitable when interacting with someone insisting on following a brain rail down the road and around the bend, it might be an enlightening act to ask the railer to define his terms.

John: "I oppose affirmative action."

Jake: "You're a racist."

John: "What is your definition of a racist?"

Jake: "You."

This is a typical example of brain railing. Rather than engaging in a discussion of the pros and cons of affirmative action, the brain railer immediately changes the conversation away from an idea and onto a person. The subsequent discussion, if there is any, revolves around the guilt or innocence of one of the speakers, who feels attacked and defensive over the charge of racism.

Eventually, I bought two Chihuahua puppies, from a backyard breeder not far from my house. We just recently said goodbye to Bear after 18 years of joy and love. (His brother, Wolf, an equal source of joy and love, passed away four years earlier.) They weren't pedigreed, certified purebreds, but one thing is for sure—they didn't come from any Arkansas puppy mill.

2676. Regarding political stunts such as handing out a hundred T-shirts with a sarcastic attack on a candidate: A stunt is not an argument. A stunt is not evidence. Unfortunately, a stunt for many people is more powerful than an argument or evidence because stunts appeal to the emotions, to quick reactions, to memorable scenes. Arguments? Don't bore me. I don't have the time to listen, much less the time to think things over. But a stunt? Call the media.

2677. Your doctor is looking at your disease, but you are living the disease. Tell him what you are experiencing in as much detail as you can.

2678. Manufactured truth creates a manufactured reality.

2679. "One thing worse than lying is confusing the truth."
— Proverb.

2680. **Summary.**
        In youth, life is global.
        In age, life is local.
        In youth, we see God in the universe.
        In age, we feel God in our heart.

[May 25, 2018; age 67]

2681. The older I get, the wiser God becomes.

2682. Many "facts" are constructed rather than discovered. Poll results are a good example. The choice of words, individuals asked (and others not asked), sample size, and so on, all influence the resulting "fact."
    Some facts, it would appear, are unknowable. How many unfaithful husbands or wives are there? How much money is spent on illegal drugs? How much child abuse is there? Why do Treadful tires outsell RiCappo tires? How can we measure productivity lost because of daydreaming at work?

[June 20, 2018; age 67]

[Going through a long-neglected cabinet, I discovered an old, blue, fabric-covered three-ring binder with a lamp drawn on the spine. Judging by the fact that my handwriting was quite legible, I'm estimating that the entries were made in the 1970s or early 1980s. Here begins some of the contents of the Lamp Notebook.]

2683. The True Book
    1. "The excesses of hope must always be expiated by pain."
                    —Samuel Johnson
    2. The two great disappointments in life are: not getting what you want, and getting it.
    3. To assume is to be deceived.
    4. "Who will believe what he desires to be false?"
                — Samuel Johnson, *Rambler* 153.

2684. Figurative Language
    1. A pile of empty nutshells
    2. A hot rod Cadillac
    3. He read that only insecure men had beards, so he shaved his off. (Q.E.D.)
    4. A as original as mud in a fruitcake
    5. Like asses who wear out their hides carrying empty pots across the barren countryside so that every house, of its three pots, may have no two that look alike.
    6. Couched in studied ambiguities
    7. He's but a moth batting his wings at the lips of a frog—he will be eaten soon enough.
    8. It's like renting gasoline
    9. Buying tumbleweed seeds
    10. Teasing rattlesnakes with your bare feet

2685. Each chapter [of a proposed book] will contain several pertinent analogues.
    1. MUSIC, a classical composition
    2. PAINTING, an Old Master painting or engraving
    3. ARTWORK, a modern print
    4. ARTWORK, a cartoon
    5. LITERARY WORK
    6. A FILM, such as *African Queen*, or *Elephant Man*

7. A BUILDING or ARCHITECTURE

8. RELEVANT OBJECT, as a typewriter, cement mixer, aerosol can, ladder

9. COAT OF ARMS

10. SCULPTURE

11. NATURAL EFFECT or THING, as geyser, place, mineral (pyrite)

12. FLOWER or PLANT

13. ANIMAL, as butterfly

14. COLOR

15. TASTE or FLAVOR

16. LOGICAL FALLACY

17. WORD

18. GEOMETRIC SHAPE, as square, triangle, hexagon

19. GENERAL, as coal mine, Stonehenge

20. SUBJECT or area of enquiry

21. CONCEPT as movement, stasis

2686. A Few Notes.

1. The difference between looking at stars on a map and turning your eyes to the heavens.

2. "Individuals with long experience in one technical discipline often tend to reject new ideas." — William Harding, *Machine Design* 9-22-77

3. "A general state education is a mere contrivance for molding people to be exactly like one another; and . . . it establishes a despotism over the mind. . . ." —John Stuart Mill, *On Liberty*

4. The gilded swill of Hollywood creeps into our psyche

5. "Ego shredding in a supportive atmosphere" — our motto

2687. Reasons I Oppose Your Plan.[7]

1. It is not a standard or accepted method of proceeding. (It's new.)

2. It lacks the necessary élan and vigor that a fresh approach would have. (It's not new.)

---

[7] Compare this list to *Glimmering* 2486, above.

3. Such a wild and sudden departure from ordinary concepts is too surprising to be considered and would never, for example, have been suggested by me. (I didn't think of it.)

4. Such a procedure appears to bypass the standard method of operation. (It enables you to do something in a way that's easier or more efficient than the way I had to do it. Or, it makes a task easy that I think should be hard because it was hard when I did it.)

5. There is always the contingent scenario that success would be unimplementable, and therefore the project should be abandoned. (It might not work, so we had better not try it.)

6. It might work.

7. No one has ever tried it and who are we to presume?

8. It has been tried already and we never try anything twice.

[a page is missing]

[Some entries from the blue binder]

2688. This impossible, visionary philosopher of the old school actually asserted that there was a difference between appearance and reality. If things are not always what they appear, why then, science is a cheat and evolution a hoax. For the former is based largely upon observation and the latter upon similarities and comparisons.

2689. Science has taught us how to see the tip of a stink bug's nose with clarity and exactness, but not how to relish it in the scheme of things, not to see beyond it to its Creator, not how to understand either intellectually or emotionally the life it represents. (Thus the well-known expression, "He couldn't see beyond the tip of a stink bug's nose.") We can see with precision but not very far.

2690. Some have argued for the necessary victory by truth over error, because truth has right on her side and is naturally attractive. Not so. Truth is more beautiful than error only to those who look deeply. Truth is a shy, reserved maiden; and error a brazen hussy. Truth has more natural beauty, but it is not always superficially evident. Truth must be coaxed to go with you; she must be adorned and dressed by you, for she scorns to do it herself. She won't be handled any way you please; you must remain a gentleman in her presence. Error, while foul and ugly at the bottom—smelly too—dresses herself in whatever costume is your favorite; she promises easy and ready access and the fulfillment of your every selfish pleasure, always agreeing to give you what you desire—eventually if not immediately. Fondle her how you will, as many have before you. Truth stands off and must be accepted on her own terms. She is rigid but constant, and once won by you, will be ever faithful. Error, whore that she is, will be in someone else's hands tomorrow, and while she may have pleased you for a while, she will eventually leave you with nothing but several diseases you hadn't counted on.

And it is a tragedy of human nature that men will fight more vigorously for a whore than for a virgin.

2691. **Aptitude Test**

Ralph is pulling a 60-foot trailer full of pianos up a steep incline in his high-mileage compact car filled with a tank of bad gasoline over the Mohave desert in August. Since the outside air temperature is 122 degrees Fahrenheit, the car's air conditioner is set to maximum. Suddenly the water pump freezes, breaking the fan belt.

Question: If Ralph continues to drive at 100 miles an hour in second gear, what is likely to occur? Explain your answer.

A. The rear view mirror will get dirty.

B. Ralph will end up selling his spare tire for a cold drink.

C. Not enough information is given to answer the question.

Student 1. Answer is B. Explanation: The fan belt, or serpentine belt, runs not only the water pump, but the air conditioning compressor. When this compressor stops, so will the cooling of the cabin air from the AC system. Ralph will get hot and will stop to get a cold drink. The fact that Ralph is driving a high-mileage compact car suggests that he doesn't have a lot of ready cash for unexpected events, so he is likely to sell the spare tire for a cold drink.

Student 2. Answer is A. The comment that the water pump freezes suggests that the car has entered a place of freezing weather (maybe Ralph has driven far enough uphill that the temperature has dropped substantially). A sudden freezing like this is bound to fog over the rear view mirror, which Ralph thinks of as getting "dirty."

Student 3. Answer is C. Too many facts are missing from this scenario to draw a probabilistic conclusion about the future. For example, how long has Ralph been driving before his water pump freezes? And how long does he continue to drive after that before one of the stated answers occurs? Nor are we told the make, model, and year of manufacture of the car. And is the radiator cooling fan electric or engine driven?

2692. "Learn to call sin sin and do not call it liberation and progress, even if all of fashion and propaganda disagree." —Pope John Paul II, March 26, 1981

2693. "It is amazing how complete is the delusion that beauty is goodness." —Leo Tolstoy

2694. "The empty words were a defense against thought, because thought was the final enemy." —Bryan Griffin, "Panic Among the Philistines," *Harpers*, August 1981.

2695. We don't necessarily like the Truth. First, it is often not quite or not at all what we'd like to believe. And if it's the truth, we can't argue or disagree. Instead of the truth, give us opinion, interpretation, or judgment, because we can disagree, rebut, and sometimes refute it.

Samuel Johnson, *Rambler* 96, says it better:

> Truth is, indeed, not often welcome for its own sake; it is generally unpleasing because contrary to our wishes and opposite to our practice; and as our attention naturally follows our interest, we hear unwillingly what we are afraid to

know, and soon forget what we have no inclination to impress upon our memories.

For this reason many arts of instruction have been invented, by which the reluctance against truth may be overcome; and as physic is given to children in confections, precepts have been hidden under a thousand appearances, that mankind may be bribed by pleasure to escape destruction.

2696. We experience our lives as a sequence of entailed events, a linear consciousness involving free choice or free will and cause and effect. (See also the theory of decision streams, where every decision both cuts off some choices and enables other choices.) This is the line of life. But eternity is a sphere rather than a line. All things are ever "present" to their observer, God. God sees existence as an all-present whole, not as a series of linear events.

Time is the linear experience of a piece of eternity; the line is the perceptual arrangement of elements from eternity. This is necessary for us even to begin to understand them. Prophecy looks across eternity.

2697. A question to ask before you act: When your life is shown on the giant screen of heaven in super high-definition, will you be glad to have this action included? Will you be able to look Jesus in the eye and tell him that you are glad you did it and that you did it for his glory?

2698. Creativity is the ability to use the scrap lumber of the mind to make something new or beautiful or useful.

2699. When we persevere through trials and tribulations, not only do we grow in our trust in God and our love for him, but we also become a beacon of light, a model of spiritual behavior, to others. Perseverance and simple trust reveal to others the solidity of our faith.

2700. Most of the ambitious hopes we formed in our eager youth are eventually converted from a wagon-load of wishes into the detritus of dreams, corroded into dust by time and circumstance. If we had been able to focus and persevere, however, one or two might have been pushed along the road to realization.

2701. Q. Why isn't life after salvation perfect and painless? God is supposed to love and care for us.

A. That's exactly what he is doing when he allows trials and disasters to visit us. When suffering arrives, we realize that we can't endure it alone. So we ask God for help. This act of realizing that we need God's help humbles us. And since pride is our greatest enemy, every act of humility improves us.

2702. Hierarchies. When we discover that we have some kind of advantage over others, we puff ourselves up with pride. Then when we discover that someone else has some kind of advantage over us, we are consumed by envy.

Both of these attitudes are wrong. There are many hierarchies in life: talents, skills, wealth, power, attractiveness, social position. No matter which hierarchy you consider, you will always find some people above you (better natural talents, superior skills and experience, more money, more power and influence, better looking, more socially adept), and some people below you.

Don't envy those above you—learn from them.

Don't feel superior to those below you—help them.

2703. I'm not lucky. I'm blessed.

2704. Our ideal choice usually does not exist, because it is a creation of our imagination made by combining the best qualities of each of many alternatives. In other words, no choice that matches our ideal 100% is available, and if we wait for it, we will wait forever. To be both wise and happy, we should choose whatever gives us 80%.

I know what you're thinking. "Oh, so we have to settle for less than we want and grit our teeth with an unhappy compromise and pretend that we are happy." My reply is that those who think this way are victimizing themselves. Their revulsion over the phrase, "settle for," is trapping them in a thought process which can have only a depressing outcome. The fact is, 80% is the best available. Remember that 100% doesn't even exist. So choosing 80% is not "settling for" less; it's smart, mature, and realistic.

Rule 1. One hundred percent does not exist and therefore is not available.

Rule 2. If you think you have found 100%, you're probably so delusional and starry eyed that you have in fact found 40%.

Rule 3. Your best choice will give you 80%.

Rule 4. If you cannot be truly happy with 80%, don't choose at all. If you choose 80%, you will always regret, resent, and repent your choice, forever torturing your psyche with self-criticism at your folly.[8]

2705. There's a guy on social media whose philosophy of life is that he should live for himself and that no one else matters, not even his relatives—because we are all dead in the end, anyway. He has had serial girlfriends for some time now. When he gets tired of a girl after a few weeks or months, he dumps her and gets another. Even though he's 40 now, he is good looking, so he has no trouble getting a new girlfriend whenever he tires of the previous one.

2706. In the Rocky Mountains of Canada, bears can show up unpredictably and be a danger to humans. As one of the T-shirts for tourists says, "Bears love humans. They taste like chicken." As a result, it is advisable to carry pepper spray designed to stop a bear attack. I heard it being touted in a hardware store, with the claim that it was effective up to 21 feet. The next day, I came across two park rangers (who were exhibiting a grizzly bear pelt), and asked about bear spray. The ranger pulled out the same item that had been for sale in the hardware store. She said it had an effective range of six to nine feet. So

---

[8] If you are interested in decision making theory, learn about maximizing and satisficing.

what happened to 21 feet? The difference, I suppose, is twelve feet of hyperbole, otherwise known as marketing.

2707. Every criticism—and every praise—involves a judgment against some standard. A criticism implies that something or someone falls short of the standard, and a praise implies that some standard is met or exceeded. It is therefore legitimate to ask, "What is the standard of measure you are using?" And, if you are cantankerous, "In what specific way or ways does this fall short (or meet or exceed) that standard?"

2708. Some people wrongly assume that what is of keen interest to them must also be of keen interest to you. I remember many years ago, my brother and I were invited over to a couple's house where, after dinner, the couple got out their slide projector and showed us pictures of horses—for three hours. Ever since then, my brother and I labeled anything insanely boring as "horse pictures."

"Want to see a documentary about which paints dry fastest?"

"Horse pictures."

"We're invited to our cousin's birthday party, where Aunt Edna will talk our ears off. Shall we go?"

"Horse pictures."

2709. To say that an action is moral is to claim that it conforms to (or does not violate) a standard of right behavior, an established code of values. To say that something is legal is to claim that it conforms to (or does not violate) an established law.

Thus, something legal might or might not be moral, and something moral might not be legal. However, in a just society, there must be a high correlation between legal and moral.

2710. Judgment involves analysis, not regurgitation. If we are to learn good judgment, we must learn how to analyze—how to think. Learning how to memorize the "right answers" is not only indoctrination, but the enemy of learning how to think.

2711. We are often too busy to learn. We don't learn when we rush from one thing to another without having time to reflect on the meaning of the previous thing. In fact, we are often so busy thinking about what is coming after whatever we are doing now that we cannot even process what we're doing now. Thoughtless experience consumes our lives. (See also Glimmering 2602.)

2712. They say money talks, but that's not true. Money shouts. In fact, money commands.

2713. Pride prevents people from learning because in order to learn something, you must humble yourself by admitting ignorance, and recognizing that someone else knows something you don't.

2714. Shame is an attack on our self image. In other words, it hurts our pride. As a result, when we feel shame, we sometimes turn it to anger against the person who made us feel ashamed.

2715. Pride way out of control: People who think every oversight is a personal affront.
    "Hey, waiter! I got no spoon in my table set up."
    "I am so sorry, sir. I will bring you one immediately."
    "You'd better. And I expect excellent service from now on. And don't expect a tip, either."

2716. "Have you read this new book?"
    "I looked at it. The author says nothing new. It's all been said before. So I put it down."
    "Did it ever occur to you that something repeated, if true, might be especially important, might be nuanced, might be strengthened or clarified? And to answer falsehood, the same answers, the same truths, must be presented again and again?"
    "Naw. Repetition is boring. I always like new ideas."

2717. Analytic thinkers ask, "Why?" Creative thinkers ask, "Why not?" And those who don't think at all ask, "Why me?"

2718. The reasons people refuse to be saved are the same as the reasons they refuse most good advice:
- It would be too difficult.
- It would make me give up something I want to do.
- It would make me do something I don't want to do.
- It would be unpleasant.
- I would have to admit I have been wrong, and humble myself to accept what is right.
- It's just not me.

2719. In *Rambler* 87, Johnson says that some people repay a favor not because they are grateful but because it is too painful to feel obligated or indebted to another. When I was at the university, a dorm mate once asked for a cup of my bottled water because he was out. Two minutes after I had given it to him, he brought me three cents to pay for it. He had calculated how much per ounce I was paying based on the cost of a five-gallon jug and paid me my cost for the cup. Just imagine how obligated he would have been had he not paid me!

2720. "You owe me one," is the sign of a selfish, transactional heart.

2721. *Rambler* 87 again. Johnson says that many people reject the advice given them, even taking a contradictory position, in order to show that they are above being taught by the giver of the advice. Once again we see pride (Johnson calls it vanity) as our enemy.

2722. In works of fiction, such as novels, you have to learn to read between the lines. In works of nonfiction, such as current event books and articles, you have to learn to read between the lies.

2723. Everyone believes in some truth, even those who are relativists and situationists. Relativists believe that relativism is true. Even though the statement, "There is no truth," is self-refuting (or self-referentially absurd), many people still believe that it is true.

2724. In recent years, asking someone why they believe something has often produced an offended look and sometimes the comment, "That's just what I feel," or "That's just what I believe." Being asked to supply a reason or piece of evidence was just beyond the pale of decency.

Now, however, people seem to understand that a reason is important for separating their claims from those of others, which remain groundless. Unfortunately, this has resulted in the proliferation of non sequitur *because* clauses, which do not supply actual or relevant reasons. For example, "May I use the copier before you because I need to make some copies." or "You know our pizza must be good because I'm Joe Thompson."

2725. As social values and behaviors continue to decline, the culture still preserves the good words that make us feel good about ourselves—individualism, maturity, empowerment—but their definitions have changed. Now individualism means selfishness; maturity means smoking, drinking, and copulating; and empowerment means breaking the law in the name of personal values.

2726. Whether you are attempting to solve a crime or develop a scientific theory, the evidence by itself does not determine the conclusion or hypothesis. Instead, the conclusion, often in the form of a story, is creatively constructed in order to account for as much of the data or evidence as possible. The best story—or theory—is the one that best meets the criteria for being the best. Which explanation includes more of the data than other explanations? Which is coherent with other conclusions in the same arena? Which is the most "elegant," as some say? I read somewhere that "theories are underdetermined by the facts," or some such phrasing.

2727. An accident is an event you didn't plan. But it might be an appointment set by God. This seems to be the idea behind the saying, "Everything happens for a reason." If that is true, then often the reason is unavailable to us.

2728. Why does God permit evil to continue? Why do bad things happen to us? One thought is that if bad things didn't occur, there would be no need for — and no way to develop and express — compassion, comfort, sympathy, empathy, pity; and there would be fewer occasions to show mercy, relief, generosity, kindness, and sacrifice, or even to build relationships.

2729. He who mistakes the truth for a lie comes to a halt.
He who mistakes a lie for the truth goes backwards.

2730. Satan reduces the service of some souls by preoccupying their attention — and time — with trivia and wasteful events. I am guilty of this folly because I love "museum shopping": going through stores and looking at all the wares just as some people go through museums and look at all the art or relics.

2731. First premise: The greatest commandment is to love God with all your heart, soul, strength, and mind. Second premise: Feelings cannot be commanded. Conclusion: Love is not a feeling.

2732. Worship should be all about God rather than about the feeling we can get from it. Worshipping God means showing respect, reverence, admiration, and submission. Bowing down (Psalm 95:6) should be an act of humbling ourselves.

2733. The academy needs to admit that every criticism, every praise, every comparison — every judgment and every conclusion — is and must be based on a standard of reference, a stand-

ard of values. In literary criticism, whether applying histori-
cism, Marxism, identity politics, or some variant of postmodernist theory, a standard of values forms the foundation and the set
of principles by which the scholar evaluates the text.

All this is to say that, if all of these standards are acceptable
and legitimate in the eyes of the academy, then the Christian
standard of values should be equally acceptable. Christian
scholars can integrate faith and learning by adopting this truth.
They need not respond to (that is, critique) other approaches, or
attempt to work from inside other approaches or try to harmonize Christian faith with other approaches. (Attempting to harmonize identity politics with Christianity is a fool's errand.)

At some point, of course, Christian scholars must contrast
both the differences in worldviews and critique the errors in the
popular approaches. Teach students what Marxism and Marxist
theory are, and then show that Marxism doesn't work because it
is based on a false concept of human nature. But then go on to
present an interpretation of the work or idea from a Christian
and Biblical perspective. Don't try to integrate Christianity with
a false worldview.

2734. Now that all the previous ways of attacking Christianity
have failed, there is a new way. Yes, persecution, denial, ignoring, diluting, replacing, offering alternatives — all have failed to
extirpate the faith from the world. So now it's time to destroy
the foundations of all knowledge so that Christianity will have
nothing to rest on. Truth has now been redefined as a subjective
commitment, one of an infinite number of claims. Facts are now
merely intersubjective hegemonic assertions kept in place by
naked power. Reason is a tool of suppression and misogyny,
employed against those with alternate voices.

"If the foundations are destroyed, what can the righteous
do?" — Psalm 11:3

2735. An inductive conclusion must (1) tell a coherent, plausible
story that explains the evidence, (2) account for as much of the
evidence as possible, (3) include or at least not contradict the

most important evidence (4) show how the evidence is linked together, in a linear fashion or in a matrix.

2736. Dialog about Hell. (From Randy Newman at a conference long ago.)

"Do you really believe that anyone who isn't a Christian is going to hell?"

"Do you believe in hell?"

"No."

"Then why do you care?"

"Okay, so what if I do believe in hell. My question still stands."

"Do you think anyone is in hell?"

"Hitler."

"How do you think God decides on whom to send to hell?"

2737. Everyone who thinks has doubts. That's a sign of thoughtfulness, analysis, and either confirmation or change. In science, philosophy, religion, and many other areas, wondering about some aspect, small or large, is normal. Usually, we end up doubting our doubts and recommitting to our belief — which is now stronger than ever because we dared to examine it and the reasons for it.

2738. The ontological components of reality are not constrained by the limitations of our epistemology. People — and entire civilizations — can possess a false understanding of reality because they are unwilling or unable to accept certain inconvenient truths that would impinge on their preferred beliefs. The chosen limitations on what we allow to be true do not in any way shape what really is true, or what actually exists.

2739. "The only real things are things we can measure."

"Then how much does that statement weigh? And how long is it? And once we know how long it is, what more do we know that can be called a useful gain in knowledge?"

2740. **Observational Hierarchy.**

There is a hierarchy of significance in the observation of events and the collection of data. We can use the Journalistic Six to show this.

1. When. Usually the easiest question to answer is when an event occurred.

2. Where. There is often a location easily distinguishable, such as a crime scene, an address, and so on.

3. What. You might think that answering the question, "What happened," is easy and straightforward, but it's not always clear. "Was this a suicide or a murder?" "Did the investment group have inside information or simply make a lucky guess?" The answer of "What happened?" often involves a network of collected facts and arguments, forming a coherent narrative of cause and effect. The evidence includes what is available, what will be ignored, what hunches (intuitive feelings) are available, previous experience, and much more.

4. Who. The answer to "Who did this?" is often both a source and a product of the constraints applied to the situation by the reasoner. And it is the question most influenced by assumptions. "Him? That couldn't be true," "Her? No way."

5. How. The methodological question can be one of the most difficult to answer because it is deeply involved with causation. Cause and effect, while among the most important avenues for exploring events, can also be very tricky. Mistaking a correlation with a cause is one of the most common errors in thinking.

6. Why. The answer to the question Why is often the most difficult to discover. Determining human motivation, whether for doing something good or something bad, can often only be guessed at. Why a natural disaster (earthquake, volcanic eruption, forest fire, hurricane) occurred just when and where it did is often the object of speculation only.

2741. **Found Proverbs.**

Going over some notes recently, I found a page marked "Proverbs," with the date of February 21, 2000. I do not know where they came from, but I thought they are worth preserving:

1. *Adversity cures the blind.* Change can be so stressful that many people refuse to see the growing evidence of its necessity. When the situation grows desperate, even the resistant can see the need. No more "turning a blind eye" to the problem.

2. *Believing is seeing.* This proverb reminds us that sometimes we are unable to understand—or even acknowledge—something because we reject the possibility of its truth or existence. Once we grow willing to consider the possibility, all kinds of supporting data floods in—data that was always there but unseen. To see God in the Chambered Nautilus, butterflies, tree frogs, crystals, you must first believe in God.

3. *When everyone speaks, none listen.* This proverb actually identifies one of the major problems with information overload's effect on decision making. With too many competing and often conflicting appeals, decisions that in simpler times would have been made quickly are now made slowly or not at all. If you have a choice of three movies on TV, you easily choose "the least objectionable program." But if you have a choice of 60 or 100, you might just toss the remote down and take a long nap. When was the last time you actually paid attention to the ads in a magazine?

2742. "But no precedents can justify absurdity." —Samuel Johnson

2743. "Whereas in truth all these names . . . are but hard words which only express a learned and pompous ignorance of the true cause of natural appearances; and in this sense they are mere words without ideas." —Isaac Watts, *Logick* (I.vi.3)

2744. "Jenkins, come here."
"Yes, your majesty."
"Bring me a snack."
"Yes, your majesty."
. . . . . .

"Here you are, Sire. Prime, dry-aged Kobe filet mignon wrapped in Applewood smoked bacon, with a garnish of woodland truffles."

"These truffles don't look fresh."

"Oh, yes, Sire. They were harvested just yesterday."

"Yesterday!! How dare you serve me this spoiled garbage. Guards!"

2745. When you request something from God, thank him before he answers, knowing that his answer is going to be the best. Even if it's "No."

2746. God created heaven as a place of purity and righteousness, a place where those sanctified and holy could live and commune with him forever. And what does he get? A bunch of leftover broken sinners clinging to the robe of Jesus Christ and hoping to share in God's undeserved mercy.

2747. "I don't see a shred of evidence for the existence of God."

"Have you tried lifting your eyelids?"

2748. Organizing lumber and nails can give you a house, or an outhouse. Organizing ink on paper can give you a book of devotions or a pornographic novel. Mere organization is important, but not enough to result in the Good.

2749. The fox that brags the loudest about his pelt attracts the furrier's eye the soonest. —from the book of *Newly Made Proverbs*

2750. If you write a controversial book and a publisher refuses to print it, that is "rejecting an unmarketable book." If it gets published and the libraries and bookstores don't carry it, that is "selecting only the more important works." If a copy gets shelved in the library and a patron objects to its being available to children, that is "censoring ideas."

2751. Sometimes a lie is exposed because it is overdressed.
— from the book of *Newly Made Proverbs*

2752. It's pride again. We are so self-absorbed that we reflexively reject anything that would require submission to authority. The end result is to exalt the entire process of criticizing, rejecting, "exposing," ridiculing, and dismissing as much more important and useful than its opposite, the process of reaffirming, praising, and recommending. To recommend an idea suggests the positive value of an authority, so both idea and recommender will be instantly condemned as patriarchal and hegemonic. "No one can tell me what I can or cannot do."

2753. "All our reasoning comes down to surrendering to feeling." — Blaise Pascal. This claim used to irritate me. More recently, however, I am starting to believe that an emotional commitment or decision often (always?) precedes an intellectual one. We often "think backwards," concluding first (based on an emotional response), and then seeking reasons to support the conclusion.

2754. Some thought of the artist as a rebel, but he saw himself as a pointer of the telescope in a better direction, a turner of the focus knob, an adjuster of the display on the screen of life.
    "Here's a better window," he says to the woman with him, as she pads over to his side of the room and looks into his eyes to see if she can see trust there before she looks out the window. Seeing both trust and the outdoor scene reflected in his eyes, she holds his arm and looks out the window.
    "Will this be on the test?" she asks, playfully.
    "This will be on many tests," he replies.

2755. Life is a single performance, with no rehearsal and no rewind. And no one can cheat on the test of life.

2756. **Rainbows.**
    You cannot touch them in the sky,

Nor always see their end;
But rainbows lovely, true, and high
Prove real, the promise of a Friend.

2757. Little lamb, little lamb, how can you feed?
Little lamb, on such a barren hill
How can rocks and sticks your hunger fill?
How can a desert ever fill your need?
"Fear not, kind sir, you see my lovely bell,
It shows how much my shepherd cares for me.
He feeds me still and ever very well
With nourishment that others cannot see.

2758. Wisdom is a generalized summary of personal and collective experience, purchased with the pain of failure, and occasionally with the analysis of success. Though these wise generalizations do not always apply to specific new circumstances, we should seek to understand them out of respect for the suffering necessary to their formulation.

2759. A roofer breaks up the solid roofing tar kegs and puts them into the kettle. He turns on the gas and heats the tar. At 400 degrees, the tar is still solid and can't be worked. At 420 degrees, the tar is just right and can be pumped up onto the roof to seal it. The tar is mopped on and swished around to cover all the cracks, holes, seams, and defects in the surface of the roof.

However, if the roofer becomes fixated on the roof and does not pay attention to the kettle, he can pump the kettle dry, requiring a lengthy start-up process. Worse, at 510 degrees, the tar will catch fire and destroy the kettle, the pump, the roofer's truck, and possibly the building he is working on.

2760. Making words work. In listening to a roofer talk to his helpers while they all mopped molten tar onto a roof, I noticed that he used the word *hot* not only as an adjective, but as a noun and a verb also.

"How hot is it now?"

"I can hot it down now."
"I need more hot."[9]

2761. The world as an amusement park, where all rides end where they began.

2762. If you parsed her sentences, you would find that 80 percent of the words she spoke were *I, me, my,* and *mine.*

2763. **Apologetics.**
    "Why is there evil?"
    "Why do you want a reason?"
    "So I can understand."
    "Do you have so little trust in God that you must have everything explained?"
    "I just want to know, to comprehend, because evil is against God's nature."
    "That's right. Now tell me, who rules the world right now?"
    "God."
    "No. Satan rules the world now."
    "Huh? No way."
    "Look at 1 Peter 5:8, James 4:7, John 12:31, Ephesians 2:2, John 16:8-11."
    "But everyone says—"
    "Why, in the Lord's prayer, does Jesus ask, 'May your kingdom come and your will be done'? Clearly, it's because God's kingdom is not here yet and his will is often thwarted until his kingdom is installed."

2764. Many of the hippies of the sixties and seventies said they wanted to get back to nature and reduce their impact on the earth. They scorned technology and made their clothes and other items by hand.
    So, no electricity. OK. No natural gas service. OK. No treated water. Are you sure that's a good idea? Going to boil all of it?

---

[9] For you rhetorical fans, the use of one part of speech as another is anthimeria.

No sewer system. Wait a minute. Going behind a bush has its limits. Did you ever wonder why ancient tribes of every nation were so nomadic?

It seems to me that hippiedom represented the rejection of all the cultural developments humanity had progressed to and the embracing of an intentional devolution toward animalistic primitivism.

2765. Genesis recounts God's creative activity including heavens, earth, and us. Verse 16 describes the sun and moon. Then, at the end of 16, almost parenthetically, it says, literally, "The stars also." (Most translations add the words, "He made.") Estimates vary on how many stars there are, so let's go with a billion trillion. That's why we call him the Creator. (And man's faith was stronger in the days when they thought there were "only" about 6,000 stars.)

2766. An epitaph. "Joe Doax. 19XX- 20XX. He ate many meals and watched 21,946 football games. He died with the remote in his hand and a slice of pizza in his mouth."

2767. An epitaph. "Jane Doe. 19XX-20XX. She read 3,224 romance novels and watched 1,277 'men behaving badly' movies. Married four times, died alone."

2768. In a kingdom filled with fools, he would be thought wise.

2769. "These two cars are the same price," said the salesman. "The dull one is made from heavy sheet steel painted with a can of spray paint, while this other is made from cardboard, covered with 27 coats of premium lacquer and six coats of clear sealer."

"*Of course* I'll go out with you," said the beautiful young woman, later on. "Where did you get such a gorgeous car?"

2770. "This is reality," said the man to his friend, as he held up to the videoconference camera a photograph of a postcard of a painting of a forest.

"That's great," said his friend. "What's it called?"

"*Imaginary Woodland.*"

2771. What does it mean to worship God? Does it mean being filled ourselves or pleasing God? Is worship something we do for ourselves (a "worship experience"), or something we do for God, to praise and thank him?

2772. Excuse me, but isn't God present when we worship him? Then why do we sing worship songs that mention God as if he is not there? Shouldn't we address him directly in praise? Instead of, "He's my rock," shouldn't it be "You're my rock"? Instead of, "His name is wonderful," shouldn't it be "Your name is wonderful"?

2773. Everyone alive now will eventually die. The only issue is when and how. Asking why is ridiculous. Why is there so much suffering, so many tsunamis, earthquakes, volcanoes, plagues, wars, diseases, cruelties? Remember that God's kingdom is waiting while Satan rules the world, showing the results of his "Defy God's rules" philosophy.

2774. Suffering is the knife that carves the question on our hearts, "Do you really trust me?"

2775. Prayer should involve intimacy with God, much more than mere communication with God. Communication with God is like talking with your spouse. Intimacy with God is like making love to your spouse.

2776. When you pray do you hold back not because you lack faith but because you realize that God's will is more important than your needs and wants?

2777. Much of our worldview is shaped by our belief that the world is either a zero-sum or an additive sum game.

Zero summers: If the rich get richer, the poor will get poorer.

Additive summers: If the rich get richer, so can the poor.

2778. Nails were made by hand for the first few thousand years. *The Steel Wire Handbook*, Chapter 9 on "Nail Manufacture," informs us that

> At about the year 1800 there were still over 60,000 nail makers employed in the Birmingham, England area. As late as 1883, long after the introduction of nail machines, there were still 24,000 people making nails by hand in England. (318)

So the introduction of nail-making machines eventually unemployed 60,000 people. Should such machines have been outlawed in order to save jobs? On the other hand, imagine how happy carpenters were when nail prices dropped. From one point of view, automation costs jobs and causes unemployment. From another point of view, automation frees workers from boring, repetitive jobs and allows them to get better jobs.

2779. Contemporary writers of what is called poetry have rejected for their works just about everything that sets poetry apart from ordinary prose: figurative language, rhyme, meter, rhythm, word arrangement, rhetorical devices, and so on. Often the result is either an ordinary sentence arbitrarily broken into lines or an incomprehensible collection of nonsense pretending to be deep.

I wish
you could
you would
have stayed
and eaten lunch
with me

That took me ten seconds to write. Think it will live forever in the minds and hearts of everyone? How about something "deep":

It was a shack
my castle
on the beach
breached
by the storm
ruined
but perfect in my memory
forgotten no more
because of her

2780. Reversal Proverbs.

1. Necessity is the mother of invention; invention is the mother of necessity.

2. Belief leads to action; action leads to belief.

3. Not everything that can be understood is true; not everything that is true can be understood.

4. To live is to choose; to choose is to live.

5. Men test gold to see if it is pure; gold tests men to see if they are pure.

6. Truth is stranger than fiction; fiction is stranger than truth.

7. Seeing is believing; believing is seeing.

8. The faithful find their strength in weakness; the proud find their weakness in strength.

2781. The only thing worse than stupidity is stupidity fueled by alcohol.

2782. Permission outranks prohibition. A traffic light with a red light on top and a green arrow on the bottom permits the motorist to turn right without stopping. You can go through a door with a sign saying, "Absolutely No Admittance" if the person with you has the key and invites you in. You can drive on through an intersection where the lights are all red if a traffic control officer waves you through.

2783. "The disciples did not understand what Jesus meant, and they were afraid to ask" (Mark 9:32, CEV). And we criticize students for not asking when they don't understand a simple comment.

2784. I fell over backwards in my workshop recently. I crushed a small, empty cardboard box and knocked over a five-gallon bucket of fertilizer. The fall reminded me of the cosmic fall that caused sin to enter and ruin the universe and that allowed Satan to run amok for a time on earth. I, through Adam, was complicit in that fall. "Every one of them has turned aside; together they have become corrupt; There is no one who does good, not even one" (Psalm 53:3, NASB).

2785. "Why me?" The fact that you have to ask the question of why you are suffering shows you the reason for your suffering. To question why you suffer means that you don't understand the serious nature of sin and the fall. No, your suffering is probably not a direct consequence of a specific sin by you. Instead, it is the result of the sinful nature we all have, together with the evil culture we live in.

2786. The purpose of our suffering:
- to soften our hearts and to show us (and increase) our dependence on God.
- to improve our empathy with others' suffering
- to be an example, both to the saved and the unsaved, that a Christian can continue to trust God through all circumstances.

2787. One of the keys to writing good instructions or any document, whether discussing a concept or a procedure, is to find the happy spot between too little and too much. I've tried to set up items when the "Quick Start" sheet left out steps, and I've puzzled to find the answer in a 500-page manual.

2788. "Every knee will bow." Some willingly and happily, some unwillingly and resentfully. The humble will find it easy; the proud will find it difficult.

2789. You've probably seen those cars with very dirty rear windows, in which someone has written in the dirt, "Wash me please." I recently saw one with the message fingered in the grime, "Wasme plase." This is Exhibit One for the case that, if you want to be taken seriously, master the English language. The car did indeed need washing; but the joke collapsed on its author.

2790. Kids can have fun with anything because their imagination is unrestrained. They can see beyond a large, old cardboard box, a stick, or an empty soda can. Instead, they see a space ship, a rifle, and a hand grenade; or perhaps a doll house, a flag pole, and the resident of the doll house.

2791. **Great Opening Lines for a Novel:**
1. By the time Elizabeth realized that the poison wasn't working, she had decided that she really did love Bertie and didn't want it to.
2. After their eleventh child was born, Althea and Norman both realized that they didn't care for each other at all.
3. Rachel's face revealed a look of surprise as she watched Jordan come out from behind the wall. "I missed you," he said, as he ejected the clip from his pistol. "But I'm reloading."

2792. At last, after 20 years of careful analysis, I have discovered the real secret to a happy marriage. Knowing the secret will not necessarily bring you a happy marriage because knowledge and implementation are not the same.
The secret to what makes marriage happy is an agreed on and practiced distribution of power.

- Who does what?
- Who gets to decide who does what?
- When agreement can't be reached, who is the Supreme Court?

Most marriages begin with a struggle for power, with each partner striving to stake out areas of authority, or in worst cases, striving to be the sole authority in all areas. This latter, "I am the boss" belief is as common in women as in men.

Some couples never quite succeed in dividing or sharing in an agreeable way, so after two or three years, they become resentful, bitter, critical, and disagreeable.

So, what is the secret to a happy marriage? Shared values and a resolved distribution of power.

2793. The power struggle mentioned above often begins again in retirement, because many wives view a retired husband as a slave, to be assigned tasks at will.

[October 13, 2018; age 68]

2794. Happy Birthday, Bob. How did I ever get to be this old, and with Parkinson's disease for about 13 years also? Praise God for all of his blessings and mercies. I don't know if the Glimmerings have gotten better or worse, or whether they are insightful or obvious, but here they are.

2795. In addition to the Bible, which you should be reading daily and continually throughout your life, here are a few books (not necessarily in this order) that deserve a careful reading and rereading.

1. Blaise Pascal, *Pensees*
2. Brother Lawrence, *The Practice of the Presence of God*
3. Marcus Aurelius, *Meditations*
4. Samuel Johnson, *Rasselas*
5. William Law, *A Serious Call to a Devout and Holy Life*
6. Aristotle, *Nicomachean Ethics*
7. Cicero, *On Duties*

8. Samuel Johnson, *Rambler* essays
9. Thomas a Kempis, *The Imitation of Christ*

2796. "They did not ask for the counsel of the Lord" (Joshua 9:14b). And so they were deceived. There are deceivers everywhere. Always ask for God's guidance in your decision making.

2797. Draw close to God to listen, not to lecture.

2798. God uses the metaphor of sexual relations to represent the spiritual relationship between himself and those who seek to belong to him. Israel "played the harlot after other gods" (Judges 2:17, and compare Judges 8:33); God says, "I saw that for all the adulteries of faithless Israel, I had sent her away and given her a writ of divorce, yet her treacherous sister Judah did not fear; but she went and was a harlot also" (Jeremiah 3:8). The sexual metaphor shows us how intimate is the relationship between us and God.

2799. "Woe to those who extend their iniquity with a chain of lies" (Isaiah 6:18a, Bob's version).

2800. Yesterday it was a staggering, joyfully welcome blessing beyond imagination. Today it is taken for granted without a thought. Tomorrow it will be an entitlement expected to be delivered on demand.

2801. God is astonishingly incomprehensible. We don't think of this because we usually reduce our concept of God to someone who thinks like us.

2802. **Love Poem.**
Sometimes love is like the wind;
It moves unseen from one to other,
But we believe it by its end,
For it flies from lover to lover

And soundlessly its message sends,
Setting the heart ablaze again all over.

Such is your love, dear heart, to me
Whose power crosses every space between us
And keeps me loving sweet Marie.

2803. Most of my life, and especially after my brother became schizophrenic, I have set my mind to watch my brain. When a thought arises in my brain, my mind asks, "Is that true? Is that real? Is that a hallucination? Is that a delusion?"

2804. When something bad happens to someone else, many people construct a rationalization that protects themselves from worrying about the evil happening to them.
    "Did you hear about the woman who was raped downtown?"
    "Well, you know, the way these girls dress these days, they are just asking for it."
    "But she was the manager of a financial company."
    "Well, she had no business being in that part of town at that hour of the night."
    "It was 2:30 in the afternoon."
    "She must have had unconfessed sin. I wonder what she did to deserve that?"

2805. This victim blaming above has precedent in the Bible: "As He passed by, He saw a man blind from birth. And His disciples asked Him, 'Rabbi, who sinned, this man or his parents, that he would be born blind?'"(John 9:1-2, NASB).

2806. Change in the mind is often easier than change in deed. I had a freshman once who told me that she had been a Christian for only three months, and while she was intellectually and emotionally committed to our Lord, she was having difficulty trying to stop swearing. Speech habits are especially intractable.

So, like, don't get into the, um, habit of, you know, using those, uh, verbal pauses most of us use, okay?

2807. Christianity is a religion of do, not just a religion of be. Why do so many Christians miss the Bible's constant call to action? We are called to serve, to do good deeds.

2808. For some people Christianity is a coat they wear on Sunday to take part in worship. For others Christianity is their very skin which holds them together every day and every night.

2809. "Chastity? It's not like that's in any movie anyone ever sees, so what's the deal with it?"

2810. What the writing teacher always hoped he could have written on some student essays:
"This is absolutely the very worst excuse for a paper that has ever been imposed on me. There is no grade low enough to fit this chaotic pile of horse manure pretending to be a serious effort. It couldn't be a bad joke because it is not good enough to be a stupid and incompetent attempt at satire. It is not even good enough to be a bungling and inept attempt at ordinary prose. How dare you offend my sensibilities with this repulsive affront to the English language. I assume you used voice recognition software to dictate a single draft off the top of your head and didn't bother to revise or even read it over before turning it in. Do you have no shame? I've seen better writing from students who spent five minutes writing papers ten times as long."

2811. Just read this in a Tom Clancy novel: "The more you sweat in training, the less you bleed in battle." These words should be on a poster placed in every English composition classroom. If you really want a future of competent communication, pay attention in class, study hard, practice every day, and learn how to write.

2812. At a meeting recently, I was asked, "How does someone like you, with Parkinson's disease, have hope when you have a terminal disease ending in death?" I said, "Life is a terminal disease ending in death." During the Renaissance, many of the well-off had human skulls on their desks to remind them of the inevitability of death. We need to consider this practice for today. Too many people don't think about death and its aftermath. There might be many more believers if they would. An advantage of having Parkinson's disease is that I don't need a skull on my desk. The progressive debilitations of the disease remind me of my mortality just fine.

2813. "Then Samuel told the people the ordinances of the kingdom, and wrote them in a book and placed it before the LORD" (1 Samuel 10:25). Writing moves the rules from subjective to objective, and the objective is the source of the principles of fairness, equity, and justice; and these principles support a safe and harmonious social structure.

2814. Saul was chosen king, and the people rejoiced. "But certain worthless men . . . despised him and did not bring him any present" (1 Samuel 10:27). Why are we surprised or abashed when God's will is opposed? Or simply when a moral proposition is ridiculed or cursed? There are always, and always have been, "certain worthless men" whose role is to oppose the good.

2815. Does it strike you as odd that today, more people than ever can read, but fewer people than ever can think? More people than ever have college degrees, but fewer people than ever can conduct a reasoned, evidence-based argument?

2816. Is society improving? Of course. In the past, when lovers kissed, the camera moved to the blazing fireplace to work as a metonymy for the subsequent events. Now, the camera zooms in on the two naked bodies merging. Wouldn't want to confuse anyone by forcing them to rely on their imagination.

2817. Notice: No running, no jumping, no fires, no dogs, no music, no dancing, no food, no alcohol, no sleeping, no tents, no umbrellas, no bicycles, no motorbikes, no skateboards, no glass objects. Enjoy your beach.

2818. For your convenience, a 20% tip has been added to all restaurant charges.

2819. As a courtesy to our customers, a $25 resort fee has been added to your room charge each day. This charge includes a complimentary copy of the local newspaper.

2820. Music is the interface between the brain and the soul.

2821. When women get together, they talk about other people (especially the shortcomings of men), or about each other. When men get together, they talk about things: cars, tools, sports.

2822. "And this is love, that we walk according to his commandments" (2 John 6). Love is not a mysterious feeling that comes and goes. Love is a verb. Love is shown by actions, by doing things that benefit the beloved. Here in 2 John, John says that love involves obedience to and concurrence with the values and rules of the loved one.

2823. **In the Faculty Lounge.**
     "Here's an announcement that the library will add weekend hours during finals week."
     "How can we unpack that?"
     "Is that a microaggression from the hegemonic administration?"
     "But is that relevant?"
     "Is it viable?"
     "Can we bifurcate that?"
     "Before we riot, we should expose the intertextual claims buried in the subtext—claims that rearm the totalizing narrative of oppression."

2824. Many places in the Old Testament, Leviticus especially, say that the sacrifices of worship and atonement, of both grain and animal, are to be burned as a "soothing aroma to the Lord." This reveals to us the closeness of God, his immediate and specific presence in the place of worship. Not just his eyes and mind, but his sense of smell, is involved. He doesn't merely observe the worship — he participates in it.

2825. Why was Solomon considered the wisest man ever? God appeared to him and said, "Just tell me what you want" (1 Kings 3:5b). What would you choose? Obscene wealth way beyond the wildest dreams of avarice? The naked power to command every soul on the planet to do whatever you demand? The extremes of sensate experience, whether in the form of taste bud ripping food or carnal indulgence? (Remember that in Greek mythology, Paris chose Aphrodite's offer of the most beautiful woman in the world, a choice that quickly entailed misery and death for thousands.)

Offered anything he wanted, Solomon asked for first, obedience and submission to God. Offered the opportunity to choose power and authority over others, Solomon chose to submit to God and to gain the ability to discern between good and evil.

Next time you are in a conversation about anything, drop in the word submit or the word obey. Note the reaction. Our prideful hearts hate those concepts. Solomon wanted the ability to gain understanding, which can be derived through processed personal experience or by learning from those who have already been down that road. Or, in God's case, Solomon could learn from him who created us, and gain understanding through the knowledge of our own design.

2826. If you seek understanding "like silver" (Proverbs 2:4), then you will "discover the knowledge of God" (2:5b). The point is, you have to desire understanding, to want it seriously, even when it threatens cherished beliefs. That's why, when people get into philosophical arguments, they resort to straw man descriptions of their opponents' ideas, mis-summarize opposing positions, and drag red herrings across every line of argument. They do not really want to understand the opposition to their own emotional commitments.

"I'm in favor of educational vouches so that parents can choose the schools they want to send their kid to."

"So what you are saying is, you want to destroy the public schools so that a handful of rich parents can send their kids to private schools where only kids they like can be admitted. You're a racist, sexist, homophobic, transphobic, climate denying evil person with hidden agendas."

2827. Over the last few decades, we have been told that our decisions should be made, not by reason, but by "following your heart." Our whole society has rejected reason and duty in favor of feeling and impulse. Consider the shift:

Thinking	Feeling
Reason	Emotion
Evidence	Passion
Evaluation	Urge
Judgment	Lust
Analysis	Desire
Need	Want
Self-denial	Self-exaltation
Others	Me
Duty	Expedience

2828. "Provoking the Lord God of Israel with their worthless idols" (1 Kings 16:13b). Certainly it antagonizes God when someone prays to a piece of carved wood for rain or a good harvest. But it must really anger him when someone thanks the block of wood for a blessing that God himself has given. None of us are grateful enough to the Lord for the blessings that continuously rain down from his hand into our lives; and to misattribute them, not to someone else, but to a piece of wood or stone—no wonder God is so disappointed with us. And whom are you worshipping when you attribute to your own amazingness the accomplishments you attain?

2829. Another way to describe the problem of pride is to say that it produces an antipathy toward restraint. Self-control becomes "unhealthy inhibition," and submitting to social rules becomes "hegemonic repression." Since Eve, the temptation to fall from righteousness has been embodied in the act of rebellion, accepting the tempter's grant of permission to have pleasure that God has prohibited.

2830. "The heart knows its own bitterness, and no outsider shares in its joy" (Proverbs 14:10, HCSB). The deepest sorrows and the deepest joys are private, even secret, experiences. No degree of empathy from another can scale the height of elation, or fully share the "music to my soul at midnight" (George Herbert), that, say a kind or supportive word can produce. Others would laugh if we told them how intensely we received the card or comment or smile. Similarly, they would tell us to "grow up" if we revealed how hurt we were at a negative comment, a failure to be chosen for the promotion, or our long continued sorrow over the loss of a pet.

Every time I think of my two doggies, Wolf and Bear, I start to cry, even though Wolf has been gone for several years and Bear for almost a year. I could tell you that I loved those two little dinky dogs (Chihuahuas), but you would laugh or smile knowingly and say, "I'm sorry," while thinking, "This guy needs to get a life."

But it's all right. If we rejoice or grieve in secret, we do so in the presence of God, who hears, sees, and feels our hearts. And he is the important audience.

2831. "Every wise woman builds her house, but a foolish one tears it down with her own hands" (Proverbs 14:1, HCSB). If you study and understand this proverb, you can skip reading Frimpkins on *The Psychodynamics of Marriage*, Beetletar on *Emotional Tone Control in Interpersonal Relationships*, Coldwyn on

Why Men Have Affairs, and Smervitz on *Bedmaking Among the Zambeezi.*

2832. Stop complaining. Complaining means that you reject what God has allowed to happen to you, and therefore you reject his sovereignty over your life. Of course, God might not—probably did not—want the situation or suffering you are complaining about. Instead, the events likely reflect only his permissive will (what he has permitted to occur), not his directive or executive will. God frequently allows the disasters caused by the corruption of the world to impact Christians while at the same time grieving over them. Our role is to be a light to the world and show that we can love and trust God through every bad experience.

Complaining about your state would mean that you are criticizing God, which means that you are sitting in judgment over God and finding him morally wrong. So you are declaring God to be a sinner while exalting your own moral code to the status of cosmic authority.

Contributing a piece to Samuel Johnson's *Rambler* essays, eighteenth-century writer Elizabeth Carter reminds us that Christians ought to be optimistic and trusting in every circumstance:

> Remember that the greatest honor you can pay to the author of your being is by such a cheerful behavior, as discovers a mind satisfied with his dispensations.[10]

There should be no, "Why me?" in the life of a believer. No criticizing of God with, "I shouldn't have this illness," or "It's wrong for God to allow this evil event," or "God, do you know what you're doing?"

This does not mean that you cannot ask for healing or deliverance, as in, "Lord, heal me of this disease," or "Lord, help me

---

[10] Published as number 44 in Samuel Johnson's *Rambler* essays in 1750. British spelling Americanized.

bear with this disaster," or "Lord, have mercy on this hurting people."

Remember that we are called to show our bodies as silent witnesses to the joy we have in Christ, and the trust we maintain, believing that "Christ gives me the strength to face anything" (Philippians 4:13, CEV).

Therefore, bring your issues before God privately and quietly, seeking to understand his will and purpose in your life, and asking for deliverance "if it is God's will."

Another way to think about this is to understand why God was so angry with the Israelites when they whined about their lot as they moved from Egyptian slavery toward the Promised Land (see especially Numbers 11:1-20). They were rescued and had the personal guidance of God and yet they complained.

In our terms, we have houses to shelter us, heating systems for the winter, cooling systems for the summer, reliable electricity, refrigerators and freezers to keep our food edible, a safe water supply with hot and cold on tap, portable phones, computers, food from around the world, allowing us to eat "summer" fruits in winter as well as summer, electric light, and on and on. And yet give us a broken leg, or—horrors of horrors—an incurable disease (like my Parkinson's), and instantly we get mad at God. How dare we. Count your blessings and praise your maker, regardless of your pain.

If pain makes you resentful, that's a sign that you need it. Try some humility and trust. Yield to the Spirit.

2833. Says the son of a wealthy magnate when an attractive young woman smiles at him: "Love is in the air."

Says the attractive young woman to her friends after the son has smiled at her: "Love is in the heir."

2834. What does it mean to "keep the Sabbath day holy"? It means to consecrate it—dedicate it—and the day's activities to worshipping the Lord, to serving him, to honoring him. Keep the day separate from the other days. Holiness is something we do, not a feeling about ourselves. In the Old Testament, the words translated *holy* mean *consecrated, dedicated, hallowed.*

> Remember the Sabbath day, to keep it holy (H6942: qadash). —Exodus 20:8

> You shall surely observe My Sabbaths; for this is a sign between Me and you throughout your generations, that you may know that I am the LORD who sanctifies (H6942: qadash) you. Therefore you are to observe the Sabbath, for it is holy (H6944: qodesh) to you. — Exodus 31:13-14

> Then the LORD spoke to Aaron, "Now behold, I Myself have given you charge of My offerings, even all the holy (H6944: qodesh) gifts of the sons of Israel I have given them to you as a portion and to your sons as a perpetual allotment. — Numbers 18:8

> For I am the LORD your God. Consecrate (H6942: qadash) yourselves therefore, and be holy (H6918: qadosh), for I am holy (H6918: qadosh). —Leviticus 11:44

Holiness and the Sabbath boil down to concentrating on God, as the King James version says, "Be still, and know that I am God" (Psalm 46:10).

2835. Dead men don't have many needs.

2836. What's the one thing, above all else, that a guy wants to hear from his girlfriend or wife? "I love you"? Nope. "You're handsome [smart, brave, wonderful]"? Nope. The one thing we want to hear (and that we hear so seldom) is, "I'm happy." Yes, guys want the girl of their dreams to be amiable, easy going, funny, smart, good looking (but not fashion-model beautiful), and so on, but foremost we want the girl to be happy — content — and show it.

2837. A Prayer to Begin the Day

Dear Lord God, creator of the heavens and the earth, and maker of my soul, your child comes to you humbly to seek your heart, to praise you for your goodness, and to thank you for the blessings you have heaped upon me every day of my life. May your truth, wisdom, and Holy Spirit be with me today in all that I do and say and think. May you be honored by everything that involves me. And may your will be done in my life. In the name of Jesus, the savior you have so graciously provided. Amen.

2838. In times of persecution or suffering, we try to persevere by wrapping our hearts with the tissue paper of courage, when what we need is Jesus to line our hearts with the steel plates of trust in God.

2839. I cannot give you happiness, but I can give you joy. Happiness must come from within, but joy comes from God.

2840. Our skepticism keeps us from believing 50% of the most dangerous lies we are told, and from believing 90% of the most important truths.

2841. Deception is the art of plausibility combined with the almost true.

2842. A lie must be very small or very large in order to be believed.

2843. Teaching someone how to detect fraud and deception also teaches them how to practice it.

2844. If you go halfway down a road, you will not arrive at your destination. — Chinese proverb

2845. Sometimes there is no shortcut. — Chinese proverb

2846. When Diogenes was asked what he had learned from philosophy, he replied "I've learned to be rich without money."

2847. The richest man is he who is least tied to the material world.

2848. Diogenes once told a customs agent, "You cannot see the treasure I'm carrying because you keep the eyes of your soul firmly closed."

2849. Monday: "Senator Frimpson's statements about government spending appear not to concur with the published statistics."

Tuesday: "Senator Frimpson is apparently advancing alternative facts not available to anyone else."

Wednesday: "Senator Frimpson seems to be maintaining a rather fluid relationship with the truth."

Thursday: "Senator Frimpson's statements are wrong."

Friday: "Senator Frimpson is lying."

2850. The incompetent worker blames his tools. — Proverb
Comment. Once again, we see how pride prevents improvement, because the worker who blames his tools rather than taking responsibility for the result will not seek to learn how to produce a better result. Unless we can force our egos to yield to reality, we will be unable to make progress.

2851. Just about every Sunday, when the offering bag is passed, I see someone pretending to put something in the offering bag. It's often the same gesture — hand flat, pointed downward as if it might be mistaken for an envelope. Sometimes there is a shoving motion to the hand, as if the donation is so large it needs assistance to get deep inside the bag.

Why do people do this? The people around them, like me, probably assume that they give online or by credit card, or on another week. We don't care. Since I give online, I can be seen every week not putting anything in the envelope, but it doesn't bother me a bit.

2852. We blame the modern educational system for not teaching figurative language. In the past, we learned about metaphors and personification in class, and we saw hundreds of examples in the Bible. Certainly, this lack of ability to understand metaphors is a new tragedy in human existence.

Actually, not. It just occurred to me that many of the Israelites of Jesus' day also were clueless about figurative language. Let's look.

Exhibit A. When Nicodemus, a well-educated man (a Pharisee), talks to Jesus, Jesus tells him, "Truly, truly, I say to you, unless one is born again he cannot see the kingdom of God."

Nicodemus takes Jesus literally and asks, "How can a man be born when he is old? Can he enter a second time into his mother's womb and be born?" (John 3:3-4).

Exhibit B. When the Jews ask for a sign, Jesus tells them, "Destroy this temple, and in three days I will raise it up."

Again, they think Jesus is speaking literally about the physical temple. They say, probably in a sneering tone, "It has taken forty-six years to build this temple, and will you raise it up in three days?" (John 3:19-20).

Exhibit C. When Jesus refers to himself as the "bread of life," the Jews take him literally, even after he explains the symbolism: "I am the living bread that came down from heaven. If anyone eats of this bread, he will live forever. And the bread that I will give for the life of the world is my flesh."

The Jews then disputed among themselves, saying, "How can this man give us his flesh to eat?" (John 6:51-52).

Jesus explains: "It is the Spirit who gives life; the flesh is no help at all. The words that I have spoken to you are spirit and life" (John 6:63).

Even after Jesus explains that he was speaking figuratively, "many of his disciples turned back and no longer walked with him" (John 6:66).

2853. **God's Power.**
1. There are more than two billion Christians in the world.
2. Christians speak more than 3,000 languages.
3. God listens to every prayer.

2854. A CEO without wisdom is a fool in a suit.

2855. Promises are the leaves, but deeds are the fruit. —Proverb

2856. If a fool has a good idea, it is still a good idea. —Proverb

2857. The beautiful city of Success can be reached only by crossing the narrow bridge of Risk. —Proverb

2858. No criticism hurts as much as the one that is justified. —Proverb

2859. "We will not be ruled by this rigid authoritarian," the sailors said. And so they threw the rudder overboard. "We are free spirits, so let us be guided by the wind, wherever it may take us." And so they unfurled all the sails. The boat sped up and turned to receive the full push of the wind.

Unfortunately for the free spirits on the boat, the wind that day felt like blowing toward the rocks.

2860. Beauty, intelligence, personality—these will help advance one in the world. But what the world really values is ability, because ability is the foundation for accomplishment; accomplishment is the foundation for service; and service is the foundation for our value to others (and also our heavenly reward). Ability is a gift, but if we don't refine it through education, training, and practice, it will be wasted.

2861. The Sultan's account of the journey is much different from those who carried his chair, for the Sultan never saw the mud or felt the rocks or noticed the hills.

2862. "Ideas not represented by sensible objects are fleeting, variable, and evanescent." —Samuel Johnson, *Rambler* 110.

This fact explains why so many cultures (especially in the past) have been idol worshippers, and why so many believers in the God of the Bible so often watch their minds wander during prayers. The mind wants to focus on a picture in order to maintain thought. Without a picture, our minds quickly move on to something else that is represented by a picture.

2863. "We seek in the knowledge of others a succor for our own ignorance, and are ready to trust any that will undertake to direct us when we have no confidence in ourselves." —Samuel Johnson, *Rambler* 110.

The great danger of recognizing our own ignorance in some area is that we too often uncritically grab on to the first explanation as the correct explanation, and then habitually reject future, competing explanations.

2864. Why is it so difficult for unbelievers to come to God? Why so difficult for Jews to come to Jesus? Why so difficult for evolutionists to change their nineteenth-century smoke and mirrors explanation for the natural world into a vision of the truth?

There are many contributing answers—unwillingness to give up control, too much pride to yield to a humbling idea and a humbling being, unwillingness to give up the indulgences of atheism ("Where there is no God, everything is permitted").

But there is an additional answer. People cannot easily adopt a new idea that requires them to give up a familiar and cherished idea or set of ideas that supports so much of their epistemology. The requirement to reject long held conclusions on which so much of their intellectual (and emotional) architecture is based is too much of an earthquake to accept.

So it's not just pride, not just confirmation bias, but self-identity issues that hold them back.

2865. Why do people turn from the only true God to worship false gods? Oh, yes, it's true that we've gotten so much wiser and more sophisticated. We no longer worship wooden or metal figurines. Instead we worship video games, social media, famous media stars, possessions of every kind, and on and on. Why? The answer lies in the nature of the so-called gods. Gods made by human hands can be controlled by human minds. Want to keep sleeping around and not be criticized by Christian morality? Just adopt Tantric sex as part of your religion. Want to continue your habit of stealing stuff? Adopt the Spartan view that getting caught was worse than the stealing itself. Like lusting after consumer goods? You are welcome among many others who will make you feel comfortable. Want to feel as if you belong? Buy something.

Make up your own deity, customized to your own likes and dislikes. None of this angry God stuff.

2866. The most negative result of the advanced technology we enjoy is that too many people believe that it eliminates the need for culture, morality, and wisdom, while it also replaces the need for God. If you live a completely comfortable life, with every physical need more than well taken care of, why do you need God? Oh, foolish and blind, that's when you need God the most.

2867. In my book on prayer, among the various ways God answers prayer is number 10, "Yes. Now get started." Reading through the Old Testament, we find this a common way God works in the lives of his people. The Israelites had to do battle with those people who occupied the land God promised to give to Israel. God was in the battles, serving as a force multiplier that allowed the Israelites to succeed where they otherwise would have failed.

This participatory answer to prayer not only involves God in our lives and in our struggles, but it also keeps us in connection with God, seeking his will and his help.

2868. Women find joy in order; men find joy in chaos. Then they marry each other.

2869. How does an expert in an area differ from an ordinary person or amateur? The expert has, not just more knowledge in the area, but

- more detailed knowledge
- better organized knowledge
- more accessible knowledge
- more knowledge based on experience

And the expert can work with his knowledge. In other words, the expert is better able to derive, adapt, and apply personal knowledge to the new situation and knows both the rules and the exceptions.

2870. The history of the world can never be a comedy because people are just too evil.

Right from the beginning there are Adam and Eve, Cain and Abel, the erasure of all the evil through the Flood, that Golden Calf episode, and the broken Tablets of the Ten Commandments. Then in the history of the Israelites, God's Chosen People divide in two, become enemies, and kill each other. As for most of their kings, fill in the blank: "_____ became king and he did evil in the sight of the Lord."

And extra-Biblical ancient history is little more than a record of conquest and the atrocities accompanying the battles. Every time I read about thousands killed in battle, I think of the resulting widows and orphans. And for those not killed, what of them? Slavery for the losers: "Are they not finding and dividing the spoil — a girl or two for each warrior? . . ." (Judges 5:30).

Oh, but we became civilized. Yeah right. Slavery becomes a commercial enterprise, and in the African slave trade, both on the east coast of Africa, where the Muslims make the slaves walk on a long death march, and on the west coast, where the brutalized slaves are packed into ships and sent to the Americas, the "inventory shrinkage" is thought to have been around 50 percent.

World War I, the "war to end all wars" starts up, and instead of meeting the enemy with bayonets, the soldiers discover they are marching into machine guns and mustard gas. Millions die, many horribly.

World War II, more millions. (How much time have you got for this?) Communism, 100 million die, and more are essentially enslaved. And on and on.

Yes, this realm can never be a comedy.

It can, however, be a tragi-comedy, if only we would all turn to the one Redeemer who can make it so. Think we will do that? Nah. We'd rather continue to refine our definition of "horrific."

2871. Jephthah the Idiot.

Jephthah makes a vow to God to sacrifice "whatever comes out of the door of my house to greet me" if God grants him the victory over the Ammonites. He wins the battle, and guess who comes out to celebrate his victory "with tambourines and dancing"? His daughter, of course. And if it had not been his daughter, it might have been a son or his wife or even some other human being. What an idiot to make such a vow. Lesson for us: Be careful when you make a vow, to God or anyone. Think, man!

2872. Growing Up.

"Papa, what does this mark mean?"

"That's an asterisk."

"An actorick? Why is it there, after 'Free'?"

"An asterisk means, 'See the explanation for this lie at the bottom of the page.'"

2873. When you pray, you open a direct path of communication between yourself and God, energized by the Holy Spirit. That is the essence of prayer. When you pray aloud, the person you are praying with benefits from hearing and participating in the prayer. If you are praying in a group setting, the path of communication is still between you and God. The words you speak are for God. It is a privilege for those hearing the payer to be present as you pray, but it is less important what they think of your prayer than what God thinks.

Prayer can impact hearers when spoken aloud by edifying, encouraging, convicting, or reassuring them. But the central event is the connection between you and God.

2874. "We snore away flat on our backs; we do nothing, we enjoy ourselves . . . as though this life of ours were not a war, but a Greek drinking bout" (The *Enchiridion* of Erasmus, 2). How easy it is for us to forget that life is limited, that we will soon be dead, and that what will happen to us next depends on how we live now, and will last for all eternity. How can we look at a flower or a rainbow and not be frightened if we don't know its meaning—how it got here with us, what it means, and what we should do about it.

2875. I can't read a book without a pen (usually a ten-cent Bic) and a six-inch ruler. (Four plastic one-foot rulers from the Dollar store, cut in half will make eight six-inch supports for underlining, in case you lose them as fast as I do or want to use them for bookmarks.) I underline what are to me exceptional comments, facts, ideas, and so on. Today it occurred to me that when we write, we should all tell ourselves, "Write something worth underlining."

2876. The ultimate thesis of many self-help books is, "You live what you believe. Expand your mind to welcome more ideas, including ones that you now consider impossible, and choose from among the new, better ones."

There are so many tragic stories about people who ruined their lives (through drugs, crime, accepting the choices presented by the toxic culture around them) that society should offer warnings about likely consequences for dangerous choices. Those who make the crucial decisions of their lives should neither be the limited ("It was all I could think of"), nor the thoughtlessly expansive "It seemed like a good idea at the time").

2877. Thinking about Glimmering 2021. I've noticed a relatively common reading phenomenon among younger people. They will read a sentence and say, "I don't understand what he's talking about." Then in the next sentence, the writer explains, defines, illustrates, or clarifies the statement in the previous sentence. The short attention span, instant gratification, or just-in-time learning, or perhaps the method of teaching now, in little bits of information at a time — perhaps these things have created the idea that a reader must understand completely what was just said before going on to the next sentence. As writing continues to decline in competence and clarity, many writers cannot reveal their knowledge without many sentences to carry the load a bit at a time.

Advice: Read on, even when you don't understand a sentence or a paragraph. In fact, read through the article or examine the book carefully in advance to see the structure of the discussion before you do a full reading.

2878. The good news about time is that things change. The bad news about time is that things change.

2879. Since we learn principally by analogy, comparisons to God can be useful. But they can only put one foot on the long path to understanding.

2880. Entry for the saddest obituary of all time: "Jehoram was 32 years old when he became king; he reigned eight years in Jerusalem. He died to no one's regret and was buried in the city of David but not in the tombs of the kings." — 2 Chronicles 21:20 (HCSB)

2881. Pride knows no limits.

2882. **Ten Questions.**
    1. Why are you alive?
    2. What is the most important thing in your life?
    3. What gives you the most satisfaction?

4. What is the purpose of life?

5. What is the purpose of death?

6. What happens after death?

7. What is the key to happiness?

8. What is the main goal of your life?

9. How have you answered the "God question"?

10. What is the most important question?

2883. Comment on Glimmering 2034. When we discuss art, since there are no standards other than novelty and anti-authority, music that gets awards is painful to endure. But when we discuss money, as in box-office profits, music (that is, the film score) is often amazingly beautiful, powerful, moving. It might win an Academy Award, but it is not highbrow enough to win a *real* award.

2884. When I first studied the structure of biological cells in high school, my response was admiration at the complexitgy and functions of the various parts, such as the nucleus and he cell wall. Later in college my admiration changed to wonder as I learned more about the DNA molecule, mitosis, and the like. Later still, my response changed to amazement as I learned about micromachines, cell transport, "doors" for oxygen to get into the cell, flagellar motors, and such. Now that I am beginning some research into epigenetics, my amazement is changing to astonishment. What once was thought by many to be about as complex as a blob of Jello is now turning out to be so unbelievably complex and interdependent that it staggers the imagination.

2885. Why is it that "Breaking News" is a permanent label at the bottom of the screen of some news channels?

2886. Quick personality quiz. Divide the following list of words into two columns. First column, "Like." Second column, "Don't Like."

The words are autonomy, control, obedience, power, sub-mission, authority, pride, following, humility, commanding, leading, compliance.

Do you want to be the boss?

2887. Is it possible that the only reason so many people reject eternal truth is that they have been programmed to expect constant novelty in ideas?

2888. Re: Glimmering 2183. Seducers of various stripes engage in a process known as grooming their victims before they actually seek conquest. Whether sexual seduction or selling someone what is really a pyramid scheme, first comes a time for making the victim feel comfortable, trusting, and valued. Grooming might take some time, but the seducer is the soul of patience.

2889. What I intended to convey in Glimmering 2102 was that to be a good actor, don't try to become the character; let the character be you.

2890. Re: Glimmering 2206 about the "I feel" hegemony in the assertion of beliefs. Have you noticed that one personal example now completely refutes decades of studies, statistics, expert analyses, and collected accounts?

For example, here is an actual interchange from a critical thinking class session.

Me: "There is a story that if a driver in a car flashes his headlights at you and you flash yours back, the driver (and his friends in the car) will murder you."

Student: "Yes, that's right."

Me: "Researchers have found that the story is an urban legend with no basis in fact."

Student: "No, it's true. My boyfriend told me he knows someone it happened to."

Me: "And they were murdered?"

Student: "All of them."

Me: "Why is there no record of any such event?"
Student: "I don't know. It was probably suppressed."

2891. Christians should be happier in their lives because they understand that they were put on earth to serve, while many non-Christians think they were put on earth to rule.

2892. As I look back on my life, I realize that it has been more failure than success. One of my most ardent goals was to support the development of a Christian intelligentsia. But I couldn't get students (or fellow faculty) interested. What does it take to get people interested in developing their minds? In learning how to think? In wanting to avoid falling for fallacies?

If I might appeal to the culture, it is no help in promoting thinking. The gold-plated excrement that fills our media consumption day actually works against thinking and analyzing. Because if you do either. you'll stop watching.

2893. Re: Glimmering 2295.

"Two books on wisdom to choose from?" asked the fool's friend. "I'll take the one with the bigger type and the fewer pages. And does it have pictures?"

2894. Re: Glimmering 2300. There is an idea that we value things that require effort to attain. I think this is a correct idea because it is used in so many situations. Requiring a certification or license in order to, say cut hair or paint fingernails not only provides revenue for the licensing government but also makes the licensee feel good for having put in the effort. So-called "exclusive" clubs sometimes have extensive membership requirements; many golf courses require, in order to join, hefty membership fees in addition to the recommendation of a current member; some young people, especially young women, play hard to get, thinking that they will be valued more by their pursuer as a result of the challenge and difficulty he has in winning them.

2895. **The Keys to Happiness.**

The order of importance or priority depends on each individual. If you don't know where to begin, this order is a place to begin.

1. Humble Yourself.
2. Honor God.
3. Listen First.
4. Practice Patience.
5. Reduce Expectations.
6. Change Yourself.
7. Always Forgive.
8. Help Others.
9. Be Truthful.
10. Be Kind.
11. Choose Carefully.
12. Avoid Shortcuts.

2896. In the days of the Old Testament, raising sheep was the way to translate work into money. See Proverbs 27:25-27.

2897. Those who reject moral constraints make fun of them. "Those who reject the law praise the wicked." —Proverbs 28:4a Have you ever read a better definition of Hollywood?

2898. There are those who fall into sin from temptation and weakness, and there are those who run into sin for enjoyment and exhibition of their autonomy. These latter delight in exposing—in drenching—the former with every evil thought and fantasy and action. "Woe to you, scribes and Pharisees, hypocrites, because you travel around on sea and land to make one proselyte; and when he becomes one, you make him twice as much a son of hell as yourselves." —Matthew 23:15

And if you dare to call them on it, they say, "Huh? We are just presenting ordinary, normal behaviors."

2899. Those who believe everything learn as little as those who believe nothing. —from the book of *Newly Made Proverbs*

2900. Re: Glimmering 2333. We also value things that give us power or make us feel powerful. Money, a person with money or possessions (fancy car, big house) or position (Vice President, Attorney) are also valued because they exude power.

2901. "He hangs the earth on nothing" (Job 26:7b). Question: If Job was written somewhere between 2100 and 1400 BC, how did the author know that the earth is suspended in space? Does "divinely inspired" ring a bell?

2902. When you have locked your doors to keep the devil out, be sure to check your windows, too. —from the book of *Newly Made Proverbs*

2903. Whither the Appliance Repairman?

Over the last 30 or 40 years, there has been a transition in the way we buy and repair technology. I remember driving to downtown Los Angeles with my mom sometime in the 1970s to buy one of the early microwave ovens. It cost more than $500. And in the late 1970s, I bought a VCR for $750. It weighed probably 20 or 30 pounds, and the blank tapes were $20 each. If either one of these expensive consumer goods had broken down, we naturally would have called the repairman.

Then, consumer electronics began to get cheaper, and formulas were developed to tell the owner whether he should have the product repaired or just buy a new one.

And then, after a while, that decision was made automatically as prices continued to drop and repair costs continued to rise. I remember buying a small black and white TV at one of those now-long-gone discount stores (remember Zody's, White Front, Disco Fair, Gemco, FedMart, Fedco?) for $39. After less than a year it went on the fritz. I talked to a TV repair shop and they said, (1) there would be a $75 charge just to diagnose it, And (2) since they were not made to repair, the cost to fix it would be high.

And so it is with most of our modern products. When the old model breaks, don't fix it; toss it. Besides, the new models have better performance and additional features.

2904. Three Types of Evidence for the Existence of God.
1. The natural world. Life is preposterously complex, even at the cellular level. The beauty of flowers, trees, grass, animals, and so on all testify to the Creator who made them. And their beauty and design persist even through the corruption caused by the fall.

2. Personal experience. Many of us can testify to the working, blessing, chastising, love, grace, and mercy God has done in our lives.

3. The record of Scripture. The Bible tells us about God, his ways, his requirements, and his leading. The book is really his word to us so that we may know his will and his heart. That's why so many people are quick to sneer at it and many more are afraid to read it. Their fear is justified, because there are many testimonies of those who set out to read the Bible in order to mock it or disprove it, but who found themselves praying the sinner's prayer and joining the faith.

2905. "I oppose the bill to subsidize buggy whip manufacture."
"That's hate speech."
"Oh, come on. The whole concept of hate speech is just a way of silencing opponents."
"What you just said is violent speech. You could be arrested for that."
"Violent speech? That's an even dumber idea than hate speech."
"Oooh, you used the phrase 'dumb idea.' I'm calling the police."

[May 17-26, 2019; age 68]

Glimmerings 2906 through 2929 were written during a vacation in Maui.

2906. A major part of maturity is knowing how to feel your hurts. Recognizing that a lost romance, for example, however painful now, will heal in time helps you process the grief more positively and aids toward a new, healthier future. With the loss of a parent, if you understand that you are most likely grieving more for yourself than for your loved one, you'll be better able to manage your pain.

2907. May you find the God you need rather than the God you want.

2908. Why are the lyrics of so many pop songs little more than two or three minutes of ungrammatical banal inanity?

1. The songwriter has nothing to say, and in spite of the joke ("He had nothing to say but he sure said it well,") he can't sing it well, either.

2. The lyrics don't matter because they are drowned out by the music anyway.

3. The songwriter is so ignorant that he can't express himself clearly and understandably. (That's why you hear so many "I ain't got no lovin' baby" lyrics.)

4. The old saying, "Things too stupid to say can still pass if they are sung," fits pop songs perfectly.

5. Postmodernism has taught us that any given lyric can embody hundreds or thousands of meanings, while highbrow culture has for a long time produced millions of scholarly articles and books predicated on the assumption that the more obscure and impenetrable a poem or lyric is the deeper the meaning and hence the more profound and valuable.

2909. **Example Modern Poem.**

LYING NAKED ON BROKEN GLASS
The mirror steak red
the bed gripped lead
a tomato
a potato

yeah baby, yeah baby come on, come on
oobie foobie goncha loobie
yeah baby yeah baby come on, come on

2910. Anticipation, waiting, experiencing, disappointment: life.

2911. If your eyes are blind, you cannot see.
If your heart is blind, you cannot feel.

2912. "Someday, you have to give up all your position, whether you want to or not" (Thomas a Kempis, 2.7). Why do we act as if everything will be ours forever?

2913, Why do we envy the rich and powerful with all their property, possessions, and people when we know that they, like us, must someday die?

2914. If you violate your rental agreement and drive beyond the smooth pavement onto the washboard, suspension-destroying road past the tiny settlement of Hana on Maui, you can eventually turn sharply down a dirt road marked with a weathered sign pointing to a Congregational church. Turn left at the bushes and bounce your way along a so-called road so narrow and curvy that the shrubbery on both sides scratches your vehicle and bangs your side mirrors out of adjustment until you eventually come to a lonely church. Park and walk around the back of the church, past a few gravestones in what is sort of a cemetery area. If you search carefully enough, you will find the grave of Charles Lindbergh. Once celebrated by millions, now virtually forgotten.

Not only that, but those who cheered him on and those who cursed him are now all dead. Such is the end of us all.

2915. Vacations and enjoyments of any kind require you to be relaxed and not brain busy. If you are brain busy you can't enjoy anything.

2916. If willingly endured for the love of Christ, suffering can be the shortcut to sanctification.

2917. We think that the more effort and trouble and suffering and pain we willingly endure or seek out, the more spiritual advancement must result. But if the focus is not on Christ and our true progress in sanctification, we might be suffering in vain.

2918. When you are called to suffer, by all means pray for deliverance. If it pleases God not to give you healing or relief, pray that he will use your hurt for his glory and your benefit.

2919. When an entitlement becomes theft. An analogy. When you get coffee from a coffee takeout, you are entitled to some sugar packets and some creamer packets, together with a wooden or plastic stir stick. But if you take a fistful of sugar packets and a handful of creamer packets and enough stir sticks to build an entry in an art contest, you have become a thief.

2920. Brother Lawrence[11], "The stone to be carved. . . ." The chisel chipping away at the sinful excrescences causes pain and distraction.

2921. "God is my rock" means just that. Those who develop a strong interior life with God are joined to the Rock in such a way that they can face the most powerful storms of life with courage, calmness, and quiet trust. They are unshakable. "We are the trees whom shaking fastens more." —George Herbert[12]

2922. The world promises little and delivers less. God promises much and delivers more. But the world's promises are sung by

---

[11] The *Practice of the Presence of God,* Second Letter. This book is well worth reading and re-reading carefully.
[12] "Affliction (V)." Herbert is the master of Christian poetry, just as Shakespeare is the master of secular verse.

the sirens of flattery and are always on sale at a discount. Why not take the easy road?

2923. The foundation of any building, project, idea, or philosophy determines its strength, durability, and resistance to attack. What is the foundation of your soul? Deep or shallow? Level or tilted? Square are skewed? Will it withstand the storms of testing? The bright sun of scrutiny?

2924. How often do you visit the foundation of your soul? Do you find it musty and awash in brackish water? Or do you keep it clean and scoured?

2925. If it rained salvation, few would hold out a hand to receive it. Fewer still would cross the street to drink from the stream of eternal life.

2926. **We See God Through Several Lenses.**
1. His creation: design, beauty, strength, and order. Structure, law, hardiness, and fragility. Creativity and imagination. What hath God wrought not only in nature but the technology he has given humans by allowing them to use the *imago dei* to advance.
2. Personal experience. Comfort, healing, experience of trust, seeing—feeling, knowing, experiencing—God in our lives.
3. Scripture. God's objective truth. Love, mercy, slowness to anger. Unchanging rules based on unchanging loving, everything in our best interest. His sacrifice (for us!).
4. Story. Vicarious experience. Hearing the stories of others to teach us about endurance, trust, faith, love.
5. The five senses plus. Living in a world accessible through multiple channels. Seeing, smelling, tasting, hearing, touching, reasoning, thinking, feeling.

2927. **A Beautiful Morning Near the Beach in Maui.**
So I'm sitting on the patio of a premier hotel enjoying the peaceful morning quiet. Then a gardener with a push mower

arrives and starts his mower up and begins to cut the grass about 50 feet away. Soon a gardener on a riding mower drives in and begins to mow right in front of me. He pauses with his idling mower about 10 feet away while he moves a kid's toy from the lawn.

Just then a gardener with a string trimmer walks over and starts trimming the grass around the palm trees. The riding mower guy gets back on his machine and starts mowing in circles right in front of me.

Soon joining this concerto of noise is yet another gardener, this one complementing the orchestra with a leaf blower. He first blows the grass off the sidewalk, then walks around right in front of where I'm sitting and just blows the grass clippings around. He then walks across the lawn randomly, blowing the grass here and there a foot or two from one spot to another.

I leave my patio location and find refuge in a walkway chair just off the quiet lobby. Ten minutes later the leaf blower guy shows up and blasts the debris off the walkway where I'm sitting, coming ever closer until he is just a few feet away. I look over to see just what he's doing and discover that he is pushing a little pile of grass trimmings back and forth.

Incredibly, one of the string trimmer gardeners comes up into the patio area and begins repairing his trimmer. He gets it going and revs it up. A second string trimmer guy shows up. Soon, however, the two string trimmer gardeners leave without further noise. The leaf blower guy continues to push his little pile of grass clippings around for another ten minutes. Finally quiet returns.

2928. In Glimmering 2656, I recounted the various times at various airports that the PA system announced, "Will the passenger who left a notebook computer at the TSA screening point please return and claim it." Now we can add San Diego airport to that list. I'm not sure how you can forget that you are carrying a PC, but apparently it is common.

2929. The latest euphemism is printed on your boarding pass for your next flight. Mine says, "Zone 5." Turns out that's a euphemism for "fifth class passengers." Now, I might be exaggerating a bit, but you will have to admit that Zone 5 passengers have to wait until those in the first four zones are seated.

2930. Re: Glimmering 2470. We have memorized the answers, but we don't understand the questions.

2931. Re: Glimmering 2613. Updated, it should say, "A fourteen-dollar keyboard in the right hands can change the world."

2932. My Parkinson's continues to slow me down and make my walking awkward. So it was with near astonishment that I recently saw a video presentation of people dancing the Shuffle. Those of us who still remember black and white TV also remember that the traditional dances we knew, such as the waltz, the fox trot, even the tango, featured a limited set of steps, danced in a set sequence, usually with a fairly slow pace.

The Shuffle represents the difference of the ages, accelerating dance speed, and including a large (unlimited?) variety of steps, presented in whatever order the dancer chooses. The steps are eclectic. I know little about modern dance, but I can recognize portions of the Charleston (from the 20s and 30s), and the Moon Walk (from the 80s), as well as aspects of Irish dancing. There is also a variety of arm movements.

What strikes me most is the speed of the dance. Few of us antiques could ever hope to move with such complex speed. All I could think of was, "That must be burning up dopamine by the gallon."

Importantly, the Shuffle reveals the change in social relationships that we see occurring in the larger society. Yesterday's dances, such as the waltz and the foxtrot, were participatory, with partners holding each other. The Shuffle is a dance of exhibition, where one (or occasionally more than one) person dances to an audience. Even in a group setting, there is no holding on.

2933. Just as stories are more powerful for changing our beliefs than reasons or evidence, so the examples we see in the lives of our contemporaries are more influential in shaping our behavior than are arguments or appeals to history.

2934. We should, by all means, avoid being influenced by bad examples; but we also should avoid, by all means, being bad examples ourselves.

2935. Another of the tragic consequences of the loose morality of contemporary culture is that women no longer feel free to be friendly or nice or kind to men. A friendly look, kind word, smile, touch — any of these formerly innocent gestures will now too often be taken by many men as "offers of availability."

2936. **It's Those Young People.**

"Listen to this: 'The mental disease of the present generation is impatience of study, contempt of the great masters of ancient wisdom, and a disposition to rely wholly upon unassisted genius and natural ability.'"

"That very well describes the young these days, especially the millennials. Who wrote it?"

"Samuel Johnson."

"Was that published this week?"

"No. It was published on September 7, 1751."

2937. Half or more of teaching involves correcting wrong belief. In the case of objective information, such as how a home thermostat works or why "her and I" is always incorrect, the correction is clearly understood and accepted. But when the belief is open to debate (philosophy, politics, religion), the "correcting wrong belief" can often mean "propagandizing for the professor's ideological commitments."

2938. Why do we spend so much time and energy trying to stand out just a bit among our friends, family, and coworkers, and so little time and energy working to improve the cosmic importance of our lives among both our larger society and the rest of global civilization?

2939. How did Israel's prophets long ago get the attention of the Jewish authorities? God told Hosea to marry a promiscuous woman (possibly even a prostitute) who would bear children by other men—all as a testimony against Israel's unfaithfulness.

God told Isaiah to go naked and barefoot for three years as an omen about the shameful future of Egypt and Cush.

Neither of these actions would stand out today. "Hosea? Yeah, he married a party girl. And Isaiah? Just some strung-out leftover hippie."

2940. As for love, we learn to love and to refine our practice and expression of it by being loved first and copying those who loved us. We need models for love because love conflicts with the selfishness of human nature. Let this be a tribute to my mother: My mom taught me how to love—not with words but by example.

2941. Without a human model, you can still learn to love, from the best teacher. Even if you had hateful, abusive parents, you can study how Jesus loved others and copy his ways. Take his principles from his word and apply them. Imitate his behavior.

2942. Love is a turn of 180 degrees:
from take to give
from self to other
from be served to serve
from me to another

2943. **The 1-2-3 Plan to Change the World.**
   Every Day:
   1. Do one Good Deed
   2. Pray for Two Strangers
   3. Give Three Compliments

1. Do One Good Deed Each Day.
- Pick up a piece of litter and throw it in a trash can.
- When you see someone in a store confused or uncertain about which item to choose, offer to help.
- At a coffee bar, offer to pay for the coffee of the person behind you (or give the barista a $5 bill and say it's for the next customer).
- Go to the bank and get some $2 bills. Then tip people who don't ordinarily get tipped: the fast-food order taker, the checker at the hardware store. I tipped the order taker at a Carl's Junior hamburger restaurant because she was so nice to my mentally ill brother. I let her know that her kindness was the reason for the tip.
- Donate some clothing to the Senior Center or the Salvation Army. (*How many pair*s of shoes did you say you have?)

2. Pray for Two Strangers.
- Almost every day you will see someone on the street, drunk, insane, sick, in pain, hungry — or as in the case of prostitutes and thieves — misguided. The next time a hooker asks you if you want to have a good time, say, "I would have the best time if you would let me pray for you. Do you any specific needs or requests?"
- Almost any conversation with a stranger can involve expressed needs or worries or problems. Whenever such an idea is shared with you, say, "I will pray about that for you," and then continue your conversation without elaboration. If the stranger asks, "Do you go to church?" then you have a permissive opening to share the things of God and what he has done for you.

3. Give Three Compliments.
Our society is much more negative than positive, making criticism much more common than praise. Praise therefore not only stands out but is remembered a long time. A sincere kind word given on a suitable occasion, can motivate and encourage better than a trophy or plaque.

2944. Quiet Evangelism.

1. Avoid drive-by evangelism. It comes across as arrogant, insincere, and manipulative.

2. Let your actions be a quiet witness.
- Pray aloud in restaurants before each meal.
- Wear a shirt with your church's logo on it.
- Wear a commercially made shirt with a tasteful Christian message on it.
  - I'm not perfect. Just forgiven.
  - To get into Heaven, you've got to know the right person. I know. Ask me.
  - I'm not lucky. I'm blessed.
  - The older I get, the wiser God becomes.
- Take Christian books with you to the waiting room at the doctor's, dentist's, auto licensing's office. Leave the book behind when you are served.

2945. In the bad old days, before we had the advantages of labor-saving appliances, we spent all our time as slaves of the sink, washing dishes, or slaves of the river, beating our clothes clean by pounding them on a rock by the side of the stream. But technology has freed us from this sort of time-consuming labor.

Now we can sit back, free to spend all our time as — slaves of maintenance. Clean the grind chute in the coffee maker, take the car in for servicing, adjust the direction and flow of the sprinklers, get new batteries for the electric toothbrush, call about the loss of signal by your Internet service provider, log on to change your appointment time with the hairdresser, get the alarm clock repaired, change the filter in the water purifier, add more rinse aid to the dishwasher, clean the stove top, get the car washed, oil the garage door hinges, renew your homeowner's insurance, auto insurance, life insurance, anti-virus insurance, fix the lawnmower (or take it in to the repair shop), replace the leaking washer on the garden hose. . . .

2946. Today is a day that will never come again. Make good use of it.

2947. Re: Glimmering 2863. The first explanation might not be the best explanation. Especially in developing areas, early explanations depend on the then available information. As the facts become clearer and more numerous, the early inferences must often be revised or replaced.

2948. Some people are deaf by birth; some people are deaf by accident; and some people are deaf by choice. They just don't want to hear.

2949. The lies were cooked and flavored well, but the host served so many and such large ones that the guests all choked.

2950. "They drank the wine and praised their gods made of gold and silver, bronze, iron, wood, and stone" (Daniel 5:4).
    "Welcome to Spiritual Sam's Affordable Idol store. We have idols for every budget. You can have your choice of gods here. If you have only a few coins, we can match you up with something from the economy room. How about this nice deity made from iron? It's sturdy enough for the kids' room, and the expression on its face is not overly angry. Or, if you want to impress your friends, this attractive polished bronze god will dress up your living room nicely. And it's available with special financing—a low down and easy payments.
    "Or maybe you are the practical type. Are you suffering from a chronic disease, and sacrificing your daughter to Molech didn't heal you? Why not try this silver god? Or if you are really serious and want some high-speed results, we have a special on this golden goddess. (She's also a god of fertility, so if you buy it, be sure to warn your wives and servant girls.)
    "So, what will it be?"

2951. Re: Glimmering 2894. The more a young woman plays hard to get, the more likely her pursuer will come to think of her as a conquest, and therefore the less enduring their relationship will be once he attains his goal.

Conflicting with this claim are some studies that show how our value of something increases with the effort needed to attain it. That explains membership rituals in fraternities and clubs of various kinds. If it's difficult to join, it must be great.

2952. Those whom God has chosen for glory he has also chosen to suffer. See Luke 9:23.

2953. With the rejection of truth, reason, traditional social (and moral) hierarchies, religion, and the governing ideas of Western civilization, all that's left is power—power by every means necessary. Hence, no need to fashion an argument or assemble evidence for or against any proposal. Those with power will inform you of the correct decision shortly.

2954. The investment with the lowest cost and the greatest return is a word of encouragement.   —from the book of *Newly Made Proverbs*

2955. The problem with friendship is that the deeper it becomes, the more of a burden it is for your friend. You share yourself more and more, until you realize that a human being simply cannot bear the load of feelings and empathy you need. You realize that you are crushing your friend with expectations he simply cannot meet.

Friendship should involve joy and happiness and fun—as well as some sharing—but human friends can carry only so much. Read the Psalms and see how God can carry any load you have. Put the weight on him, and lighten up on your friends.

2956. The more dazzling the bargain, the less closely the buyer looks. —from the book of *Newly Made Proverbs*

2957. Does the suspicion ever run across your mind that all of the events brought to us through the media—and many in "real life"—are fake, prepackaged? We read that "reality shows" have scriptwriters; many "news" stories are actually product promos supplied by industry groups as public service announcements (with spots in the video to put the reporter in, asking questions, so that the story seems real); many news stories consist of a reporter reading a script while the supposedly supporting pictures are just stock video.

Have you ever watched an "amateur video" of people dancing to a new song, only to suspect that you are watching professional dancers pretending to be caught on camera? (The video looks to be professionally edited, the dancers give camera looks, and they are all physically fit, attractive, and coordinated with each other.)

[Glimmerings 2958 to 2978 are taken from a document, "The Wisdom Project," created December, 2016. With emendations June 6, 2019; age 68]

2958. **A Word to the Wise.**

A word to the wise is seldom sufficient, so here are a few comments on wisdom: what it is and how to apply it.

1. Wisdom is knowing how to apply the decision making principles drawn from personal and vicarious experience.

2.Wisdom is the ability to apply optimally and constantly the decision making principles gathered from an analysis of personal and vicarious experience.

3. Wisdom is knowing when to act and when not to act.

4. Wisdom is the ability to make the right choice at the right time, applying the right values.

5. Wisdom is identifying multiple scenarios and planning for each of them.

6. Wisdom is thinking down the road to identify unintended and unanticipated consequences.

7. Wisdom is understanding the world through a realistic view of human nature.

8. Wisdom is the ability to avoid being conned. Wisdom is a skill that keeps the wise person from falling for disinformation,

slanted and selected narratives, fake or distorted claims, logical fallacies, lies and half-truths.

9. Wisdom is knowledge gained by studying the successes and failures in the area where wisdom is needed. Without studying mistakes, wisdom is impossible.

10. Wisdom is the appropriate application of general knowledge to a specific situation. "The young men know the rules, and the old men know the exceptions." What is the tested, standard answer? Does the standard answer apply? Does the standard answer need modification?

11. Wisdom is discernment, separating truth from falsehood. It must be more than tossing a truth claim into one bin or the other. "True or false?" belongs to a past era. Now the question often is, "What degree of truth or falsehood is in this claim?" or "How have the true and the false been intermixed?" or "How has truth been distorted, or watered down?

2959. Wisdom is critical thinking, confronting fact claims with analysis, evaluation, and a healthy degree of skepticism.

2960. Wisdom is circumspection, examining and accounting for context. Take off the blinders and look around.

2961. Wisdom involves intuition. If it doesn't feel right, keep looking before you decide.

2962. Wisdom takes into account agreement, consensus — and disagreement.

2963. Wisdom is the realization that you cannot say, "If I were you, this is what I would do," because you are different from the other person.

2964. Wisdom is the understanding that other people are not like you. You shouldn't criticize others based on yourself.

2965. Shortcutting wisdom is an oxymoron. Wisdom is making the right or the best choice. Choosing means decision making. Decision making involves identifying criteria, weighting criteria according to values, identifying alternatives, weighting alternatives according to the degree of match to criteria, and considering possible negative consequences.

2966. Wisdom is knowledge of human nature so that the wise one can predict the effects that will follow each alternative choice.

2967. The wise man sometimes acts against his own self-interest.

2968. Wisdom is being initially skeptical toward all knowledge claims.

2969. Wisdom is a compendium of lessons learned by making mistakes.

2970. Wisdom derives from reality—seeing the world as it really is, understanding human nature and human motivation.

2971. Wisdom is telling others what not to do—after you've found out by doing it.

2972. Wisdom is the circumspection that allows you to see through confidence schemes, fake news, urban legends, and disinformation.

2973. Wisdom is accumulated good judgment.

2974. Wisdom is sharing your mistakes.

2975. Wisdom is paying it forward.

2976. Wisdom is knowing when to hold on and knowing when to let go.

2977. Wisdom is knowing God by observing his creation.

2978. Wisdom is realizing that your ego makes you think that you are three times as smart as you really are, that your contribution to the project is four times as good as it really was, and that the credit you think you deserve for the final result is five times what is actually the case.

2979. The Ten Commandments in Two Words Each
     1. Worship God.
     2. No idols.
     3. No blasphemy.
     4. Revere Sabbath.
     5. Honor parents.
     6. No murder.
     7. No adultery.
     8. No stealing.
     9. No lying.
     10. No coveting.

2980. From the lips of love to the eyebrows of hatred requires only a small movement on the face.

2981. "Do what is right, not what you want to do." "Follow your head, not your heart." "Humble yourself." "Serve others, not yourself."
    No wonder wisdom is unpopular.

2982. Re: Glimmering 2979. Some people complain that the Ten Commandments have too many "do not's" in them, too much negativism. Okay, so here are the Ten Commandments expressed positively.

    1. Worship God only.
    2. Making statues of gods, which are fakes, will harm your soul.
    3. Use God's name only with reverence.

4. Revere the Sabbath.

5. Honor your parents.

6. Murder is wrong.

7. Remain faithful to your spouse.

8. Respect the property of others.

9. Tell only the truth.

10. Forget what your neighbor owns and pursue the things that will help you serve God better.

2983. Solomon the Romantic.

The appropriateness and beauty of the images we choose for the figurative language of poetry and song are affected by culture and technology. In the Song of Songs Solomon writes a love poem to his bride, telling her that

> Your hair is like a flock of goats streaming down Mount Gilead.
> Your teeth are like a flock of newly shorn sheep coming up from washing, each one having a twin and not one missing.
> . . . .
> Your neck is like the tower of David, constructed in layers.
>
> —Song of Songs 4:1b-2, 4; HCSB

Do you think Solomon's bride heard these lines and sighed, "Oh, Sol. You shred me"? And what did she think when he told her that he already had "60 queens and 80 concubines" (Song of Songs 6:8)?

Did he perhaps use his most tender voice of allurement to whisper to her, "Come to me now, my darling. You are one of the only 140 girls I have ever loved"?

2984. Re: Glimmering 2890. Lessons we learn from students' attitudes about truth:

1. Stories are much more persuasive than data

2. It's difficult to prove a negative. If you assert that there are no documented cases of something (such as the headlight

flashers or Halloween razor blade criminals), it can always be claimed that there are suppressed cases.

3. We all pay attention to stories and remember them because they are more interesting than a recital of facts.

2985. When your lips praise you, people laugh; when your actions praise you, people cheer. —from the book of *Newly Made Proverbs*

2986. We are so committed to indulging our pleasure habits that we set up walls to guard them against God.

2987. Many young people (teens, twenties, thirties) appear to have been harmed by their lack of education and by the shortening of their attention span by the visual media. There seems to be a tendency to see every sentence as an independent element, unconnected to the other sentences around it. As a result, song lyrics, essays, and conversations are all exercises in non sequiturs. So many students will read a sentence and then say, "I don't understand this book." When asked where the confusion lies, they will point to one sentence or one word — that is clarified in the next few sentences.

Advice 1: When you don't understand something, don't stop and quit. Keep reading and see if the matter doesn't become clear.

Advice 2: Look for meaning across paragraphs, chapters, and the entire book or article.

Advice 3. Don't look at prose as a collection of independent snippets. Instead, look for interrelated expressions, sections of text that provide transitions and connections.

2988. It's always easier to tell others how to control their emotions than it is for us to control our own.

2989. It's especially easy to give excellent advice to others — when they are not around.

2990. What packaging tells us; or, On the value of competence in one's area of claimed expertise; or, On paying attention to details in product manufacturing; or, On the perfect storm in the self-diminishment of imported goods.

Many manufacturers, especially of Chinese products, seem to neglect the truth that the perception of product quality is in part dependent on the presentation of the product—that is, the packaging. Is the product, say, placed nicely in a box that contains some accessories, such as batteries? And is a clear, understandable instruction manual included?

Semiotics is the study of how things send non-verbal messages to a reader or viewer or hearer. Quick example: When the user of a radio turns the switch on, does the sound of the click and the feel of the knob convey the sensation that this radio is a high-quality, durable, well-engineered item, or does it say that the radio is a piece of ephemeral junk that probably won't last a week?

Test: In a store, you pick up a pair of scissors shrink wrapped to a piece of thin cardboard. On one side is a description of "Product Characteristics and Usage." The description begins with, "The body of Scissor is Make of High-Quanlity Stainless Steel." The scissor is also said to be "Defending the Rust Enduring."

Question 1: Are you most likely to be standing in (A) Macy's, (B) Saks Fifth Avenue, (C) Home Depot, or (D) The Dollar Store?

Question 2: Why did you choose the store you did?

2991. What packaging tells us, Example 2. You walk into a store and notice a nicely packaged bottle of brown shoe polish, just what you have needed. Flipping the package over, you note that half the back is printed with an area marked "Notice!" followed by five bulleted points in Japanese. Fortunately, below that are five bulleted points in English. The final two points are:

- Please keep it where the child out of reach, do not keep it in the high temperature and the direct rays place.
- Please do not use it for any purpose.

Of course, you probably recognize that the final point is something of a typographical error, and you understand that the intended meaning is not to use the polish for *any other* purpose.
But, according to semiotic theory, a prospective purchaser will
transfer the message of the back language — the message being
that the manufacturer is careless or has incompetent employees — to the product itself — that the shoe polish is of low quality.

2992. Odds are that the giant casinos win more often than the
gamblers.

2993. Using fish for sandals will slow you down unless you first
step into the water. — from the book of *Newly Made Proverbs*

2994. The hierarchy of evil:
- those who do good and resist evil
- those who resist evil but don't do good
- those who don't resist evil but do good
- those who do evil but also do good
- those who do evil but don't do good
- those who do evil and persecute those who do good

2995. When we pray for God's will — and we always should —
we usually don't consider that we might not like what God's
will is for the thing we are praying about. "Come see the works
of the Lord, who brings devastation on the earth" (Psalm 46:8).
We like to frame our prayer requests in a way that a Yes answer
will be something we like. That's human. Even Jesus did this,
asking for deliverance from crucifixion — before he subordinated
his own preference to God's will (Matthew 26:39).
    So we should pray, "Do your will, Lord, even though I
might not like it." Or, "May it be done to me, dear Lord, according to your will and not mine."

2996. **Read the Instructions.**
    "Hello, DuraBest Razor customer service. How may I help
you?"

"Yeah. Your razors are junk. I bought six of them and not a one of them works. They just push the shaving cream around on my face."

"I'm sorry you're having a problem with our razors, sir."

"When I'm done shaving, if you could call it that, with your crummy excuse for a razor, not a whisker on my face is one bit shorter."

"That's not right, sir. Again I'm sorry."

"Well, what are you going to do about it?"

"Let me understand the situation a bit more. Can you tell me the batch number printed on the "Take Six" card?"

"Yeah. It's 2109020733. You're thinking the whole batch is probably defective?"

"I don't know, sir. But we want to find out. Thank you for that information. So tell me now about how you shave. You put on the shaving cream, and then—."

Of course I put on the shaving cream. What are you getting at?"

"Then, let's say you take a brand new razor out of the package."

"I hope you're not patronizing me, because if you are—."

"After you remove the plastic blade guard, do you shave with the handle up or with it down?"

"Wait a minute. Blade guard? What the—. Oh, never mind."

[Click]

2997. **The Lawsuit Model of Moral Health.**

The moral (and spiritual) health of the people of the United States can be measured by the ratio of lawsuits filed in a year to that year's population. A lawsuit implies a real or imagined lapse in an agreement, a perceived lack of moral behavior. Thus, the more lawsuits filed per capita in a year provides us with an index of the population's moral (and by derivation, spiritual) health.

Lawsuits are necessary to resolve actual and perceived wrongs. A nation with many lawsuits shows that its people are corrupt:

> Their hearts are devious. . . . They speak mere words,
> taking false oaths while making covenants. So lawsuits
> break out like poisonous weeds in the furrows of a field.
> —Hosea 10: 2a, 4

2998. The proverb, quoted elsewhere, that "The expectation of gratitude is the first mistake of the human heart," can be applied with double force when someone gives a present that he would like to have received, only to learn that the recipient seems to dismiss it as of little value, use, or importance. Thinking, "I'll give one of these things to Joe, because I think they are just so cool and useful," sets you up for an emotional fall.

The lesson here is to stop expecting others to have the same tastes and values as you. You think a pulseoximeter or a laser distance measurer would be welcome by any of your friends or acquaintances. The more fool you are. If you do give such a gift, the look on their face will be about the same as if you had given them a pancake maker that puts an outline of Mickey Mouse in the pancakes. Or maybe Goofy.

2999. There will always be chronic liars. By telling a lie, the liar not only seeks to gain some advantage that he couldn't have gained with the truth, but serving you a lie, hoping that you will swallow it, makes the liar feel superior to you, even though you may be smarter, richer, taller, and better looking. Liars feel an internal smirk when they think you are buying their line. You are a chump and only they know it. The liar's enjoyment from taking you for a ride explains why many of them lie for no practical reason. Lying for its own sake: What an ego boost.

3000. The prophet's role is to foretell future events, often in the form of coming judgments or disasters of some sort, but sometimes blessings. However, their promises or threats are nearly always conditional. That is, bad things will happen unless you mend your ways and turn back to God. Or blessings will attend you—as long as you remain faithful. To face a conditional challenge, there is choice and hope. To face a conditional blessing, there is perseverance and commitment.

3001. Aristotle puts every virtue in the middle of a scale, between two extremes, which are vices. If discipline is the virtue, what are the extremes? An excess of discipline would be cruelty or child abuse or authoritarianism. A deficiency of discipline would be abandonment, anarchy, chaos, or irresponsibility.

3002. Repentance is the belated triumph of the mind over the body.

3003. We owe it to civility, honesty, and integrity to summarize fairly the position of those we disagree with. Unfortunately, whatever follows, "So what you're saying is . . ." almost never fairly or accurately summarizes the position of our opponent.

3004. The curious person picks up a new object and asks, "What is this supposed to do?" The curious and creative person asks, "What can I make this do?" [from a TEDx Talk]

3005. Why are new ideas so often opposed by the establishment? We often think that "the authorities" oppose new ideas because they have settled the issues and are defending the truth according to their understanding. But a closer look reveals that at bottom, the opposition comes from a fear of loss of power, prestige, and position. The power struggle is couched in terms of truth standing up against error, but as history eventually shows, the real battle was between the upstarts and the entrenched. The disagreement was described as a question of science, but in fact involved a political struggle more than a scientific one.

"Science is the pursuit of truth wherever is leads, as long as it doesn't lead to truth that threatens us." Once again we see the pernicious nature of pride.

3006. Re: Glimmering 2464. Another example of God's mysterious ways. In the book of Luke, we read that Zechariah and Elizabeth were both "righteous in God's sight, living without blame according to all the commands and requirements of the Lord"

(Luke 1:6, HCSB). But in spite of their praying from their youth into their old age, they were unable to have children. And lack of children in their culture was seen as a badge of shame, a withheld blessing.

But then, when they are aged beyond hope, they are chosen to give birth to John the Baptist, who comes in the role of Elijah, to announce the coming of the Messiah.

⌘⌘⌘

A note on *The Book of One Hundred Lies*
Entries from the book may be found as follows:
Lies 1- 13, Glimmering 806
Lies 14-18, Glimmering 816
Lies 19-20, Glimmering 848
Lies 21-22, Glimmering 901
Lies 23-25, Glimmering 1095
Lies 26-27, Glimmering 1106
Lies 28-31, Glimmering 1136
Lie 32, Glimmering 1216
Lie 33, Glimmering 1632
Lies 34-35, Glimmering 1851
Lies 36-40, Glimmering 1901
Lies 41-44, Glimmering 1976
Lies 45-47, Glimmering 2225
Lies 48-52, Glimmering 2234
Lies 53-61, Glimmering 2254
Lie 62, Glimmering 2321
Lies 63-64, Glimmering 2323
Lies 65-66, Glimmering 2436

All three Glimmerings books, together with Robert Harris' other books, are available through Amazon, Barnes and Noble, and other fine stores.

Colophon

Glimmerings III was set in Book Antiqua 11-point Roman, italic, and bold. Book Antiqua is Microsoft's version of Palatino, a famous typeface created in 1949 by Hermann Zapf, influenced by 16th century calligraphy. Book Antiqua's high x height makes it more readable than typefaces with low x heights.

At the same time that the x-height contributes to ease of reading, the typeface itself presents an "intellectual" appeal, helping to render the content slightly formal.

www.ingramcontent.com/pod-product-compliance
Lightning Source LLC
Chambersburg PA
CBHW061425040426
42450CB00007B/907